Exploring the Economic Opportunities and Impacts of Migrant Entrepreneurship:

Success Stories and Case Studies

Meena Chavan
Macquarie University, Australia

Sheba Nandkeolyar
Multiconnexions, Australia

A volume in the Advances in Business Strategy and Competitive Advantage (ABSCA) Book Series

IGI Global
PUBLISHER of TIMELY KNOWLEDGE

Published in the United States of America by
IGI Global
Business Science Reference (an imprint of IGI Global)
701 E. Chocolate Avenue
Hershey PA, USA 17033
Tel: 717-533-8845
Fax: 717-533-8661
E-mail: cust@igi-global.com
Web site: http://www.igi-global.com

Library of Congress Cataloging-in-Publication Data

Names: Chavan, Meena, 1959- author. | Nandkeolyar, Sheba, 1957- author.
Title: Exploring the economic opportunities and impacts of migrant entrepreneurship : success stories and case studies / by Meena Chavan, and Sheba Nandkeolyar.
Description: Hershey, PA : Business Science Reference, [2022] | Includes bibliographical references and index. | Summary: "This book highlights the population growth fueled by migrants coming to Australia, bringing with them much more than bags packed full of their belongings but rather how they stimulate the economy, bring fresh new ideas and a unique perspective on business, offering a huge variety of positive and intangible benefits from enhanced productivity to innovation and more"-- Provided by publisher.
Identifiers: LCCN 2022008800 (print) | LCCN 2022008801 (ebook) | ISBN 9781668449868 (hardback) | ISBN 9781668449875 (paperback) | ISBN 9781668449882 (ebook)
Subjects: LCSH: Immigrant business enterprises--Australia. | Immigrants--Australia. | Entrepreneurship--Australia. | Australia--Emigration and immigration--Economic aspects.
Classification: LCC HD2360.5.A8 C43 2022 (print) | LCC HD2360.5.A8 (ebook) | DDC 338.6/4220994--dc23/eng/20220223
LC record available at https://lccn.loc.gov/2022008800
LC ebook record available at https://lccn.loc.gov/2022008801

This book is published in the IGI Global book series Advances in Business Strategy and Competitive Advantage (ABSCA) (ISSN: 2327-3429; eISSN: 2327-3437)

British Cataloguing in Publication Data
A Cataloguing in Publication record for this book is available from the British Library.

Advances in Business Strategy and Competitive Advantage (ABSCA) Book Series

ISSN:2327-3429
EISSN:2327-3437

Editor-in-Chief: Patricia Ordóñez de Pablos, Universidad de Oviedo, Spain

MISSION

Business entities are constantly seeking new ways through which to gain advantage over their competitors and strengthen their position within the business environment. With competition at an all-time high due to technological advancements allowing for competition on a global scale, firms continue to seek new ways through which to improve and strengthen their business processes, procedures, and profitability.

The **Advances in Business Strategy and Competitive Advantage (ABSCA) Book Series** is a timely series responding to the high demand for state-of-the-art research on how business strategies are created, implemented and re-designed to meet the demands of globalized competitive markets. With a focus on local and global challenges, business opportunities and the needs of society, the **ABSCA** encourages scientific discourse on doing business and managing information technologies for the creation of sustainable competitive advantage.

COVERAGE

- Value Creation
- Strategic Alliances
- Strategic Management
- Differentiation Strategy
- Entrepreneurship & Innovation
- Ethics and Business Strategy
- Customer-Orientation Strategy
- Foreign Investment Decision Process
- Competitive Strategy
- Economies of Scale

IGI Global is currently accepting manuscripts for publication within this series. To submit a proposal for a volume in this series, please contact our Acquisition Editors at Acquisitions@igi-global.com or visit: http://www.igi-global.com/publish/.

The Advances in Business Strategy and Competitive Advantage (ABSCA) Book Series (ISSN 2327-3429) is published by IGI Global, 701 E. Chocolate Avenue, Hershey, PA 17033-1240, USA, www.igi-global.com. This series is composed of titles available for purchase individually; each title is edited to be contextually exclusive from any other title within the series. For pricing and ordering information please visit http://www.igi-global.com/book-series/advances-business-strategy-competitive-advantage/73672. Postmaster: Send all address changes to above address.

Titles in this Series

For a list of additional titles in this series, please visit:
http://www.igi-global.com/book-series/advances-business-strategy-competitive-advantage/73672

Analyzing the Relationship Between Corporate Governance, CSR, and Sustainability
Ayberk Soyer (Istanbul Technical University, Turkey) and Umut Asan (Istanbul Technical University, Turkey)
Business Science Reference • © 2022 • 315pp • H/C (ISBN: 9781799842347) • US $215.00

Handbook of Research on Digital Innovation and Networking in Post-COVID-19 Organizations
Ana Pego (Nova University of Lisbon, Portugal)
Business Science Reference • © 2022 • 539pp • H/C (ISBN: 9781668467626) • US $315.00

Antecedents and Outcomes of Employee-Based Brand Equity
Muhammad Waseem Bari (Government College University, Faisalabad, Pakistan) Muhammad Abrar (Government College University, Faisalabad, Pakistan) and Emilia Alaverdov (Tbilisi State University, Georgia)
Business Science Reference • © 2022 • 297pp • H/C (ISBN: 9781668436219) • US $250.00

Cases on Emerging Market Responses to the COVID-19 Pandemic
Raj K. Kovid (Sharda University, India) and Vikas Kumar (Central University of Haryana, India)
Business Science Reference • © 2022 • 332pp • H/C (ISBN: 9781668435045) • US $240.00

Impact of Digital Transformation on the Development of New Business Models and Consumer Experience
Maria Antónia Rodrigues (Polytechnic of Porto, Portugal & CEOS.PP, Portugal & SIIS Porto, Portugal) and João F. Proença (Faculty of Economics, University of Porto, Portugal & Advance/CSG, University of Lisbon, Portugal & ISEG, University of Lisbon, Portugal)
Business Science Reference • © 2022 • 347pp • H/C (ISBN: 9781799891796) • US $240.00

Cases on Survival and Sustainability Strategies of Social Entrepreneurs
Charles Oham (University of Greenwich, UK)
Business Science Reference • © 2022 • 312pp • H/C (ISBN: 9781799877240) • US $215.00

For an entire list of titles in this series, please visit:
http://www.igi-global.com/book-series/advances-business-strategy-competitive-advantage/73672

IGI Global
PUBLISHER of TIMELY KNOWLEDGE

701 East Chocolate Avenue, Hershey, PA 17033, USA
Tel: 717-533-8845 x100 • Fax: 717-533-8661
E-Mail: cust@igi-global.com • www.igi-global.com

Meena Chavan

This book is dedicated to my brave, entrepreneurial mother – a compassionate, lively, and resilient woman who taught me to be accepting and respectful of all cultures – as well as my mentors Prof Elizabeth Christopher and Prof Lucy Taksa for their wholehearted, enthusiastic, and passionate guidance and direction in my academic career. This book would not have been complete without the inspiration that I have derived from my inspiring husband Sharad my wonderful, supportive sons Amit and Anuj and my vivacious daughter in law Prachi. Last but most importantly the book is dedicated to all those who dream of being a successful entrepreneur.

Sheba Nandkeolyar

This book is dedicated to my husband Sanjeev, my son Sanchay, my daughter-in-law Vesna and my grandson Leroy. You are my strength, motivation, and inspiration for all that I do.

I would also like to dedicate this book to all new migrants coming into Australia from around the world under different circumstances. We are united by a common dream to prosper and thrive despite whatever challenges are in front of us.

Table of Contents

Preface

If you don't give up, you still have a chance. Giving up is the greatest failure… Never give up. Today is hard, tomorrow will be worse, but the day after tomorrow the sun will shine.

– Jack Ma, Alibaba Founder & CEO

I'm convinced that about half of what separates successful entrepreneurs from the non-successful ones is pure perseverance.

– Steve Jobs, Apple Co-Founder

I must be prepared to endure tremendous trials and tribulations for the benefit and betterment of my family, and the same spirit must extend to my business – it's all about love.

– Laiwa Chan, China's 17th richest person and one of just 19 self-made female billionaires in the world

I knew that if I failed, I wouldn't regret that, but I knew the one thing I might regret is not trying.

– Jeff Bezos, Amazon Founder & CEO

Whatever you do, throw yourself into it. Throw your head, heart, and hands into it.

– Indra Nooyi, former CEO of Pepsico

Australia is one of the world's major migration nations, with new Australians fuelling our country's population growth. We are home to the world's oldest continuous cultures, as well as Australians who identify with more than 270 ancestries. The most recent Census (2016) found that 28.5 per cent of the estimated resident population (ERP) was born overseas (6.9 million persons). If we consider those in Australia who have at least one parent born overseas, the multicultural reality becomes even more apparent.

But beyond fuelling population growth, migrants coming to Australia from abroad bring with them much more than bags packed full of their belongings. They stimulate the economy; they bring fresh new ideas and a unique perspective on business. They bring a huge variety of positive and intangible benefits from enhanced productivity to innovation and more.

The 2016 Census found that 14 per cent (just over 1.5 million) of all employed people in Australia identified as owner managers of businesses. A CGU study found that Australia's 620,000 migrant-owned small businesses collectively employ a staggering 1.41 million people. Further, one in three of these migrant-owned businesses have plans to employ new staff, leading to the creation of 200,000 jobs within the coming decade.

Australia is not short of highly successful Immigrant business owners. John Hemmes left the Netherlands after WWII with just $20 to his name and built a billion-dollar entertainment empire. Maha Sinnathamby came from humble beginnings in Japanese-occupied Malaysia and established the largest privately owned master-planned city in Australia. Polish-born Richard Pratt was renowned for acting and philanthropy and was worth more than $5 billion when he passed away. Russian-born IT entrepreneur Zhenya Tsvetnenko made a home in Perth and accumulated a net worth estimated at more than $100 million after humble beginnings. "High-Rise Harry" Triguboff, a Russian, escaped China's revolution and came to Sydney to find modest work before finding his true calling in real estate and accumulating a net worth of more than $4 billion. Frank Lowy grew up in Cypriot and Palestinian detention camps before coming to Australia and developing shopping centres – accruing wealth of $5 billion with Westfield Group. The examples are boundless.

Dancing with Destiny is a compilation of the true, biographical stories of ten Australian migrant entrepreneurs who danced with destiny.

It was compiled and written by two women who were migrants to Australia themselves - Dr Meena Chavan and Sheba Nandkeolyar. The authors aim to shine a light on some of these amazing migrants' stories and inspire others to achieve big, succeed in business and life, and overcome obstacles against whatever odds.

The authors met a few years ago when Meena got in touch with Sheba to invite Sheba to speak to her university students about her bilateral business experience. After the initial contact and meeting, the pair clicked instantly and bonded over a shared passion for cross border business and the contribution of migrants to the economic fabric of Australia. Since then, Sheba has become a regular speaker at 'India Immersion' sessions for Meena's international business program.

This book is the result of the pair's shared passion and enduring friendship.

So, what does it mean to dance with destiny?

In these ten stories, the phrase has come to mean a variety of different things for each person interviewed by the authors.

It might mean they took a chance that paid off. Or they survived and thrived against formidable odds. They tapped into their inner strength. They tapped into the support of those around them. They got lucky. They made their luck. They used their street smarts. Or they used their book smarts.

But what each one of the successful migrants interviewed has in common is they left their beloved homeland, lives, friends, family and culture with a leap of faith to start a new life in Australia, the so-called lucky country. They all refused to give up in the face of adversity, and they overcame their various and unique challenges.

They have all shared their incredible stories with the authors in the hope that it would inspire others who might themselves be in similar situations – whether the reader is a migrant themselves, a budding entrepreneur, an established business person, or perhaps someone who sees parallels between their own journey in life and the themes and issues faced by the interviewees in the stories.

Early on in researching for this book, Meena and Sheba faced challenges in locating successful migrant business leaders who were open to sharing their journey and its difficulties. Sometimes it can be painful or shameful to be brutally frank – warts and all. Sheba and Meena also wanted to locate stories of migrant business leaders who had actually learned from their journey and were thus able to frankly share their learnings with others.

Each of the migrants interviewed has been brave and candid in sharing details of their business and secrets to their success, making for compelling reading.

This carefully curated collection of stories features:

Pauline Nguyen – A down-to-earth and philosophical Vietnamese-origin restauranteur who faced seemingly insurmountable challenges and has since achieved remarkable success alongside her business partners

Diem "Yim" Furggersberger – An elegant, sophisticated and humble Vietnamese-origin packaged food producer who credits her family and values as being key to her success, despite a difficult start in Australia

DD Saxena – A charismatic, bona-fide (edible) oil baron of Indian-origin, whose razor-sharp business acumen particularly in the agri-business field has seen him make an indelible mark across borders

Cristina Talacko – A Brazilian-origin former lawyer whose homesickness and undying love for her native country led her to set aside her legal ambitions to pursue her passions and lead a highly lucrative Brazilian-inspired food empire in Australia

Rustom Kanga – A highly educated man of Indian origin, whose unwavering belief in artificial intelligence has seen him push the boundaries of what is possible and build a global footprint based in his new country, Australia

Michelle Lam – A gutsy businesswoman from China who has built an outdoor furniture empire in Australia through her networks in China

Joseph Assaf – A Lebanese-origin entrepreneur and visionary who arrived in Australia in someone else's shoes (literally) and went on to yield tremendous influence particularly in the field of multiculturalism in Australia

Marina O'Neill – An Italian-origin queen of architectural hardware with an uncanny knack for seeing business opportunities and capitalising on them

Kananjar "Kan" Shivaram Shetty – An Indian-origin former accountant who overcame humble beginnings and a struggle to find his feet in a new country to build and head an enormous global paint empire with his family at his side

Kam and Reet Phulwani – International student couple who came with dreams that came true through their persistence and hard work through a Global Pharmeceutical company

In sharing these stories, Meena and Sheba hope to create a momentum where migration is celebrated. They hope more migrant entrepreneurs come forward and set up businesses.

Migrants have a strong need and passion to realise their dreams. The success of migrant businesses is a testimony to their passion and aspirations.

Migrants deserve to be celebrated not only because of the diversity of cuisine or cultures but also because of the excellent contribution that migrants make in the business world and to the economy.

Migrants create jobs and industries and have a huge, positive impact on the fabric of Australia and our economy.

Meena Chavan
Macquarie University, Australia

Sheba Nandkeolyar
Multiconnexions, Australia

Acknowledgment

Meena Chavan

First and foremost, I would like to give a huge thank you to the 10 successful entrepreneurs who gave us their valuable time and narrated their stories for this book. Thank you very much! My heartfelt thanks to my co-author Sheba Nandkeolyar who despite her busy schedule of managing a multinational corporation made time to engage with the respondents.

I am grateful to both our research assistants Katrina Hall who helped us with the copy editing of the book and to Sapna Khiani Kumar who helped during the interviews.

I am thankful to the many individuals who helped us with the review process and gave us their time with the reiterative review of versions along the way as this book took shape. I would like to acknowledge Macquarie University for the scholastic support in writing this book. I would like to thank staff and students from the Macquarie Business School who inspired us to write this book.

I would like to convey my profound thanks to Prof Elizabeth Christopher who gave me my first lessons in Cross Cultural Business and cultivated my passion for the subject. I am grateful to Prof Lucy Taksa for being so generous with her time and for her constant mentorship over the last ten years. A big thank you is also merited to my PhD students who explored the many facets of Intercultural Business Management in depth, bringing new insights to light.

Many thanks to the editorial team for their patience and professional support in working diligently to get the book published on time. Finally, I would like to thank my partner and kids for their support and sacrifices during the many hours spent editing the book chapters.

Acknowledgment

Sheba Nandkeolyar

I would like to thank each of the entrepreneurs interviewed in this book for sharing your story with us. Your candour, humility, and willingness to share your story for the sake of helping others who may be in a similar situation as new migrants are inspiring.

I would like to thank my dear friend and co-author Dr Meena Chavan for her positivity, resilience, perseverance, and tremendous knowledge throughout the process of putting together our book. Your sincerity and passion are truly infectious.

I would like to thank our editor Katrina Hall and researcher Sapna Kumar for your dedication and attention to detail. Your advice and inputs have driven our book forward to an outcome we can be proud of.

I would like to thank the editorial team.

And last, but certainly not least, I would like to sincerely thank my family for your encouragement and support.

Chapter 1
Joseph Assaf AO

ABSTRACT

Founder of the Ethnic Business Awards, Joseph Assaf faced many challenges before he became the renowned entrepreneur he is today. Arriving in Australia from Lebanon, Joseph went from carrying a suitcase full of dreams to becoming a highly successful business and multicultural marketing leader. Although he initially confronted cultural and language barriers and the difficulty of navigating a new country, Joseph fell in love with Australia's diversity and multiculturalism. Joseph has gone on to accomplish many more things in his life including becoming a Member (AM) in the Queen's Birthday Honours list for his work in the field of multicultural communications, being bestowed the Lifetime Achievement Award by the Australian Migration and Settlement Council in 2014, and being appointed as Officer of the Order of Australia (AO). This chapter tells the story of a man who danced with destiny and chased his dreams with perseverance.

DOI: 10.4018/978-1-6684-4986-8.ch001

Figure 1.

Joseph is an Australian entrepreneur and communications professional of Lebanese origin. Assaf is the founder of the Ethnic Business Awards.

Joseph was awarded the Order of Australia in 2010 and he became a Member (AM) in the Queen's Birthday Honours list for his work in the field of multicultural communications. The Lifetime Achievement Award was bestowed on him by the Australian Migration and Settlement Council in 2014, and in 2018, he was appointed an Officer of the Order of Australia (AO) for distinguished service to multiculturalism and for his contribution to the linguistically diverse society.

From a Lebanese-origin migrant arriving in Australia with nothing but a suitcase full of dreams, to a highly successful businessman with multicultural political policy influence, Order of Australia recipient and author of two books among many other accolades, the story of Joseph Assaf is truly that of a man who danced with destiny.

EARLY LIFE

Joseph Assaf was born in a mountainous village in Lebanon into a big, close-knit farming family, with two brothers and three sisters. In Lebanon at the time, it was compulsory to study Arabic plus a second language of either French or English. Joseph took French. When he finished school, he wanted to attend university, but his parents did not have enough money to pay for the faraway coastal institutions. To save for university, when he left school, he worked for two years doing odd jobs including manual labour and waitering and finally commenced his first year of university, studying economics. Around this time, Joseph's older brother developed a major heart problem and passed on at just 24 years old, devastating the 22-year-old Joseph. Struggling to cope with the loss, Joseph wanted to have a fresh start, so decided to migrate to Australia from Lebanon.

Joseph explained the unique circumstances of October 1967, when he came to Australia.

He wanted to come by boat, but after the Six Days War, the Suez Canal was closed for ships. People coming from Lebanon to Australia either had to go around the Horn of Africa by boat or fly. Joseph elected to fly. Australian authorities sprayed planes before they landed in case the plane's exterior carried diseases like foot and mouth. They also asked everyone to have a brand-new pair of shoes to avoid carrying diseases in their shoes and not to put them on until boarding the aircraft.

Joseph said, "I arrived at Beirut Airport and they asked me to put on my new pair of shoes, which I did. They took my old shoes. An hour or so later, they told us that the flight was cancelled so I had to go home and come back the next day. When I checked in the next day, they again asked me to put on my new shoes. I said, 'These are my new shoes'. They said 'No, these are not new now because you used them to go home'. I said, 'But you took my old shoes! I couldn't go barefooted'. They said, 'Sorry sir, you can't travel'."

"I sat in the corner, devastated, until one of the officers took pity on me. He went behind the counter and started opening other suitcases for other passengers, until he came across a brand-new pair of shoes, double the size of my feet. He gave them to me and told me to put them on and get on board. That's how I landed in Australia in someone else's shoes."

'In someone else's shoes' is the name of Joseph Assaf's first book. Joseph Assaf is the author of two books, *In Someone Else's Shoes* - about how to communicate with people of different cultures and backgrounds and *When Up is Down* - the title of which arose from his early English language confusion in Australia at hearing someone say 'hurry up' to him as he was descending the stairs at the train station. Joseph thought to himself, "Why is up, down? Is it because we are down under?"

ARRIVAL IN AUSTRALIA

Soon after Joseph arrived in Australia, he fell in love the country. He was fascinated by Australia's diversity of faces, races, languages, cultures, religion, and cuisine and quickly decided to settle and call Australia home.

He was desperate to learn English, so took on work at a local factory intending to learn from his colleagues but soon realised none of his co-workers were from an English-speaking background! He befriended a few South American Spanish-speakers at the factory because they could communicate a little, Joseph being a French-speaker and the two languages being so similar. He soon gained a reputation for his language and communication skills, and his boss gave Joseph a pay increase from $20 to $25 per week to add on-the-job translating to his job description.

Joseph realised there is an economic advantage in diversity and money to be made in communicating in another language.

While working, Joseph commenced a Bachelor of Arts at Sydney University.

"It was hell for me because I struggled to catch the words coming from my lecturers' mouths! While others would spend five or seven hours, to write an essay it would take me one or two weeks because I had to learn the meaning of every word, then write it and check it. I used to comfort myself by thinking when I finish my degree, no one would know how long it took me to write my essay, and I would have an equal opportunity to everyone else with the same degree. No one ever asked me how long it took me to write my essays. I had a BA like everybody else."

He met and fell in love with his wife Angela soon after arriving in Australia. The pair started Australia's first multicultural communication agency together.

"The work of that agency took us everywhere. Not only to all the communities that make up Australia, but quite often to the countries of origin too. We ended up doing work with our clients locally and globally. It was not always me making my clients aware of many things, but I also learnt from all of them. I learnt from every community."

BUILDING A BUSINESS

"My love of multiculturalism is where we started. In multicultural communications, you have to understand your target audience and ask yourself 'how can I connect with all of these communities?' I always say you have to tap on people from within that community to create a strong message for you, because sometimes words can be misleading, or even offensive. I always told my clients, 'Don't translate it, create it'."

In the beginning of his career, Joseph found achieving first successes to be hard work. When Joseph and Angela began their business, they did not have much cash. Joseph was introduced to a Russian Canadian man who helped them start up. They found a suitable office in North Sydney, and the friend charged them $2 a week to put a phone on a desk so they could present as having a business address.

"When we finally moved from there to an office, we did not have any money to buy furniture, so we bought old furniture and some cheap material to cover it. We fixed the material on with a stapler. We did not need to borrow money – we managed with cheap cloth."

Despite these early hardships, Joseph considered himself fortunate to have clients coming on board.

He recalled often going for an urgent job pitch in Canberra and working all night to complete the presentation with no sleep. He would fly down and wait for the committee to come, present his ideas to them, and fly back to Sydney. Often, the committee would then want changes to his work so he would have to work all through the night again.

"At times, it would be almost 48 hours before I got to sleep," recalled Joseph.

"In terms of expansion [of my company], I was very conservative. My office in Toga House, York Street did well after one or two years so we moved to a beautiful office in Market Street. Then from there I moved to MLC after my success with Lifesavers (the mints)."

"Their product QuickEze was not selling well in Sydney's multicultural western suburbs and they requested me to find out why. I did the research and found out that consumers there see it placed amongst all other confectionary. They don't read the pack, assume it's sweet, put it in their mouth, then spit it out. I said, 'Well, you can't put it amongst the sweets, because they assume it's a lolly, and it doesn't taste sweet'. I produced small explanatory brochures and distributed them in western suburb shops, pharmacies and so on. Immediately sales went up."

After this initial success, Lifesavers were keen to delve further into multicultural and global markets with their Mastercraft chocolate and lollipops, among other products. Joseph negotiated an excellent commission and commenced research on Arabic-speakers particularly in the Gulf region. It proved a highly lucrative market, earning Joseph some excellent renumeration in return for his business savvy, relationship skills and Arabic language skills.

"I did work for the Electoral Commission for at least 25 years. Now you have to tell the people when the election is, but you have only one week to develop the ads in different languages. You have to tell them how to vote, when to vote, absentee voting, all that, and create ads. We created ads for everybody to understand them. In the advertising industry, deadlines can be stressful!"

Joseph cites successful campaigns for environmental agency, anti-smoking, cervical cancer, the Kidney Foundation, HIV prevention and many more.

"I had hundreds of companies in various industries that I was helping in different overseas markets – some in Asia, some in Europe - because they came to me as an expert on how to get into those markets. I was good at finding people and making connections. In business, your name is important. If you fail with one, they tell each other. Success always brings success."

As time went on, Joseph deepened his relationships with government, manufacturers, and businesses through trade fairs and a variety of networking opportunities. Joseph continued to tap on these relationships whenever he had business in the various countries, to his benefit and the benefit of his clients.

Joseph says relationships are also key to success. It is important to find a way to connect with people. You never know what a relationship can bring you in the future if you spend the time to connect with people in a meaningful way. His relationships and support for multicultural communities went beyond the transactional.

"I learnt one thing, right from the beginning, that if you want to be effective in your communication, you have to understand the culture and the language of your target audience. Australia is made up of 200 different communities or language groups."

"In the early days, there were language communities in Australia that didn't have newspapers, television programs, or radio. I bought equipment for them to typeset the copy for the newspapers, I bought television antennas for community TV, and I invested $100,000. People asked, 'Why would you do that?' There were benefits for me too. If I set up an antenna, then I can advertise on television. If I can advertise on television, then I can invite all my clients to spend on TV advertising. You have to have that initiative."

"I would never, ever just translate a message from English straight to another language. Why is that? Well let me give you an analogy. Aspirin is for headaches. But can you give it to every person suffering from a headache? No. Some people are allergic to it and you could kill them. In a similar way, you can never translate an ad from English, put it in Chinese. You could kill your relationship with that person."

Joseph continued over the years with his formula of success, and it worked. It became a large and successful agency and eventually Joseph sold it to WPP Worldwide.

ETHNIC BUSINESS AWARDS FOUNDATION

Joseph observes that migrants are often the most successful in many aspects. But he laments that unfortunately, when something goes wrong, the community and media are quick to blame it on migrants, on multiculturalism, on the Lebanese, on the Chinese, on the Italian, before that on the Greek, on the Vietnamese. Joseph has long believed this is not the truth about migration.

"I wanted to educate Australia about the benefit of migration. Migrants inspire me. I created the Ethnic Business Awards as a role model to show people what migrants have done and can do. From day one 30 years ago, when SBS put the Ethnic Business Awards on air, people watched the awards and were fascinated by it. But at the same time, other migrants started watching it and said, 'I want to be like that migrant'. So, these are the people who also inspire me."

"If it wasn't for migrants, Australia wouldn't have had many things. EBAs allows the country to see successful migrants in Australia. This is how you fight all the bad things that they say about migration. Now we have the former Governor General, Michael Jeffery, as a judge. He announced publicly he wants to make an alumnus of that, and do it, right."

It is difficult to find successful migrant stories, but not because they are not there. Joseph explained that there are huge numbers of successful migrants in Australia who are often too shy or don't want the attention or don't want people to know how much they're making, or how much they are not making.

With the Ethnic Business Awards, entrants have to show audited evidence of their business success. To unearth the stories, Joseph has a team who are out talking with the communities - liaising with every business council, chamber of commerce, and community in Australia. The stories are profound and inspiring.

In terms of his future plans and potential retirement, Joseph is beginning to pick and choose to spend his time on things that he likes to do – EBAs among those things! The Ethnic Business Awards continues to grow as Joseph and his team enjoy unearthing amazing stories.

"I see how the Australian government invests billions of dollars a year on initiatives focussed on indigenous communities. I would like to encourage indigenous people to be in business and I thought the best way for me to do this was to create role models from the indigenous community, so I started the Indigenous in Business Award. This is the first one in the country, the only one. Nominations came streaming in and people look at the indigenous business leaders as role models."

"I asked the indigenous footballer Adam Goodes to be a judge of the awards on the indigenous category. He said, 'Of course, I will'. Adam loves it and says it's fascinating. Many people say, 'But the indigenous are not ethnic!' To them I say, 'We are all ethnic, because we are all different people. The indigenous were the first to migrate onto this continent! I thank them for looking after this land and making it welcome to us."

POLITICS AND INFLUENCE

Joseph is widely acknowledged as a thought-leader and expert on multiculturalism in Australia and has had profound influence on government policies at a local, state, and national level.

"Whether you like a policy or not, if you really believe in what you're doing, you can influence every policy. I can show you my influence on policies."

At this point Joseph grabs some documents from his office shelf and shows us the title, '*Productive Diversity in Business. Profiting from Australia's Multicultural Advantage – Discussion Paper*'.

"This is during Paul Keating's era in 1992."

He reads from the paper, "'The significant contribution of Joseph Assaf here and throughout this paper is greatly acknowledged'. My speech became a discussion paper and then a policy."

Joseph was a Director on the Constitutional Centenary Foundation. Joseph shows us several other influential policy documents on migration and immigration.

"If you are conscientious of society around you, and you want to influence, you want to make change, go ahead and do it. I believe in the benefit. This is the biggest thing that I do believe in, the benefit, the profit from multicultural.

There is often talk of wanting to reduce the number of migrants to Australia and people say it's because it's a burden on the government. I fight against this kind of rhetoric because migrants contribute more than what anyone can see."

SECRETS OF SUCCESS – RESILIENCE AND PERSEVERANCE

Joseph Assaf today frequently gives lectures and speaks at business leadership forums and social programs. When quizzed on his secrets of success and advice to new migrants coming into Australia, Joseph summed it up rather aptly in just a few words - Be resilient and persevere.

"In everything - whether it's your education, your business, growing your career as per your dreams, or whatever - the two most important qualities to have are resilience and perseverance. We all dream, and then try to make our dream a reality. Of course, in life you will immediately encounter obstacles, handicaps… so a lot of people would give up. But people who succeed don't give up. They keep going."

"I treat my business like my family, and I treat my family like my business. With your business, or your family, you don't take risks. Every business is like a child – the way you look after them, invest in them, treat them and so on is so important. So, I advise others to not take risks with your business. You also have to spend time with your family – there are not shortcuts. It is the same with your business."

We asked Joseph if he struggled with finding the time, and he responded quite philosophically.

"The only price that you pay for success is that your time is no longer yours. I could go and spend all my time with my grandchildren or my children. In my work there are hundreds of ethnic communities too with various events and activities across the year. You do what you can. The more you give, the more you receive. The more time you give to people, the more time you find you have. I believe that. There is something special about giving. If you see someone feeling sad and you go and you try to do something that makes them a little bit happier, that's giving."

Isn't that what life is all about?

NOTE

The information in this chapter is based on a series of interviews with Joseph Assaf AO conducted on January 15, 2019.

Chapter 2
Diem "Yim" Furggersberger

ABSTRACT

Ever since she was a child in Vietnam, Diem Kieu Yim Furggersberger's family instilled within her traditional values of discipline, resilience, and entrepreneurialism that would follow her in her successful career as CEO and Founder of Coco & Lucas' Kitchen, an Australian manufacturer of fresh, frozen, and homecooked meals for kids. At 7 years old, Diem overcame incredible odds to survive. With the fall of Saigon in 1975, Diem and her family risked everything and left all they knew behind, sailing miles across the ocean to seek refuge in Australia. In her new home, Diem would face many more challenges including culture shock and severe bullying. This chapter explores how the refugee experiences of a young girl shaped her to become the strong and resilient woman she is today – one who is guided by the compass of her family and cultural values to conquer challenges and strive for success.

DOI: 10.4018/978-1-6684-4986-8.ch002

Figure 1.

COCO & LUCAS - Australia's First Junior Foodies

World's first frozen meals for JUNIOR FOODIES®. Manufacturer of fresh & frozen ready meals, sauces, soups, cereal and toasted muesli, marinades, pastes, seasonings, premixes for value-added meats & smallgoods. Coco & Lucas' kitchen was born out of entrepreneur Diem Fuggerberger's vision to nourish fussy little eaters. Their product is a range of healthy, nutritious, home cooked frozen meals for kids.

Imagine losing everything not once, not twice but three times. Imagine being threatened, bullied and bereaved all before the age of seven years old. These kind of trying circumstances sound like the beginning of a tragic fairy tale, but it is the true story of Diem Kieu "Yimmy" Fuggersberger, CEO and co-founder of Berger Ingredients and creator of the Coco & Lucas' Kitchen brand, who overcame incredible odds to survive and thrive.

Looking at the elegant woman in a tailored black dress, Louis Vuitton belt, huge diamond ring and expensive heels who came to meet us for the interview, it is difficult to imagine any struggles in her life. But when she begins to tell her story - that most of us in Australia would not know about or understand – we realise she is a true heroine winning against all odds.

CHILDHOOD IN VIETNAM

Diem's family hails from Vietnam, inheriting the traditional and cultural traits valued by many Asians - hard-working, family focused, practical and intelligent. But the traits that truly set her family apart are their spirit of survival, resilience and entrepreneurism.

Diem's grandfather was a businessman with two wives – typical at the time - and an impressive 14 children to support. He had nine children with his first wife and five with his second wife, Diem's grandmother from Guangzhou, China. He managed this daunting task of caring for his family without the benefit of a formal education. However, he was streetwise and strong - characteristics that Diem would inherit.

Diem's Grandfather passed away when her Mother was only 3 years old, finances were very tight for the family. They lived a hand-to-mouth existence in the early days. Her Grandmother could not afford to keep her children fed and housed and they grew increasingly desperate. At one stage, they even briefly considered adopting out her brother because they could not afford to look after him. Diem's mother was horrified at the thought of being separated and dropped out of school to save money and keep the family together.

Like so many families today, her mother went to work for her family, so her grandmother did most of the mothering. Her grandmother, who called her 'Yimmy', essentially raised her and Diem confesses was more of a mother figure to Diem than her own was.

Her mother owned a butcher's stall at Bac Lieu Main Markets, earning around four nuggets of gold a day. Her father ran a tailor business with 20 employees and typically earned seven nuggets a day. Diem was one of six children in this well-to-do family, by comparison to others. Her parents invested their money wisely, and the family had one of the grandest houses in the province of Bac Lieu, a source of envy among their peers despite the family's generosity.

Her grandmother raised her with a strong civic mindedness; strong values, traditional Buddhist values of giving back to society where you can.

"For every ten dollars I earn Yimmy, we give back three. The rest is for the family," Diem recalls her grandmother often saying.

"This money is not my own to keep, and it is not a gift from me. It is a gift and duty from our family and only the remainder belongs to the family. To be a good person, you always have to give back to society."

These values would follow Diem into her business. Personal sacrifice for the good of others was a key value in binding her family to survive the trials ahead.

The other defining trait was fearlessness. Diem traces her lack of fear back to one day when she was very young and fell into a pond. She cried out for her family to help but nobody heard her, and she was forced to save herself. Something awakened in her that day as she reeled herself to safety.

It was a tumultuous time. After the fall of Saigon in 1975, the realities of war came to impact people's lives. Diem does not dwell on this part of her history, saying only that she and her family were forced to escape with very little time to prepare or plan.

REFUGEES

Diem's parents mulled over the decision to escape by boat for at least six months. It was a big gamble as none of the children could really swim and the risk of the boat sinking was very real. However, the conditions in Vietnam were unbearable and Diem believes in hindsight the decision was right at the time.

Diem recalls the dislocation with sorrow. She said a short and tearful goodbye to her beloved grandmother, her dog named KY and her life as she knew it. She was confused and sad to lose her emotional rock and friend, her grandmother, without fully comprehending why or what would come next.

For the regime officers to turn a blind eye and allow their escape from Vietnam, her family had to give them their beloved house, valued at more than 1,000 gold nuggets.

To escape from Hai Phong, a major port city in North Eastern Vietnam, they also had to pay a boat operator the sum of five gold nuggets per person. There were 15 members in their family's group, which included three cousins and three employees who had worked for Diem's parents for many years. The group left with only what they could carry with them, a few pieces of clothing.

Destined for Indonesia, their boat '0010', was a 25-metre-long wooden craft with just two toilets to accommodate 504 people. Although they had no privacy, she did have a tiny space to sit for the long journey. Perhaps inevitably, it wasn't long before disaster struck.

Malay pirates raided the boat on the second day at sea. Armed with guns and machetes, they began to board the boat. Amidst the chaos, Diem's mother assessed the situation quickly, calmly and rationally despite the fear. She had heard about the dangers of the Malay pirates from other refugees who had travelled the escape route by sea before her. She knew there was a real risk of rape and abduction for her young girls. She quickly cut all the girl's hair to look like boys.

The pirates were after gold, diamonds, gems and slaves.

They discovered a passenger on board who had gold teeth and were going to rip them out. Other passengers intervened to stop them and gave the pirates the gold they had sewn into the hems of their belts and clothes. Fortunately, the pirates left as quickly as they came, leaving the passengers rattled but largely unscathed.

A thunderstorm rolled in – perhaps why the pirates left so quickly. The sea swelled into enormous walls of dark green, bigger than a house, and terrified her. The boat almost capsized many times. To this day, Diem is afraid of water of any kind, especially open sea.

A larger boat drew closer in the storm and rescued the passengers of 0010 from the treacherous waters. Diem recalls being carried on the shoulders of her brother up the side of it.

"My first loss was my beloved grandmother and my precious dog. Then I lost everything to the pirates. Although we suffered enormous losses - both personally and financially – there is no point dwelling on the past. You shouldn't hold on to hate; you have to let that go. I believe in forgiving and not holding grudges as it will lift a huge heaviness off your shoulders," remarked Diem.

After arriving in Indonesia, Diem and her family were transported to a refugee camp to await visas to a safe country. The accommodation, one long house for five or six families, was better than the boat according to Diem. For privacy, the refugees erected makeshift walls using string and curtains. There were home cooked meals, a joy particular to her culture. However, the situation was still far from ideal, with malaria claiming the lives of many refugees – particularly children.

Diem learned to play on her own.

She also learned not to complain or beg for things. She passed the time by playing with branches, leaves, sticks and stones she found around camp. To this day, she remains connected to nature and loves nature.

The family's visa was approved, and they were transported to Singapore, which Diem describes as, "an extremely good place with good people."

This paradise of polite civilisation amazed her. It was the first time she had seen a shopping centre in her life. Charity workers came and helped her family.

"Singapore's laws are very strict. You are not allowed to steal. Behave with honour at all times," a female charity worker warned.

Behaving with honour is something that Diem really took to heart.

"In order to succeed in life, you have to be honourable. You can fail but be honourable in failing. I believe you should keep your promises, keep your words. This is a very major thing and I am very firm on it. I like to be an honest, open book. It made me who I am today. Keeping your word can be difficult, but you have to do it always."

On 20 June 1980, Diem and her family were accepted to live in Wollongong, NSW in the suburb of Broadmeadow.

"I felt that because I was now in a Caucasian world, I was safe," she laughs.

AUSTRALIA

This was her first time out of an Asian society, and the culture shock she felt was enormous. She spoke no English and they now had no contact with any other refugee families. The food was strange to her. People ate cereal and not congee. She remembers eating her first sausage sizzle with a smile.

After a month in Broadmeadow, the family was moved into a house in Punchbowl, Sydney with 15 other families under the one roof. It was a three-bedroom home. The only rooms not in use for sleeping were the bathroom and the kitchen.

"Even the garage was made use of as sleeping quarters!"

Although today Sydney is Australia's most multicultural city, at the time the arrival of the Chinese refugees was considered such an anomaly they ended up being featured in the newspaper back in 1984. The Salvation Army and St Vincent de Paul Society furnished the house and helped the family get used to the Australian lifestyle with practical help and advice.

To this day, Diem is grateful for their help and supports the two charities.

Unfortunately, this kind of kindness and charity doesn't always extend to school playground. Her fellow students at school taunted her relentlessly for being different. 'Ching-Chong' and other racial slurs were hurled at her daily by all her classmates. Weighing just 16 kg in Year 4, she was a tiny and vulnerable victim.

"How can you tell the teacher you were being beaten up when you can't even speak English? I realised I had to be fearless and pretend I was not scared," Diem said.

Despite her struggles at school, not all things were bad. Her home life was a refuge, with a loving father who taught her to work and study diligently and "take responsibility fully into your heart as if it's the last thing you would ever do." Her father taught values like humility, persistence, thirst for knowledge, respect for elders, respect for learning, and not to rely on handouts. Diem says he taught her, "to have good manners and always be warm hearted so the door will open wider for you."

As she grew a little older, she began helping her mother run the family restaurant including everything from front of house serving and cashier/accounting to back of house cleaning and preparing wontons.

Running back and forth between front and back of house on any given day taught her multi-tasking and fulfilling different customer demands. Her mother taught her to treat every customer like family, even the most difficult ones as they can become loyal customers.

Even though she was very young, she wanted to work more and begged her family to allow her to take another job selling various items at the markets on Sunday. They allowed her, and she began working 12 hours on a Sunday for $50; a fortune for someone so young, earning her place for the family. She took the train to and from the markets alone and befriended some older girls to keep her safe. She had already learned the vital lesson from her schoolyard bullies, never be alone.

Diem described other roles she had as a young person. These included a call centre, which she says taught her time zones and provided a foray into cross border business, and a telecommunications PA, which taught her time management, organisation, KPIs and business goals. This corporate discipline provided strong scaffolding for her own business in the early days, where many other nascent companies falter and fall.

Diem met her husband Werner Fuggersberger and decided to marry him after just two dates.

"I don't believe in overanalysing when it feels right," she explained simply.

The couple went on to have two children, and her husband proved to be financially successful and loving. Her husband's income was enough that she didn't have to work. The new family had a brief period of happiness and security.

However, it was amidst this happy interlude that tragedy struck once again.

DOWN, BUT NEVER OUT

The year was 2008 and the global financial crisis was about to hit the world, inflicting bankruptcy on her husband and wreaking havoc on their peaceful lives.

By 2009, Diem and her husband owed hundreds of thousands of dollars and they were bankrupt. They lost their family home. That same year, both her father and father-in-law passed away.

Once again, she experienced losing everything.

Swallowing her pride, she had to go to her family and mentor to borrow money. Her mother took a second mortgage on her house to help them. A loyal former employee of their old business quit his job to join her in business, taking a 30 per cent pay cut and mortgaging his own house to contribute capital.

"[The loyal former employee] never asked for anything in return as he trusted and had faith us. People you give to will give back. I think it's important to always give back. Always give back and always be kind, someone else will pull you up and help you on your way. I believe in good karma," said Diem.

With this capital and even more debt, she and her husband established 'Berger Ingredients Pty Ltd', a dry foods and sauces company. It was a bold move at a very difficult time, but it was a leap of faith.

"Food has been a major part of my ancestry, and my most precious family memories. Both my grandmother and mother have instilled in me a love of good food; the creation of unique flavours; and the joy of sharing a home prepared meal with family and friends. Perhaps it was inevitable that my husband and I would build a food business that incorporates our family values and love of the science of flavour creation," said Diem.

This fearless refugee found herself again starting from scratch – but not for long.

COCO & LUCAS' KITCHEN

Berger experienced early success, and Diem wanted to push further. The brand expanded into wet food, culminating into her own project, 'Coco & Lucas' Kitchen'.

"The namesakes and inspiration behind the Coco & Lucas range are my daughter Coco and nephew Lucas, who remind me of the importance of nourishing our children," explained Diem.

Coco & Lucas' Kitchen came about after extensive research on Diem's part, which included analysing market gaps to find her niche, better understanding parents' needs and children's preferences.

She researched flavours and found that 3-12-year-olds did not appreciate bland baby food, but they also did not enjoy strong or spicy adult flavours, so she went with something in between.

Diem realised that it was rare to find correct portion sizes for this age group both at restaurants and on supermarket shelves. She aimed to deliver a child size portion but, because it is her tradition, she always gives a little bit more.

"It is dishonourable to cheat your customer. I like to be generous with food," she explains.

For her pricing strategy, she took inspiration from Steve Jobs of Apple, who stressed that a product must be the right price and convenient. Diem realised that parents don't typically want to spend more than $5.00 per meal for their children so she set her prices accordingly.

She delivers on convenience by providing customers with multiple ways to heat/ cook her products, with easy-to-read instructions.

"I created these meals to help families like my own, who want quality, home-cooked meals, but don't always have the time to create them," said Diem.

"Today's consumer wants all the information and all the different ways to cook something and the story behind the product. Savvy parents are now watching MasterChef and becoming interested in food. They tend to know more about good nutrition and good produce. One expression is, 'You eat with your eyes,'" she said.

Diem's packaging is full of quirky embellishments to tease and delight the eyes.

Diem listens to her customers, with her first and most important customers being family. Diem realised that parents want easy food and the less complaints from kids the better.

"Coco is a fussy, discerning eater and has high standards for how her food should be presented on her plate. When Lucas was born, he had a lot of problems with different allergies. It was a battle to cook food that would not cause him to be sick and eating out was very difficult. This was the inspiration for me to spend nearly a year developing a range of recipes, that would be tasty for the discerning kids like Coco and allergen free for children like Lucas. But most importantly, I wanted the food to be nutritiously balanced in terms of protein, carbohydrates and vegetables," continued Diem.

Coco & Lucas' Kitchen products contain all-natural foods, with no chemicals, and are completely lactose and gluten free.

"Ever since I launched my kids' range, parents have been asking me to create something for them. I wanted to bring something new and exciting to the family table. I worked hard to create delicious, plant-based tastes, textures and smells," said Diem.

In July 2019, Diem launched a range of meat-free, plant-based ready meals for adults, now available in nearly 1,000 Woolworths stores nationally. They taste like meat, smell like meat and have a meaty texture.

"It is ironic that I am a Butcher's Daughter and I am making food for vegans, vegetarians and flexitarians!" laughs Diem.

"Although I am not a full-time vegan or vegetarian, I do believe in swapping our diets for a day or two because of what this would mean for the environment, our health, non-animal cruelty, greenhouse gas and energy. It would make a huge difference! Global warming starts with oneself and it is quite simple to change our actions with baby steps."

HONOURABLE IS PROFITABLE

Diem has adopted Australia and, with that, is fiercely proud that 90 per cent of her products are sourced locally and manufactured in Sydney. She says she could halve her costs if she went overseas and used other ingredients, but this would not be contributing to the Australian economy. It is not "as if it's the last thing you would ever do," she explained, echoing the words of her father.

"It is crucial to produce all our products within Australia. I wanted to build a brand that is Australian owned, sourced and made. I would like to employ Australians as this great country has done so much for my family and me.

All her packaging is biodegradable, which is more expensive too.

"I could have gone another route, but I would like to know that my contribution does not poison the world for over a hundred years in the form of plastic drowning our oceans," said Diem.

Her moral principles flow into her food. Her products have a high nutrition rating and they have been environmentally conscious in their company's growth. Being responsible, caring, sustainable and honourable has led to being reputable and that has led to demand and profitability.

MARKETING AND GROWTH

Perhaps a little surprisingly for such a big brand, Diem manages her marketing herself. She explained this choice. When she spoke to some advertising agencies, she was not impressed and felt she knew more about how to market her brand than they did as they knew little about her customers.

"You need to do deep research to understand your customer's needs. You must be persistent and listen," said Diem.

She also believes in sharing her story from her heart as 'everyone wants to hear a story that is real and raw', as she puts it.

She regularly checks Google Analytics to stay abreast of her consumers and diet trends. She also travels abroad twice yearly to gain fresh inspiration that could be adopted for the Australian market.

The majority of Diem's business comes from word of mouth and referrals, but social media has also played a strong role – particularly internationally - through professional social media platform LinkedIn. Diem regularly reads the analytics of her LinkedIn page, and places importance on Instagram and Facebook also.

She has focused on her own story and identity as a part of her brand, which has worked well for her.

The industry has taken notice of her brand's success too. After a few years of success, she was approached by several different partners - all wanting to launch her brand overseas.

Instead of taking the first or second offer, she did her own research. When listening to her describe her process of vetting the offers, it strikes me that she sounds like a President meeting another Head of State for a politically sensitive meeting! It is clear that Diem is strategically and tactically prepared before every meeting.

"Always go to the boss and don't deal with agents. It is very important to work with Middle Management of your clients. You have to know who you are talking to. I know before any meeting who I am connecting with, their net worth and their infrastructure worth to my products," she said.

This careful planning and research allowed her to pair with a strong overseas distributor that, whilst not as flashy or as well recognised here in Australia, has a logistical arm which is a powerful asset to Diem for future expansion.

"My father was a highly trained, well-known tailor and knew how to measure clothes exactly. Perhaps that's why I always measure everything carefully - including risk, my products... everything!"

Her products, which inhabit a position on the most expensive real estate in the retail world - a shelf at a chain store, fit exactly five packets wide and two deep, maximising sales.

MANAGEMENT AND REPUTATION

When we start to discuss her management style and human resourcing philosophy, Diem explains the value of reputation – both for herself and for her staff.

"I hire my staff for their good hearts and 'can-do' attitude. I always look for honourable people. I empower them and turn their weaknesses into strengths. My staff are my biggest investment," said Diem.

"My staff get paid before me even if I haven't taken a salary for years. I do not try to hold onto them if they decide they need to fly to go to big corporations. I am happy for them to do that as it means I have trained them well.'"

Diem's staff loyalty is high as is their efforts in helping the company run. Her mentors taught her everyone must eat, and for Diem this means her staff's job security and happiness are key.

Diem strongly believes in being hands on. Whilst she has seven departments with trusted and empowered managers who she says are key for "owning and being responsible for their departments", but she still likes to walk through the kitchen and research and development.

One of her strengths is her innovation. In her mind, it is key to her success. She recognises opportunities when she can bring a product to market quicker and in a more affordable manner but realises when her competitors can too.

RECIPE FOR SUCCESS

Coco & Lucas' Kitchen owns the '3-12 year' category – named Junior Foodies. She creates and produces for large, highly visible brand names and celebrity labels.

Along the way she has picked up awards like nuggets of gold, including World Food Innovation; PETA Vegan Food Awards; Ethnic Business Awards; APAC INSIDER Business Excellence Awards; Optus Businesswoman of the Year and a few others.

Diem says her strong values originate from both her family and her religion have kept her going through her troubles. She explains she would pray and pray and pray when on that tiny boat and still prays to this day.

She also believes in having a hobby. Hers is fashion and art, not surprisingly since her father was a tailor.

She tries to instil her values in her children, believing that studying STEM subjects (science technology engineering and mathematics) is not negotiable.

In the years since restarting business with her husband, her businesses have had some setbacks but fortunately there have been none of the tidal waves of tragedy of her past.

"When tragedy happens, have a little cry then fix it. Be honourable, kind and courteous, but be extremely firm and fearless," said Diem.

Fearless Diem doesn't allow herself to be bullied anymore. She even swims now! Bronte Beach is her favourite. No water or challenge will hold her back.

NOTE

The information in this chapter is based on a series of interviews with Diem "Yim" Furggersberger conducted on January 3, 2019.

Chapter 3
Rustom Kanga

ABSTRACT

Taking risks and having patience – this was the ethos that would propel Rustom Kanga into unparalleled success as the CEO and Founder of iOmniscient, a global technology leader in automated intelligent video solutions. Rustom established iOmniscient in 2001 after seeing a gap in the market for artificial intelligence-driven security analytic technology. In his journey to grow the company and develop commercially viable products, Rustom faced many obstacles, namely in getting venture capitalists to fund his business selling a completely new innovation that was first on the market. Through hard work and discipline, however, Rustom grew iOmniscient, and now it is the longest standing AI security systems organisation in the world, operating across 12 countries. This chapter explores how Rustom persevered to grow his start-up into a multiple-award-winning organisation and the valuable lessons he learnt along the way.

DOI: 10.4018/978-1-6684-4986-8.ch003

Figure 1.

TECHNOLOGY LEADER IN AUTOMATED INTELLIGENT VIDEO SOLUTIONS

Artificial Intelligence For Autonomous Systems

iOmniscient has been a leader in using Artificial Intelligence technologies to create solutions for a host of industries- from Oil and Gas to Smart Cities. They have pioneered AI techniques that have created a new paradigm to analyse data from crowded and complex environments and provide the user with real time responses. Artificial intelligence enables our systems to have high levels of accuracy and low false alarm rates even in difficult situations. Bringing together a number of different video, sound and smell analytics technologies, iOmniscient systems can automatically find the nearest responder with information on where to go and what to do. This can reduce response times significantly which is important for Mission Critical Applications. Such systems enhance your productivity and increase the return on your investment.

COMPUTER VISION

iOmniscient is the only provider of intelligent systems that can simultaneously perform Behaviour Analysis (for a multitude of behaviours) and Recognition (Face and License Plate Recognition) in crowded and complex environments. The Face Recognition system can recognize faces at a significantly lower resolution than any other system. Our intelligent systems can recognise license plates for 130 countries. These capabilities are modular and can be combined to solve complex problems.

ENABLING DATA ANALYTICS

All Big Data analysis is based on "text data". Their systems can convert everything that is seen, heard or smelt by the system into Meaningful, Multimedia Metadata (MMM) – which is essentially text. This enables very fast analysis of data for forensic investigations. As the system is able to eliminate noise which is usually 90% of the data, it helps to speed up the search and analysis even further.

EDUCATION, WORK & LIFE

Dr Rustom Kanga was born in Mumbai (formerly Bombay), India. He studied chemical engineering at IIT (Indian Institute of Technology) Bombay. Upon graduating, he went on to earn a master's degree in management at the London School of Economics; then whilst working for ESSO, and then British Petroleum he completed his PHD at the London School of Economics.

Rustom credits his extensive education as a great asset, not necessarily for the specific skills he gained through it, but for the understanding of how to solve problems and act with confidence.

At ESSO, Rustom was exposed to some very early and primitive computers for process control and learned some skills that were to become valuable to him throughout his career.

He met and married Dr Marlene Kanga who, like her husband, has profound knowledge and similar interests in high-tech artificially intelligent innovations.

After completing his education, Rustom worked in chemical engineering positions at ExxonMobil (ESSO) and British Petroleum in England before making the move to Sydney in November 1977.

The search for work began. Despite Rustom's lack of training in computer science, due to computer science not being taught in the colleges at the time, Rustom was taken on by the computer technology company, Computer Sciences of Australia (CSA). Rustom attributes their hiring of him to his early computer exposure whilst working at ESSO.

Within a few months, he joined another company called Digital Equipment Corporation (DEC), which was to be his employer from 1977 till 2000. It was DEC that gave him challenges and varied his roles. DEC was purchased by Compaq in 1998.

During this time, Rustom helped design new technologies, new business models and start several new ventures, one of which became multi-billion-dollar business. Much of the work he did was within international operation, giving him insight to the challenges associated with such activity.

The hands-off approach of his bosses at DEC and Compaq allowed him to do what he wanted, particularly in regard to creating new business ventures for the company. By 1998 Rustom was the vice president of a specialised group called Computer Special Systems that built specialised computers such as those for submarines and fighter jets and now had a vastly stronger understanding of computer technologies. In 2000, he learned that the company was going to be acquired by Hewlett Packard. This was to prove a turning point in his professional career.

FOUNDING IOMNISCIENT – PATIENCE AND PERSEVERANCE

The seed for Rustom's company, iOmniscient, was really already planted in 1977 during his time at DEC, where he began a proper understanding of computer technology. However, when he learned of the acquisition by Hewlett Packard, Rustom took the opportunity to begin the iOmniscient journey in earnest.

Rustom, a fellow former employee of DEC Ivy Li, and two other employees decided to leave the company and band together to push the boundaries of computer technology with their own venture.

Rustom explains, "I had a belief that we could use artificial intelligence technologies which up to that time had been used in very limited ways, for commercial applications. I was at a point in my life when I did not just want to do a job for the sake of doing a job. Developing this new technology soon became quite a passion for me."

Although his wife possessed natural leadership capabilities from an early age, Rustom's interest for entrepreneurship stemmed from him wanting to branch out and do something different and impactful. The support of his wife made it easier for Rustom to balance work and life. Beginning the business required a huge time investment as well as risks and challenges.

"It requires one's focus 24 hours a day seven days a week. This does take a toll on one's health, one's family and on friendships. In all these types of ventures, family support is extremely crucial. We were fortunate that I had the support of my wife who runs her own independent business. Without her ongoing support in many dimensions, I don't think this venture could have got off the ground."

Like all smart entrepreneurs, Rustom made sure to analyse all of the strengths and weaknesses of not just himself but the small team he founded iOmniscient with – they were a strong team together. Partner and co-founder Ivy Li had great technical prowess stemming from having a degree in computer science. Dr Marlene Kanga later joined as a Director on the board.

Originally, the four were working on a mobile payment system like PayPal but, due to the unfortunate timing of the dot-com burst, they put this idea to rest. Rustom and the team worked on their idea for about a year before two members left, leaving Rustom and Ivy Li to persevere.

They moved on to the idea of artificial intelligence with iOmniscient in 2001. The company began with a single product for the Security Industry.

He saw a gap in the market for artificial intelligence driven security analytic technology being sold on a commercial level and realised he could take advantage of research and development grants provided by the Australian government, as well as tax offsets.

Despite this, Rustom laments that Government support for entrepreneurs in Australia lags behind countries such as the US, Singapore and Korea. These other governments will purchase a start-up's product/service, attempt to implement it and if it works, the start-up then has a reference for the validity of their product or service. This was not available to iOmniscient, making it hard for them to address the challenge of their technology being recognised.

They faced difficulty in getting venture capitalists to fund their business as they were reluctant to invest without being able to foresee their success factors. Most of them assumed that their vision and goals were unrealistic and unachievable as most of the world were not familiar with the sort of solutions iOmniscient were preparing to provide. The company struggled to find it's footing as there was commercial wariness of the technology with most people viewing artificial intelligence as some kind of 'magic'.

Rustom explains, "Most [Venture Capitalists] thought that what we were proposing was impossible to do. So, we were not able to raise any money. In retrospect that was blessing in disguise and one of THE BEST things that happened on our journey because when the Global Financial Crisis hit, many of our competitors were wiped out by their own VCs who pulled the plug on them. As we did not have VC funding, we were immune from their knee jerk reactions."

"Today we are essentially customer funded which means we are profitable. We also found that VCs have a short attention span. They expect to exit within a few years. This means that VC funded companies have to develop their technology very quickly, make a few sales and get out. This meant that our competitors were forever building very limited technology. Their investors just did not have the patience to build the type of advanced products that may take five to seven years to build and perfect. This too worked in our favour in that today our product capability is way ahead of anything else that is available in the market."

It was a difficult and prolonged process getting the first few contractors to invest as they were trying to introduce a completely different innovation and first in the market. Although they were praised for their ideas, most contractors did not go through with their proposals as the risks involved were foreign to them. The venture took around three or four years to become recognised as a serious and innovative company. It took eight years to break even.

"We had to educate the market both on what was possible with the technology as well as the limitations of the technology. Being pioneers with a totally new concept was not easy as we had to create the market. In the early days people would often say 'your concepts are fantastic' and that is where it used to end. Many were too conservative to actually try it out. It took us many years to establish our brand and get people to trust that the technology would actually help them. I believe all entrepreneurs in such a situation need patience and perseverance."

They had faith in the technology and believed with further development that industries would come to understand and desire what they were working on. Luckily for iOmniscient this is just what happened.

MAKING A MARK

Heightened interest in national security following the September 11 attacks propelled iOmniscient forward. The technology existed before iOmniscient's inception in 2001 but did not find commercial life until after September 11.

In 2003, iOmniscient was named the winner of the government funded 'Secrets of Australian IT Innovation' award. The following year they won the prestigious 'International Fire and Security Exhibition and Conference' (IFSEC) award for 'Best Product in Intelligence Surveillance', which is presented by the British Security Industry Association. The IFSEC is one of the largest security shows in Europe and offered a great deal of exposure to many industries that could utilise iOmniscient's technology. iOmniscient has won awards all over the world including "Best CCTV System of the Year" for its Face Recognition in a Crowd and the Global Security Challenge for Crowded Scenes.

Following the recognition, sales came in quite strong with the Royal Ontario Art Gallery in Canada being one of the first large purchasers using their systems to protect paintings. This further stimulated interest in iOmniscient from many other businesses and governments leading it to be one of the most respected suppliers of intelligent video analytic technologies. Their success has allowed them to partner with lucrative organisations such as, Intel, Microsoft and Huawei.

Today, they benefit from great public relations from newspaper and industry journal coverage when they introduce a new development or move into a new country. The company is now one of the most respected developers of artificial intelligence security solutions and is running 17 years strong.

The company has solved numerous problems for more than 30 enterprises including Retail, Health and Banking.

Rustom Kanga always had the intention for the iOmniscient to be a global business and the way it operates is indicative of this. Rustom operates out of Sydney dealing with any issues that may arise for half of the time and then when he's asleep Ivy Li manages the business from Canada of which she is a native. They also have support teams set up in Singapore and Dubai to ensure that there is always a team to handle any customer service issues that tend to arise when dealing with any software technology. The business operates in 12 countries, five of which it has legal entities in. There are a further 55 countries in which they have resellers and distributors of their technology. iOmniscient has a noteworthy mark in the Middle East, Asia and North America. Rustom aims to make his mark across other markets. They offer clients 24×7 assistance wherever they are in the world in multiple languages.

iOmniscient's success owes to the combination of careful, analytical planning and proper implementation of Artificial Intelligence under a skilful team.

Rustom explained, "A key critical success factor for us has been the architecture that we developed from the beginning aimed at large complex environments."

"From the start, our systems have been designed to be totally open, totally distributed and totally scalable. The system can handle any mode of transmission, any type of cameras, any location of storage and so on. It does not matter whether the client system is in a control room or on a wireless PDA. It does not matter whether the network is local or worldwide. The system is designed to cope. This has been a major strength of ours for the larger sophisticated customers."

ABOUT THE COMPANY

iOmniscient is an Australian, private limited liability company. Dr Rustom Kanga is Chief Executive Officer, Ivy Li is Managing Director and Pathy Pathmanaban is Chief Operational Officer. Dr Rustom Kanga's wife, Dr Marlene Kanga, is a Director on the board and Ji Hao Lou is a project manager. There are overall 51-200 employees spread across 12 countries. Of those 12 they have legal entities in five countries.

iOmniscient is a developer and provider of security video analytic technologies/surveillance solutions as well as, and including, the use of artificial intelligence for autonomous systems. They have created an artificial intelligence platform, which consists of modular, technology building blocks allowing iOmniscient to combine these parts in a multitude of ways, providing what they describe as "multi-sensory solutions" for the purchaser.

The artificial intelligence is achieved through a hybrid of heuristic, neural network and deep learning algorithms, which is the unique selling point of iOmniscient's technology. The main aspect of what these systems do in basic terms is offer solutions to security issues through allowing surveillance cameras to recognise faces, analyse behaviours, smells and sounds; and subsequently inform the closest relevant authorities of any issues that have occurred or could occur in real time.

The technology can be reworked to handle tasks such as analysing meta-data. Another significant way the venture operates is to create what are called smart cities. Using the same technology cameras monitor city requirements from traffic lights and public transport to clean up of overflowing bins, allowing for greater efficiency. It is these possibilities that make the venture such a diverse SME.

The main vision behind the inception of iOmniscient, is to be an international solution to modern security concerns.

The world's first remunerating artificial intelligence system was made under Rustom's leadership, remunerating artificial intelligence system at digital corporation system.

iOmniscient targets companies, governments and institutions in over 30 industries. It does not have a set list of products a business can purchase but rather a series of building blocks that the purchaser can choose to include in their product. These are parts such as automated response, multilingual licence plate recognition, data analytics, behaviour analytics in crowds etc. This allows for a flexible product that can be utilised by law enforcement to healthcare to retail and many more industries. The cost of the product varies on what capabilities the purchaser requires and the scope of the operation it needs to be applied to.

As an innovator in Video Analytics with nearly 18 years of experience, iOmniscient is the globally the longest standing autonomous Analytics organisation.

The organisation has broadened its officially exhaustive Analytics capacity to give an Artificial Intelligence based Multi-Sensory Analytics Platform that incorporates human senses, such as, hearing and smelling and in video graphics to mimic human behaviour. Businesses and governments in over fifty countries nationwide have made use of their technology. They have over 40 international patents, which gives them an upper hand in expertise in utilising cases that exceed expectations in great detail by performing tasks no other businesses can do.

Their frameworks are intended to take into account various applications like from basic interruption and tallying frameworks to one of a kind question discovery in a group, multi-lingual License Plate Recognition, world's first non-co-agent Facial Recognition for Crowded Scenes, Detection of uncommon behavioural patterns exhibited by individuals and numerous other technological solutions.

The organisation is an innovation pioneer in the worldwide market and has survived testing periods including the Global Financial Crisis.

While the main purpose of iOmniscient technology is security, it can be applied to a myriad of industries. As the company stands now it has deployed their technologies in over 30 industries including law & order, healthcare, retail and financial services. Asides from security their technologies have been implemented in areas such as railway transportation, allowing high-speed trains to automatically slowdown and stop where cameras detect people in danger on the rails, where a human conductor could not observe and react to the danger in ample time.

iOmniscient have also been able to help create Smart Cities such as in Singapore where the technology can be used to reduce crime, increase cleanliness and better handle traffic. This broad target market presents great opportunity for iOmniscient particularly with their goal to be an international business, although it also increases the likelihood of competition.

COMPETITORS, REVENUE AND GROWTH

Despite being the first establishment of its kind in the world, iOmniscient now faces competition from AI companies that are constantly entering the market or getting better. Today, there are numerous competitors and the market is increasingly fragmented. The company has 38 employees, a small number compared to its competitors. Despite this, iOmniscient remains unthreatened as Rustom believes their achievements are well above sufficient. He believes, "Size is less important than sophistication."

Among their many accolades, the organisation earns an impressive $1,552,200 per employee and generates around $5.8 million in revenue. However, this does not mean that they will rest on their laurels. He understands an organisation need to keep improving and innovating their products and services as technology becomes more advanced with oncoming years. In addition to that, finding more feasible solutions to existing problems and coming up with solutions that are better than their lasts. He gives a small overview about how businesses should always work.

"In a competitive world you can never sit back and let the business run on autopilot. You have to continuously improve your products and build new customer relationships. I suppose we are not burning money with no return which one tends to do in the early years but at the same time one should not assume that any business can stop building. If you are not building, you are going backward."

This competitive strategy is practical and smart and can be implemented for all kinds of organisations. Furthermore, it indicates that they have a coherent idea about their strengths and weaknesses, what they need to focus on and prioritise. That is, to be versatile, innovative, continuously making positive changes and problem solving using their field of expertise.

Rustom does not view the expansion of the company to be a priority and believes that if they are satisfied with their rate of expansion and do not revolve around development accordingly and it is a bonus to not be subsidised by Venture Capitals. They centre more around having the best innovation and on giving great administration.

They were able to expand their services to countries like Dubai, UAE and Cairo, Egypt in 2010, Kuala Lumpur, Malaysia in 2012 and even partner with Dell in 2017.

What makes their organisation unique from others is their expertise and advancements in artificial intelligence. Therefore, focusing more on R&D rather growth had and continue to give them an advantage over their competitors in staying ahead. They prefer not to view their competitors as rivals, but rather focus on enhancing their existing expertise by thoroughly investing on research and development.

SMART SOLUTIONS THAT GUARANTEED SUCCESS

iOmniscient provides their services and solutions to a vast range of organisations and audiences that are made use of in various combinations. The technology can adjust to make any city 'smart'. Their innovations come in three variations, that are products, applications and industry solutions.

IQ-series is a commonly used product by iOmniscient. It offers Face Recognition and License Plate Recognition. Acknowledgment includes catching the face or tag in a group and coordinating it with a database to distinguish the person of particular vehicle. iOmniscient's Face Recognition is the world's first framework which can work in swarmed scenes to give a 'many-to-numerous' match. The tag Recognition is multilingual and bolsters more than 120 nations.

Detection and Identification had already worked independently as they required distinctive kinds of cameras and camera situation. iOmniscient's iQ-Hawk and iQ-Driver Match unite the two abilities on a similar camera to work at the same time and give huge operational adaptability and lessen the expenses of capacity and system data transfer capacity.

The second is applications. This organisation is the overall pioneer in Video Analytics with the most complete arrangement of location, recognisable proof and merging frameworks. The frameworks are globally protected to at the same time play out different identifications in swarmed and complex scenes. All iOmniscient frameworks are furnished with a Nuisance Alarm Minimisation System (NAMS) to decrease false alerts. These adaptations have enhanced security systems and enabled working in these areas less difficult and more efficient.

Some plausible examples would be intruder detection, behaviour analysis, slip & fall detection and more smart services. For instance, in case of accidents, it helps identify the severity of the incident and send information back to a control room where workers can analyse whether extra help and at the same time if the severity of the incident is low, the system is smart enough to solve it on its own, as a result, saving a lot of time for workers.

Lastly, they provide industry solutions. This falls under a huge range of services that best fit each industry. iOmniscient delivers comprehensive and concise industry solutions for more than 30 one-of-a-kind industry prerequisites. Every association has numerous partners and different offices, for example, security, wellbeing, activities and promoting. Every industry arrangement is a far-reaching arrangement of utilisation that can satisfy every office's particular prerequisites while working as a solitary coordinated framework guarantee prompt disposition of data at any instance it is required.

All these solutions help make a city more secure and aid in solving numerous problems such as crime detection and prevention with their smart technology which were otherwise difficult to depict with just manpower. Others include, finding lost children through facial recognition system or enhancing security regarding privacy issues. Privacy concerns among people regarding social media algorithms and breaches have been growing over the years. iOmniscient has taken notice of that and provides a feature that their video investigation framework is planned in a way than secures protection of people by redacting faces, that just enabling access to them with an uncommon key that can be utilised by approved personals in crisis circumstances.

They are all important requirement for any city to become smart or advanced. Therefore, there is no doubt about the obvious success of the business. In addition to that, they also operate by using cost effective measures such as, the Face Recognition system is intended to give exact outcomes with a picture determination that gives just 22 pixels between the eyes. For covering vast territories this implies one low resolution camera can cover the work of five to ten cameras required by others. The Smart Compression can decrease stockpiling and transfer speed necessities by a ninth. They aim to get the most done at the lowest costs.

FUTURE PLANS, PHILOSOPHY AND ADVICE

Rustom continues to search for more opportunities where their technology can be made use of. iOmniscient has changed the world and opened innumerable opportunities for developments of Artificial Intelligence and its possible uses in daily lives and activities. Innovations are continuous and fast. Moreover, iOmniscient and Dr Rustom Kanga are good representatives of how an organisation should operate and be piloted. He has good values and is an intellectual human being who has definitely made his big mark in the AI industry

He expressed his concern about how there are many countries that have little to no security systems or proper surveillance. This is because many of these cities go for low cost options without doing proper research of the benefits they may provide, or if the underlying problem are getting solved. He wants these cities to seek proper consultants first without jumping to decision that takes effect on the whole city and its people.

"Often cities do not have access to expert advice and end up spending money on technologies that are not able to deliver required results."

"If [a city] uses consultants, it needs to ensure that these consultants have had experience with sophisticated technologies. It will be inappropriate to ask them if they have been involved in large city projects. There are many large city projects with virtually no intelligence. It would be more appropriate, for example, to ask if they have implemented systems with an automated response capability."

Rustom has always focused on solving a problem completely when the means to it is already available rather than going for any inexpensive means. He plans on seizing as many opportunities that are possible to make cities adopt AI and make it smarter and safer.

Despite hardships throughout the venture, they have remained rational, aware, ambitious and optimistic. Rustom's advice to future entrepreneurs who have feasible and smart ideas that could work out is that they should not feel discouraged. He compared ambitions between graduates of Australian and American universities and observed that Australian graduates were less inclined to go for start-ups.

He adds, "The US business environment is certainly more "entrepreneur friendly" [than Australia] but it does show a very different attitude and self-image among the young people in these two environments. We need to encourage our youth to be more creative, to take more risks and essentially to take responsibility for their own destiny."

Indeed, if young people displayed even a tenth of the bravery, resilience and entrepreneurial spirit that Dr Rustom Kanga and his wife did in their newfound home of Australia, Australia would be well placed to take on the world.

Today this migrant business is a pioneer in Video Analytics with almost 2 decades of commercial experience (since 2001) iOmniscient is the longest standing independent Analytics company in the world. The company has recently extended its already comprehensive Analytics capability to provide an Artificial Intelligence based Multi-Sensory Analytics Platform that includes sound and smell as well as video to better replicate human reasoning. These technologies are proven and iOmniscient's systems have been implemented by commercial and government users in 60+ countries around the world.

With 70+ International Patents, iOmniscient specializes in use cases that excel in complex, extremely crowded and realistic environments – doing things that no one else can do.

Based on the company's comprehensive and extensive industry experience, solutions have been designed for particular use cases to solve specific problems that exist in 30 different industries – hundreds of use cases in all. These can easily be customized for a specific environment by combining the appropriate Analytics from iOmniscient's comprehensive portfolio of over 100 capabilities.

The unique technology foundation has enabled the company to remain a technology leader in the global market and to survive challenging periods including the global financial crisis. This has been possible because of the unique capabilities and robustness of the technology that remains ahead of tis time.

iOmniscient's brand is recognized worldwide winning numerous international awards on EVERY continent including the "Best CCTV System of the Year" for its Face Recognition in a Crowd and the Global Security Challenge for Crowded Scenes.

The company has 70+ interlocking, international patents and a significant amount of trade secret Intellectual Property that ensures that there are certain things that no one else can do.

The range of patented technologies cover areas such as:

- Behaviour Analytics in a Crowd (including the detection of abandoned objects, theft, graffiti, vandalism and car accidents despite obscuration)
- Face Recognition in a Crowd
- Dwell Time Analysis
- Automated Response systems which can locate the nearest appropriate responder and tell him where to go and what to do
- Video Utilities where multiple stake holders can use a common infrastructure to extract different types of information relevant only to themselves
- The use of depth sensing cameras for Security and Safety application

The company has published the first books on 'Automated surveillance', 'Smart Cities' and 'Facial Recognition in a crowd' helping to educate its customers and provide guidelines for their digital transformation.

NOTE

The information in this chapter is based on a series of interviews with Rustom Kanga conducted on February 13, 2019.

Chapter 4
Michelle Lam

ABSTRACT

Michelle Lam and her husband, Michael, are the owner proprietors of OSMEN, one of Australia's most popular outdoor furniture businesses. OSMEN was previously known as Contract Casual Furniture, importing outdoor furniture from China for dominant Australian retailers. Over time, OSMEN built a name for itself as a strong outdoor furniture retailer with six homemaker centres across Sydney, in Belrose, Smithfield, Alexandria, Artarmon, Auburn, and Penrith. With more than 12 years of combined experience in the Australian market, Michelle and Michael's knowledge and expertise would prove vital to the success of their company and entrepreneurial partnership, leading to OSMEN capturing a significant share of the Australian outdoor furniture industry. This chapter delves into Michelle and Michael's establishment of OSMEN and how they expanded the business through a relentless pursuit of opportunities and an effective and comprehensive marketing strategy.

DOI: 10.4018/978-1-6684-4986-8.ch004

Figure 1.

This is an intriguing story of Michelle and Michael Li's journey in the outdoor furniture industry. They are the owner proprietor of OSMEN the popular outdoor furniture business in Australia. who's built a strong outdoor furniture business twice over, after overcoming a dramatic turn of events in 2012 that sent her business in an entirely different direction.

OSMEN was previously called Contract Casual Furniture and imported outdoor furniture from China for retailers such as Harvey Norman and Domayne. Currently, OSMEN is a successful retailer six homemaker centres across Sydney.

OSMEN outdoor design is a trading company gone, successful retailer. Today they import outdoor furniture from all over Europe and Asia It is a partnership, originating from married couple Michael and Michelle Li, to introducing employees at partners. Although it is a franchising structure, Michelle implicitly states that she does not view it in this way, the "franchisees" are partners but do not operate their stores without an input.

OSMEN furniture's inception came far before the founding day, Michael Li was a first-generation producer of outdoor furniture in China. Michelle met her husband Michael in 1999 to be married in 2001, shortly after, she moved to Australia to be with him. They had their two children early in their relationship. The inception of OSMEN begins with understanding that the 30-year relationship that Michael already had with producers was an overwhelmingly beneficial starting platform. In 2002 they were a trading company, they started oblivious to the benchmark provided by competitors. The funding level of the project was shallow, selling plastic chairs and benches ranged between $26-$49, upon attending and nothing of sale at their first Australian furniture fair in 2002 they began to understand the differences in an Australian market compared to a Chinese.

In 2002, they met their agent who became a pathway to their relationship with Harvey Norman. Gerry Harvey, the founder of Harvey Norman and other ventures, took a look in their recently developed showroom in early 2002 and agreed to present an umbrella to his buyers. Their agent soon after alerted them of a 'big order' of 1,000 pieces and $110 each. Retail wise this may seem significant, but Michael was frustrated by this at it would only be three containers full, and the profit was only 20-30 per cent. They faced a conflict as the price was low and quality was high which is what buyers desire, yet they were operating on no money. At the time they were the top three of four trading companies in China so they would get large orders but with profits of about three cents on a $3.05 item.

Over time Harvey Norman refused to use their direct importing model as it was not as their standard procedure, they were required to have a warehouse. After a few years, Michelle would design collections to present to buyers with eight to ten per year. Through this technique, they began to understand their place in the market and where they would fit in. For ten years they became the biggest umbrella supplier in Australia. They started to introduce interesting pieces that hadn't entered the Australian market such as the hanging egg chair which opened them up to a collaboration with Domayne. Around 85 per cent of their sales came through Domayne and Harvey Norman. Their span of supply also involved Freedom Furniture and Barbeques Galore. Despite the onset interest from Harvey Norman, the Domayne customers were more suited to their style of design, in Harvey Norman their collection was the premium range whereas in Domayne it was their mid-range.

Eventually, in 2013, they had $2.2 million worth of stock on hand, many collections that were exclusive to their suppliers and had to negotiate their terms. Domayne was requesting they were to have $4 million worth of stock on hand but no guarantee to sell it. After discontinuing the B2B relationship with both Harvey Norman and Domayne they opened their warehouse with their $2.2 million worth of stock on the 1st of July, making $300,000 on the first day.

Over the next four years they opened up six more stores, the flagship being in Belrose, Smithfield the same year, Alexandria and Artarmon after then the following Auburn and Penrith in 2017. Today their range is not primarily from China; they have expanded their relationships with suppliers. Products produced in China targets the middle-low collection, the luxe collection is Italian. They have suppliers also from Holland, Spain and Indonesia.

From its inception as OSMEN, the brand had a strong start and continued to perform due to a variety of factors. Primarily, both Michelle and Michael Li had 12 years' experience in the Australian market; they had gained an understanding of the customers' needs and trends within the markets when they were suppliers. Additionally, Michael was the first generation of outdoor furniture production in; therefore, they had relationships with and access too successful factories throughout China. Due to starting out as a manufacturer, they understood how the process works and how to work with producers to maintain relationships productively. Their organisational structure can be considered a strength, through holding the majority share in all their stores they retain control and therefore their brand image. With the majority share, they also get maximum profits, along with creating loyalty with their partners as everyone has a vested interested in the success of all six stores. Along with their six stores they also have their factory, although this is a non-current asset which bears a lot of risks, it increases control they have over their brand and encourages the ability to expand. They have a proven history of quality and design, their relationship with international designers allows their range to be up to date and of the highest quality.

As with all retail ventures, seasonality is an issue that needs to be attended. Outdoor furniture is a seasonal item which results in an inconstant interest stream month to month. Along with the seasonal nature comes the requirement to warehouse stock during the off-peak season, and this is a costly activity. Despite the varied product ranges, high net worth customers are unlikely to order even their high-end range; they are more likely to shop at prestigious retailers such as the Coco Republic or Pottery Barn. The location of their stores being near other major homeware retailers such as Home HQ in Artarmon may hinder their sales due to the ease of access to other potentially cheaper alternatives that larger stores can provide due to economies of scale.

The proven success in OSMEN's current six stores could provide expansion opportunities. The ability to expand interstate could be explored, potentially to areas with a similar climate and outdoor lifestyle as those in Sydney, such as Queensland. Expanding to other areas in NSW such as the Central Coast could be advantageous as there are fewer premium outdoor furniture suppliers, despite the coastal lifestyle. Another means of expansion which OSMEN has begun to explore in moving into indoor furniture. As indoor furniture is not as influenced by the seasons, providing existing customers with this option will continue to create loyalty and ultimately increased sales. With growing pressure for consumers to buy locally and consciously, introducing an eco-friendly range produced in Australia would not only expand their client range but additionally address competitors such as Tait, a premium Australian brand based and manufactured in Melbourne.

Although a robust, established brand, OSMEN is not averse to risks, being aware of increasing competition and a changing economy is essential. With flat or apartment dwellings accounting for 80.2 per cent of Sydney housing in 2016 (Australian Bureau of Statistics [ABS], 2016) compared to 25.7 per cent in 2006, outdoor living is decreasing, and as a result, the need for alfresco furniture is too. Michelle discusses how the Chinese customers are aware that the furniture is cheaper in China yet of the same quality, therefore, are less likely to buy in Australia but would instead import their own. Through moving from a supplier to a retailer, the inconstant revenue becomes a threat, before detaching from the big chains, they had a regular payment every week. Currently, she expresses that there is never any guarantee, and there are personally liable for all their stock. Ongoing to this, due to their refusal to expand under a franchising structure, they remain in a partnership meaning they hold personal liability for the failure or debt of existing stores.

With each store location comes a new set of competitors. All OSMEN stores currently trading are positioned within a home centre or are surrounded by similar retailers. Aside from large corporations such as Freedom Furniture or Domayne comes smaller the competition of smaller entities such as OSMEN and its competitors. Although an online store as well, being placed within a home centre means they are guaranteed to be targeting the right audience. By covering different price points while still maintaining quality, OSMEN has acquired an extensive portion of the outdoor furniture industry. OSMEN targets homeowners or renters with a mid to high-income household. Although OSMEN has numerous price points, those starting out or on a lower salary tend to purchase their furniture from low price retailers such as Kmart, Ikea or Target, who collectively dominate the homeware retailers market.

The OSMEN design was trademarked on the 25/09/08 as an Australian Private Company. She outsourced the role to a design company to create the logo and slogan one year before opening their first retail store, although it was not expected that they would go to retail at the time. At this time, they began to advertise in magazines as a wholesaler to create brand awareness. She explains the limited knowledge at the time of individual furniture brands of the general public as most sourced their furniture from large retailers such as Harvey Norman.

Michael Li initially perceived that the Australian market was too small, as their first order for umbrellas as Contract Casual being disappointing, he did not want to continue. Despite the desire to give up they continued to push the umbrella; as a result, they became the largest umbrella supplier in Australia for ten years, soon after 12 years selling their product and presenting globally, the couple was able to gauge the demand for their products. They experienced market peaks-and-troughs, such as a decreased demand over the winter months. Coming from a Chinese background a gained understanding of the Australian market that was enabled through their relationships with Harvey Norman and Domayne proved priceless. After ending the supplier-buyer relationship with both companies, they opened their warehouse to the public, making $300,000 sales on the first day.

Starting out as a supplier under the name Contract Casual, Michelle was required to strategically move from being a mid-high price brand under Harvey Norman and Domayne to an independent retailer with a variety of price and quality points. The primary source of promotion in 2002 was a physical presentation to prospective buyers of their stock. Over time this presentation in the warehouse became larger scale and ultimately the set for future catalogue photo shoots and displays. They initially differentiated themselves from other brands by creating this showroom through spending thousands of dollars on accessories to build a set-in-order to present their stock in a way that it would be displayed in the store. The provision of custom catalogues for Harvey Norman and Domayne distinguished themselves as a supplier from their competitors.

Their marketing strategy was always to go the extra length, providing the buyer with not a sample of the collection but instead it in its entirety.

As a result of their failed first range of cheap plastic furniture, their strategy changed to provide what wasn't in the market. Unique pieces such as a hanging egg chair were unusual and often laughed away from retailers such as Harvey. Domayne was more open to the exciting pieces as it matched their clientele more. Today they have 17 different versions of this egg chair on their website. Their awareness of incoming trends was due to their attendance at all international furniture fairs and understanding the products through research on "every single magazine related to the home in Australia as well as the world". This was to be ahead of trends and understand what they needed to design and produce to remain relevant in an international market.

PROMOTIONAL STRATEGY, ADVERTISING MEDIUMS AND PUBLIC RELATIONS EFFORTS

As an independent retailer, Michelle was required to change her marketing strategy and advertising mediums. She understood the need for an online presence within social media; they use Instagram effectively through keeping their page updated with sales, and relevant and aesthetically pleasing posts. They use techniques of interacting with their audience such as asking them questions such as, "What will you miss most about summer?" along with using related events as a form of promotion such as Australia Day. Through using a platform such as Instagram, Twitter and Facebook to share photographs and videos of their inventory range, potential customers can envision the pieces in their home, a similar strategy as used previously in the showroom. They have continued their promotion in catalogues and have expanded to magazines. Michelle is also the Editor-in-Chief of New Land Magazine which is the largest Chinese magazine in Australia displaying Australian art, culture and lifestyle, an appropriate gateway for brand awareness. The Li family are active in their community on the Upper North Shore of Sydney with their children attending the local private schools; she effectively uses this as a platform for promotion. Exemplifying this, OSMEN provided outdoor furniture for Pymble Ladies College's Centenary Project Garden Party on a voluntary basis, and as a result, many parents along with the Principal of the school purchased sets themselves. Similarly, OSMEN has continued to sponsor events such as the North Shore Black & White Charity Ball supporting special needs schools and foundations such as Variety – The Children's Charity, these are a way to give back to society but also create brand awareness as an additional benefit.

Using the B2B platform Bartercard, she holds sale days for their members to purchase pieces with trade dollars typically individuals paying in cash attend as well. Such events are put on to sell surplus stock at the end of the season; these sale days can result in the sale of $400,000 of stock. Overall, these exclusive sale days have sold in excess of $2.5 million of discontinued and redundant items that would alternatively create storage costs.

PRICING STRATEGY AND PRODUCT AVAILABILITY

OSMEN started with their manufactures from China, but to increase their market share, they needed to have a variety of prices and collections. In the first year, they were required to clear their stock it soon after they introduced ranges from Spain, Holland, Italy and Indonesia, along with their original manufacturers in China. Through expanding in such a way, they can provide different price points. Michelle works closely with all the suppliers; although she does not provide the designs, she advises on the Australia market trends to create an in-demand product. As OSMEN started out as a supplier, she is acutely aware of how to select good suppliers and maintain quality relationships. She explains that Italy provides the high-end product range but are slow with their shipments as they need to get the quality right, this is tolerated as quality is essential in maintaining a quality image. For their midrange products, they use their Chinese supplier whom they have produced with for thirty years and a constant with their shipments and quality, always meeting their KPIs. Currently, they stock eleven brands including their OSMEN Exclusive range.

ORGANISATION

OSMEN Furniture is a retail partnership. They have stores all over Sydney with stock provided internationally. Although it appears as a franchise structure, the Li's always retaining 51 per cent of any store that is opened. Shareholders are sort out from loyal employees who are interested in reinvesting in the company. All shareholders have shares in each store. The goal in this is to minimise failure, and as a result, all of their stores continue to make a profit. They share 51 per cent of the profit and keep the other 49 per cent. In 2013-14 they looked into starting a franchising structure but did not continue with this restructuring. The solicitor examines their potential contracts encouraged the chain of thought that the franchisees might succeed, but there's a high chance of failure due to their limited experience in that industry. Michelle and Michael required control over their stores beyond the means of training the franchisees.

They do not have numerous offices but rather one central so that they can control everything from the same place. Holding OSMEN furniture in a partnership encourages the use of combined skills and knowledge, and therefore better business making decisions.

OSMEN furniture follows a flat hierarchy organisational structure, meaning the span of control is wide thus increasing collaboration and communication. Michelle Lam holds the role of Managing Director and she is an active participant in all aspects of the business. Based on the form of ownership, the chain of command ends with herself. Managers at all locations report to her and perform under her direction; there is a unity of command. Unity of command instructs inferiors to report to one boss only; this is to create an efficient workplace which limits confusion and incorrect information provided. Causal and part-time employees report to their managers, and their managers communicate with Michelle. At the current time, there are three managers all who are partners, they include the warehouse manager, account manager and another for a different store, they all story to her and are expected to know their allocated tasks and roles in depth.

FINANCE

Michelle and Michael funded OSMEN without any outside investors. Due to the banks' requirement for a property as collateral, they were unable to be granted a bank loan to open a new store. The money required to open the first retail store they were needed to fund themselves. After a period, they were able to finance their property and use this towards expansion. A bond was required, to ensure security on a store, this can cost between $50,000 and $60,000 to cover three months rental. Additional to this cost is the floor stock which can be up to $80,000.

OSMEN's three managers all have between 5-10 per cent equity in all of the stores, and each has the ability to invest as much as they can afford. As previously discusses, the Li's own a 51 per cent share in all of their stores, yet they only hold 49 per cent of the profits allowing the remainder to be split appropriately between investors.

As a private company, financial report and statements are not disclosed, although Michelle shared a few points regarding profit margins as Contract

Casual and current upselling techniques. Contract Casuals first successful product being outdoor umbrellas only brought in a profit on the $110 RRP of 20-30 per cent. With the first order being for only 1,000 umbrellas, they were operating on approximately AUD$2,200 – $3,300, she explained, "our price was good, but we were making no money". Eventually their order sizes became more considerable, but as a result, their profit margins fell smaller as well due to the fact they were a supplier for major retailers such as Bunnings, who bought bulk for economies of scale. To exemplify OSMEN's upselling technique she explains that through importing luxe furniture from Italy, they were able to sell a $6,000 product for a minimum of $20,000 to the Australian market, this is a 333.33 per cent margin. A profit margin as such, not only increases revenue but also assist in covering the cost of importation and necessary storage. OSMEN places themselves as a financial competitor by frequently holding sales and additionally matching delivery fees such as that of Freedom Furniture.

Organisational structures of small business can vary according to the industry and other factors. Having a structure that enables the ability to react to market trends and needs along with seasonal changes is essential in the retail sector. A flat arch structure allows trust and communication between partners and managers. Ongoing is the financial motivation OSMEN managers have for success due to their ownership incentive. This structure is unique and would not be suitable in all other ventures, as the influence of a company's external and internal environment impacts on the culture required for an entity to run successfully. The motivating and inclusive culture within OSMEN expands beyond their employees to their suppliers resulting in a successful and profitable partnership.

NOTE

The information in this chapter is based on a series of interviews with Michelle Lam conducted on October 1, 2018.

REFERENCES

Australian Bureau of Statistics. (2016, September 26). *2071.0 - Census of Population and Housing: Reflecting Australia - Stories from the Census, 2016.* Australian Bureau of Statistics. https://www.abs.gov.au/ausstats/abs@.nsf/Lookup/by%20Subject/2071.0~2016~Main%20Features~Apartment%20Living~20

Chapter 5
Pauline Nguyen

ABSTRACT

Fleeing the Vietnam War with her family at only 3 years old, Pauline Nguyen endured a tough and terrifying childhood before her family was accepted to live in Australia in 1978. Through her persistent drive and discipline, Pauline overcame her odds to become the owner of Red Lantern, the most awarded Vietnamese restaurant in the world located in Sydney, Australia. Pauline is renowned today as one of Australia's most successful and talented entrepreneurs. She is also a best-selling and award-winning author, winning the Telstra Award for Medium Businesses and Australian Book Industry Awards – Writer Debut of the Year in 2008 for her book, Secrets of the Red Lantern. Pauline's philosophy of spiritual entrepreneurship has empowered countless professionals to command self-mastery and achieve exponential business growth. This chapter explores Pauline's incredible journey and shares her unique personal, business, and life philosophy driving her to become one of Australia's most inspirational business leaders.

DOI: 10.4018/978-1-6684-4986-8.ch005

Figure 1.

RED LANTERN

Pauline is the owner of RED LANTERN the most awarded Vietnamese restaurant in the world located in Sydney, Australia which she started with her brother Luke Nguyen and Mark Jensen. In 2012 the team opened their second restaurant Red Lantern on Riley and Red Lily Cocktail Bar. She is among Australia's most successful entrepreneurs. She has a high performing Western business background with an Eastern slant of spirituality.

A CHILDHOOD FRAUGHT WITH STRUGGLES

When Pauline Nguyen was just three years old, she and her family were forced to flee the Vietnam War raging in her country of origin. The terrified young family boarded a boat and spent an astonishing nine days at sea before arriving at their temporary destination - a refugee camp in Thailand. Although the typical expected time to stay in the refugee camp was around three to six months, due to poor luck this camp was to be the family's home for almost a year. The dreary monotony of waiting at the camp was only broken by the joyful birth of Pauline's baby brother Luke Nguyen – making them a family of five (later six) living in the camp together.

The year was 1978, and Pauline and her family had finally been accepted to come and live in Australia.

Although there was a sense of relief at being able to leave the camp, the family's struggles were far from over. The family made their home at Westbridge Migrant Hostel in New South Wales alongside many other refugees in similar situations. Pauline's father secured a job at a Sunbeam factory and worked the graveyard shift – eventually opening his own restaurant, where Pauline worked from the age of seven.

Pauline reflects on her youth as a very difficult time.

The family came to Australia with no home of their own, few possessions, no money, no English and with no knowledge of the local culture, laws and customs of this foreign land. Compounding these struggles was the psychological and emotional trauma each of them carried with them, having lived through the horrors of the war and the dreary refugee camp.

Pauline's father frequently took out his frustration on his wife and young children. Pauline grew up in a violent and harsh household with both physical and verbal abuse commonplace. She was pressured to get good grades at school or face terrifying consequences. From a young age, fear followed her everywhere. At the age of 16, Pauline could not bear the torture any longer and left home to begin an independent life.

Despite a start to life which was far from smooth, it is evident that Pauline would not accept defeat and was courageous and driven to succeed. Her past would not define her future. Her courage and ambition served her well, and she remained committed to self-improvement and her studies – knowing that education opens many doors in life. Pauline explains that when facing difficulty, what helps her most is looking for the learnings and the positives to move forward.

This is a philosophy and mindset that would later guide her in her business too. She explains, "Whatever you learn on the other side of overcoming an obstacle is going to be your pot of gold."

She eventually was accepted to the University of Technology in Sydney to pursue a Bachelor of Arts - Communication. As well as a love for food and hospitality gained from her time working in the family restaurant, through her education she discovered a passion for film and writing. As such, it only made sense that while studying at university she took on several part-time jobs at various restaurants. She was fortunate to gain experience at some of Sydney's best dining establishments and under the supervision of several top chefs and sommeliers.

"If there's one thing my education taught me, it was discipline."

– Pauline Nguyen

After graduating from university, Pauline set off to live overseas in London and Paris for five years and found employment at the third largest post-production company in Europe. After coming back to Australia, she continued in a similar professional vein and worked in the field of film and television.

RED LANTERN BEGINS TO SHINE

In 2002, Pauline's brother Luke floated the idea of opening a restaurant and asked for Pauline's help. Pauline's interest and enthusiasm were piqued. Red Lantern, their very own restaurant serving aromatic, fresh Vietnamese cuisine in a chic French-Indochina-inspired setting, was about to be born.

Luke and Pauline teamed up with Mark Jensen, a talented chef and entrepreneur that Luke had met at the Olympic Hotel in Sydney.

In the early days, Luke, Pauline and Mark worked for about 80, 90 or sometimes 100 hours a week. While many Australians in their early twenties are slogging it out with fledgling internships, tertiary education or even still enjoying gap years abroad as they find their path in life, the newly forged business partners were so engrossed in their start-up that they had no time left in their lives for anything else but realising this new ambition. In fact, the work became so intense and the stress levels so high that Pauline began to lose her hair.

But Pauline discovered the entrepreneurial skills which were hidden in her. The love for business and especially for the food business gave her the chance to grow her passion. The trio had accomplished their dream of opening their first restaurant.

Today, Red Lantern is the most awarded Vietnamese restaurant in the world.

THE THREE RED LANTERN PARTNERS

Luke Nguyen is author of four best-selling and award-winning cookbooks and recently joined the Sydney Morning Herald's 'Food Hall of Fame' – an honour bestowed for his cooking and travel programs. Luke is also an ambassador for award-winning travel group APT and has introduced culinary discovery trips to Vietnam, Japan, Cambodia, and China. He is now the face/ambassador for Vietnam Air.

Mark Jensen is the executive chef at Red Lantern. He has been in the hospitality industry for about 25 years and has worked in Sydney's best restaurants. For six years, Mark was a regular chef on Network Ten's 'Ready, Steady Cook' and has also appeared at various times as a guest chef on the wildly popular 'MasterChef Australia'. He is the author of 'The Urban Cook: Cooking and Eating for a Sustainable Future' and developed the famous casual seafood concept of 'Salmon and Bear'. Mark and Pauline have two children together.

Pauline Nguyen is a best-selling, award-winning author and award-winning businesswoman. Pauline is an original 'Rare Bird' – one of Australia's top 50 influential female entrepreneurs – and is included in Blackwell and Hobday's global recognition of 200 Women Who Will Change the Way You See the World. Her personal awards include the Telstra Award for Medium Businesses and the Australian Book Industry Awards' Writer Debut of the Year in 2008 for her book, 'Secrets of the Red Lantern' which became an international bestseller. Pauline is also a coach, and mentor. She is an international speaker on Spiritual Entrepreneurship – her keynotes are inspirational and transformational, focussed on sharing her personal philosophy of self-actualisation. She believes it's important for people to know what their 'best self' is and work towards the goal of becoming one's best self.

Following on from her success with 'Secrets of the Red Lantern', Pauline has penned a new book, 'The Way of the Spiritual Entrepreneur' which contains seven of Pauline's secrets to becoming fearless, stress-free and unshakable in business and in life. Pauline describes her new book as 'a no-bones, honest and forthright methodology of business, life and spiritual practice designed to disrupt standard ways of thinking, bringing the unconscious into the conscious and catapulting the reader into an optimistic mindset of abundance and possibility'. The book recently won 'Best Entrepreneurship and Small Business Book of the Year' – 2019 Business Book of the Year Awards.

PAULINE'S PHILOSOPHY

With such a unique and challenging start to life under incredibly trying circumstances, it is no wonder that Pauline has developed her own unique personal, business and life philosophy.

Pauline believes that if people can truly design and access 'a more elevated mindset, heartset, healthset and soulset' (spirit), they can be free of the stories of the past that keep them imprisoned. She believes in order to find true freedom; no area can be ignored. She credits this philosophy as playing a key role in the success of her business and her own personal success.

Pauline views her philosophy as her own personal brand.

Her vision and leadership are based on her motto, 'If we can learn the tools of self-mastery, we can better practice the art of influence over others.'

"On the Enneagram scale, I think my mother is a classic personality type two – a 'Considerate Helper'. This means she is people pleasing, kind, generous and compassionate. From my mother, I tried to learn her kindness, compassion and sense of femininity," said Pauline.

Pauline believes it's important for women to have these traits. Growing up in a violent household, she was forced to become tough – a typically masculine trait – to protect herself from further exploitation. Pauline believes in women empowerment and feels that today many women strive to be masculine and tough but, as Pauline puts it, "It is only when they can discover and access their 'Divine Femininity', that they will unlock their true power."

"Strong women are meant to dance, sing and flow. It's about love and showing kindness to each other. We should praise each other rather than just pulling each other down! Women need to help women. Putting on a masculine, tough mask is incongruent with one's true feminine self. It is inauthentic and thus we lose our power. A woman can move mountains with the gentlest of touch," said Pauline.

Pauline says the person she is today is no mistake. She decided who she wanted to become and has deliberately designed the person she is today. She lives her life deliberately and not by default. Yes, she has had a tumultuous upbringing, "and that was my training!" says Pauline.

"Being an entrepreneur and coming from a different culture, it is very important to learn from your past experiences and make improvements accordingly. Education taught me discipline, which is a very significant part of life. It helps you grow and live an enhanced life. It helps you evolve along with your life experiences," said Pauline.

THE GROWTH OF PAULINE AS AN ENTREPRENEUR

Pauline has overcome her unpleasant beginnings by re-structuring her beliefs, questioning the status quo and adjusting to a new culture. Her life experiences have given her insight into the minds of individuals and businesses alike, permitting her to deliver on the vital and valuable skills of self-mastery, courage, resilience, and grit. After growing through experiencing suffering, Pauline has a passion for understanding humankind and holds a great respect for human beings.

At this stage of her life, she also wants to help people who are ready. It was the desire to help others that drove her to venture beyond her restaurant business and explore coaching and mentoring, and eventually her professional speaking business. She healed herself through helping others. Her mission in life is to alleviate suffering and to magnify human potential.

'From extreme adversity to success' is a much loved and appreciated topic that Pauline speaks about in her inspiring keynote.

HUMAN RESOURCES - 'FIND EMPLOYEES WHO ARE SMARTER THAN YOU, AND ENCOURAGE THEM TO DO WHAT THEY LOVE'

Pauline's personal philosophy goes hand in hand with her philosophy towards people and customers in the workplace. Pauline laughs as she says when looking at hiring new employees, she prefers to find people who are 'smarter than her' and can work much better than she can. She believes that everyone is different and has their own special skills and thus a good boss should be able to see and tap into the best in everyone.

Pauline likes to do the big picture thinking and let her other employees do the work that interests them. She evidently understands the importance and different characteristics of employees and gives them chance to grow which is a great quality of leadership.

When Pauline is in town on the weekends, she is very hands-on and adores interacting with her customers. She is fond of polishing the cutlery as she hangs out in the kitchen observing the customers and the front of house team. She loves connecting with people by serving them their food. This brings out the sense of belonging and passion for the business which is a remarkable characteristic of a successful entrepreneur. Pauline says she knows every bit of the work the employees do as she has learned it by doing it herself first - but now she has people who can do the same job more efficiently so she can concentrate on other major areas.

Pauline and her employees have established a beautiful and intensive feedback loop. She believes her business has survived where others failed because they are uplifting the human spirit of their employees and their customers.

"It is not only about the transaction or, 'Here's your food'. It is about the way we welcome our customers and how we make them feel. It's about lifting the human spirit through the alchemy of flavours, hospitality, and heart. Hence, in the end, it's all about developing and maintaining relationships with your customers, employees, suppliers and talking things out if it seems to be not working. This magic formula for success is the weapon of reciprocity and authenticity and authority and then of course with the customers because they keep us in business. So, as they see us evolve, we also see them evolve," says Pauline.

Relationships with employees are deepened by providing bonding activities. They give employees empowerment, listen to their thoughts, views, and voice. Sometimes even if Pauline knows the solution to a problem, she prefers listening to the ideas of employees, as it gives them the opportunity to speak up and think through it. She also finds they often come up with more feasible, fast and efficient options. The work environment is very friendly and empowered. If employees are not happy or have any issues they can go to Pauline and sort it out.

Despite the inclusive, attractive work environment and opportunities for growth, training and mentorship, Pauline confesses that resourcing people is still difficult. When Red Lantern job advertisements are published, she often finds the only people who apply are immigrants or those on tourist visas.

"Australians don't like working in the restaurants," said Pauline. "The government promotes Australian hospitality, tourism, and restaurants but on the other hand makes it hard to sponsor people from overseas who are looking for work – especially countries where there is excess of human population with low wage rates," she continued.

Although they have managed to find loyal and hardworking people in the kitchen and on the floor, Pauline feels that the only people benefitting from Australia's unique situation are the immigration lawyers who charge hefty sums to people to be sponsored from overseas. She laments that no aid is being provided by the government to the business owners or the workers in that regard.

CHALLENGES

As of 2019, the restaurant has been going for 17 years strong and the honours, achievements and accolades have rolled in. Today, Red Lantern is one of the most awarded Vietnamese restaurants in the world. In 2012, the team opened their second restaurant, Red Lantern on Riley as well as Red Lily Cocktail Bar. But the success of Red Lantern has not come without challenges.

The hospitality industry is renowned for being very difficult. Customers can be fickle. Tastes can change rapidly. Food fashions and fads come and go. It is a saturated industry.

Pauline confessed that despite being an award-winning restaurant, it still does not make a lot of profit. They do it for love and passion. Pauline notes that many other restauranteurs have other businesses to boost their personal profit and income. Red Lantern, like other restaurants, has to contend with rates, terms, conditions, and policies. These factors make it harder to stay in the business as wage costs are high and there are rules and regulations to abide by.

"It is our responsibility to do things in the right way, but it has not always been easy," said Pauline.

Relationships with restaurant suppliers are critical, particularly as they have been doing business with each other for a very long time. Trust has been developed.

"If the product we receive from suppliers is not up to the mark sometimes, this is where it becomes important that you have been good in keeping relations with suppliers. If you do the right thing (such as paying on time) these kinds of things help you when you might need product exchanges immediately. It is a relationship of reciprocity, give and take," said Pauline.

The last challenge that Pauline discussed in the interview was preconceived notions of what Vietnamese cuisine is or should be. Some customers need to be educated a little about Red Lantern's premium dining experience as they may feel that Vietnamese food should always be 'cheap and cheerful'.

"Red Lantern chefs use only premium products in our dishes. Our dining experience is also premium as we offer the finest services," said Pauline.

"What has helped Red Lantern survive is staying true to what we stand for and what we stand against. Even if that causes short-term pain, we need to be authentic to our brand without compromising - no matter what," said Pauline.

It does seem that patrons truly appreciate this authenticity.

To overcome these challenges, the trio have had to find grit where others may have lacked it. They needed to be both flexible and courageous.

MINDSET CHANGES ALONG THE JOURNEY TO SUCCESS

Pauline recalled a critical time in the journey of Red Lantern that brought about a mindset shift among the three entrepreneurs.

"When the restaurant was in Crown Street, Mark, Luke, and I had finished a hard and difficult service. It was actually a very difficult time, and I had lost a lot of weight, with my hair falling out because of the stress. My body ached all the time and I felt no peace from the hard work. It was two o'clock in the morning when we finished work and I had flashbacks to the time when we were kids and our parents used to work through the day and night."

"Then and there, the decision was made to do things differently. We decided that although we wouldn't be able to stop working hard, we should focus on working smarter. Working smarter does not mean we are not working hard."

The team rethought things - including their focus on secret family recipes. They realised that if you have secret family recipes, you are the one only one working till two am to maintain the secrecy of the recipes. This came with the realisation that they would have to let the initial control go.

"People think no one can work better than them or influence better than them, which is not true. There are always going to be plenty of people who are better than us in something and as a leader, you need to allow expertise and skills to grow in your team," said Pauline.

Pauline remembers fondly a teacher who taught a very valuable lesson - that every business needs an artist, a manager, and an entrepreneur.

"One needs an artist whether you are a seamstress, writer, graphic designer, chef or cook. You also need a manager to manage the little things for you, to get things together, and most importantly the need of entrepreneur who can push it forward. If things are aligned you will enjoy working, otherwise, everything will be a chaos," said Pauline.

In Red Lantern, Luke and Mark play the role of the artists. Luke is a manager as well as he manages a lot of things better. Pauline sees herself as the entrepreneur as she thinks of the bigger picture.

"People should be proud when they have accomplished something. I think we should be proud of Red Lantern too," said Pauline.

We can't help but agree.

Today Pauline Nguyen is one of Australia's most impactful speakers and developmental coaches. Combining science and spirituality, she teaches others how to design the life of their dreams, marrying material success with deep fulfilment and a great sense of play.

A multi-award-winning best-selling author as well as the co-founder of the world's most awarded Vietnamese Restaurant, Red Lantern; Pauline teaches from direct experience to help others command self-mastery.

Her coaching and mentoring are available exclusively to those who are ready to uplevel, leading her clients through self-transformation which ripples through both professional and personal spheres. Drawing from both contemporary science and ancient modalities, her teachings have helped countless professionals experience exponential business growth, greater health, deeper intimate relationships and spiritual awakenings.

NOTE

The information in this chapter is based on a series of interviews with Pauline Nguyen conducted on March 20, 2019.

Chapter 6
Marina O'Neill

ABSTRACT

Despite coming from a conservative and traditional Italian upbringing that discouraged women from working, Marina O'Neill defied expectations by forging a successful career in the banking industry, climbing the corporate ladder and eventually starting her own lucrative architectural hardware business – Unique Architectural Hardware. During her career, Marina encountered countless challenges including the glass ceiling and gender bias, but it was her determination to prove herself that allowed her to break barriers. After discovering her passion and creativity in home renovation, Marina started Unique Architectural Hardware. She encountered even more obstacles in her entrepreneurial journey including initially securing sales and finding suppliers who made small-batch production. However, Marina never lost sight of her goals and values to succeed. This chapter delves into Marina's inspirational story and how she was able to take her business, Unique Architectural Hardware, from a personal passion project to new heights of success.

DOI: 10.4018/978-1-6684-4986-8.ch006

Figure 1.

Marina

Isles

Marina Isles - Unique Architectural Hardware is a small, family operated business now located in the iconic Nicholas Building in Melbourne. Originally founded in 1993, with a vision to source unique products for the renovation and building industry it remains a small establishment, however, is substantially larger than its humble beginnings in the home of Marina O'Neill in Italy. Owners Marina and Gary O'Neill stumbled upon a local craftsman making handpainted ceramic knobs and basins. 25 years later, the business has grown into a wholesale and retail supplier of fine architectural hardware to designers, architects, joinery and furniture companies. (Marina Isles, 2022)

Now with over 1000 products on offer, Marina Isles can provide almost everything you can imagine for your kitchen and bathroom needs – from industrial hardware, to French country farmhouse sinks, and ultra modern taps and baths, you can find everything to suit your taste.

For kitchen and bathroom design ideas, follow on Pinterest and Instagram. For in person great advice on choosing the best options for your kitchen and bathroom visit Room 7, Level 7, The Nicholas Building at 37 Swanston Street, Melbourne VIC 3000. The story of the business and how it has developed is an interesting one, although an equally intriguing story is how Marina O'Neill herself came to be a small business entrepreneur.

BACKGROUND

Marina comes from a strong Italian upbringing which gave her a distinct set of values and views which she has now made all her own. She describes her early life as being pre-determined by her parents, her father in particular. Being a very traditional Italian family, it was believed that women did not need further education, nor to work. Marina was a bright and creative girl. She loved gardening, theatrics and art from an early age.

Despite this, Marina set about forging a career in the banking business as a bank officer, the industry in which her father worked. She slowly began to climb the corporate ladder, picking up education and valuable training along the way, proving she was a capable person in this industry. Dealing most with the corporate lending and some marketing aspects of this industry provided her with good experience which would prove quite useful in the future when she opened her own business.

But the working world for woman at the time was not as free and unbiased as it perhaps is today. She was subject to a constant barrage of negative comments about her being at work and not at home with the children. Marina was a woman who valued and wanted to retain her independence. After remarrying, maybe it would have been financially possible to stay home with her children, but she wanted to prove to others that she was capable of doing these jobs and doing them extremely well.

"As bad as it sounds, there was a glass ceiling; a level within a company that women could reach and go no further," she said.

She finally was fed up with the comments and realised she did not enjoy where her career was taking her, so she simply left. At this point her life took a sharp turn.

She began pursuing an acting career, which she describes as being very difficult in Australia.

When her husband was transferred to New York, she and her children moved as well, this gave Marina the opportunity to expand her acting credentials to levels difficult to reach in Australia.

Acting began to take more and more of her time which, for Marina, meant increasing feelings of guilt about her children suffering being left with caregivers for much of the day while she and her husband worked.

She forced herself to make a choice, her acting career, or her children. She chose her children and says she has no regrets whatsoever regarding this.

Following this she returned to Australia with her family and briefly contemplated the idea of opening a restaurant. Realising this would quickly be a seven day a week job, she thought about where her true interest lay - horticulture.

Wondering why she never thought of working in this industry before, she quickly began earning her way with this business, while still having the time to spend with her children during their important years. While running her horticultural business, Marina also had the free time to undertake home renovation projects including rebuilding their family kitchen.

When building her kitchen cabinets, she found the task of choosing small details such as handles and doorknobs to be fascinating and an outlet for her creativity. She decided she wanted unique small details in her home – not the dull, mass-produced products found in most stores. The task had woken up her innate creative side again!

"Inspiration comes from all around! It was the home renovation project rebuilding the kitchen that gave me the inspiration to open the business I run to this day. I knew if I wanted something unique and new in my home details, I was not the only one in the world. There would certainly be demand," said Marina.

She decided to design her own unique, architectural hardware and search for someone to produce it.

MARINA ISLES – UNIQUE ARCHITECTURAL HARDWARE IS BORN

When the first order arrived at her home, she and her husband were ecstatic, and Marina felt a boost of confidence and pride in her work. Marina and her husband thought for the first time that their business venture may be a success.

In the early days of setting up her business, Marina revelled in the task of trekking around town to find people who were willing to either purchase or display one of the products she had designed and produced.

She received two orders in their first month of being open and made barely enough to pay for the expenses incurred. Still, these early sales were a boon as they gave Marina and her husband strength and the motivation to carry on. Once she realised that there would be a demand for her handles, she decided to put into motion the beginnings of what is now known as Marina Isles – Unique Architectural Hardware.

As her business grew, Marina came across many obstacles. She struggled finding suppliers who would be willing to produce small batches. Many suppliers would only manufacture a minimum of 10,000 units; an unacceptable number for such a small, family-based company.

"Just when things seemed to be at their worst, something or someone can come along to prove, not everyone is out to just make money. I believe in karma, and that if you are a good person, good things will come back onto you," said Marina.

In today's cut-throat business world, it is rare to find examples of competitors being benevolent or doing favours without expecting some sort of payment in return. But in Marina's case, her philosophy of karma and believing in the goodness in others rang true. A fellow entrepreneur saw what was happening to Marina and offered to add her orders to the end of his order with no surcharge.

Another obstacle Marina faced was as she began producing greater volumes of product. Suppliers began overpromising about their ability to execute orders just so they could win her business. Suppliers would promise that a product would take just six weeks to arrive, when in reality it wouldn't arrive until 12 weeks later. This was a source of endless frustration for Marina as she found it hard to separate the truthful and straightforward suppliers from the untrustworthy and misleading suppliers.

As her customers' only connection to the product, it was Marina's company name and reputation on the line.

Fortunately, with slow and steady growth, she was able to iron out the supplier issue before it became an extreme problem. They were able to keep suppliers that were accurate with their time frames and discard the suppliers who were unable to deliver the goods in a timely manner.

GROWTH AND SUCCESS

As the company continued to grow and orders became bigger, Marina realised that she would no longer have enough space in her home to operate the business. She decided it would be a good time to move the company into a more commercial setting, so she set out to find a building.

She found a great location in Castle Hill, NSW in an industrial area alongside many other bulk goods retail stores - beneficial for customer exposure.

She checked out the council zoning and external building restrictions put in place by Strata and found it was zoned for bulky goods retail, which is exactly what her business is classified as.

In 2000, they purchased the location with a commercial loan secured against their family home.

She submitted her paperwork to request council approval. This cost the organisation money and time, but Marina wanted to do everything by the book because she did not want to cut corners - a key philosophy of 'doing the right thing' that has been present throughout the company since its beginnings.

Next, it was time to place a sign outside her building so people would know where her business was located. This was another hurdle for Marina! Despite many companies in the industrial area having large signs and advertisements posted on their buildings, the council would not allow her to place overhead signs.

"This is a sore spot for me because large organisations seem to be able to get away with this by-law! I think that large corporations have an advantage over small individually owned businesses because governments tend to cater to larger businesses," said Marina.

Next, Marina discovered that even though Strata did not own her business unit, they still had the right to tell Marina what she was allowed to do with the structure and interior of her unit. She discovered she was not able to paint the interior any colour but eggshell white. On the face of it, this may seem like a trivial fact, but for a company involved in interior design, the ability to easily display products on various coloured backgrounds would have been very useful!

The way Marina and her company have been able to get around this issue is with clever thinking. They erected faux walls, which show handles on different backgrounds along with what they would look like on applications. There is a wall with eight to ten different cabinet door styles and handles to give the customer an idea of what the finished product will look like.

GOALS AND OBJECTIVES

Today, Marina Isles – Unique Architectural Hardware provides unique decorative cabinet hardware products from across the world. Products include:

- Hand-painted decorative ceramics from Agra, India - ideal for interiors and available in brass and chrome
- Simple, vibrant algrave cabinet hardware from the southern coast of Portugal
- Anodised classics range of cabinet hardware products like aluminium handles and knobs
- Artisan from Marina Isles – a range of hand decorated knob, painted by Australian artists
- Crazed, a type of cabinet hardware (early French and English glazes)
- cabinet hardware including country, glass, crazed ceramics, federation, French provincial, modena, shaker, stone and earth

Marina explained when she started her company, she had goals. She always had goals - whether it was travel, building a home or starting a business. She also had hope. She hoped people would like her product, and she felt it would work. This hope has fuelled both her and her husband to go to great lengths to see the success of this company.

They had an objective when they started to not have a debt that was not manageable. Marina and her husband both feel they need to be able to control the business from the bottom up, and the top down. They did not want any banks telling them what they had to do, and they did not want to have any worries about paying their debtors.

Their decision to mortgage their family home to purchase the building in which the company operates shows a great deal of dedication to the company. Not many people would be willing to put a large debt in place with an asset as large as a house to see a vision to fruition. Marina and her husband both have the hearts of true entrepreneurs.

As the company has grown, Marina has re-evaluated her goals and has decided if Marina Isles does become an international company, they would embrace it. They have built a great website and embraced social media with help from their daughters. Their online shop allows customers to order and ship their products around the world.

Marina would like to see operations start in North America and Europe. She believes the key is to stick with the core philosophies of being a small company that deals with small quantities of products with little to no mass production and a product that is unique and specific for its design.

She would like to expand, but only if she would be able retain the control she has now. A fear of having people tell her how to run her business is a fear she has always dealt with.

Marina believes people often lose sight of their goals and values with expansion and growth, which is why she has elected to grow her company organically since the beginning. Her growth has been the biproduct of a well-run business.

NOTE

The information in this chapter is based on a series of interviews with Marina O'Neill conducted on January 19, 2019.

REFERENCES

Marina Isles. (2022). https://marinaisles.com/contact/

Chapter 7
Kam and Reet Phulwani

ABSTRACT

Founded in 2007 by couple Kam and Reet Phulwani, Medsurge is among the fastest-growing family-owned pharmaceutical companies in Australia, supplying specialised life-saving medicines to healthcare professionals across Australia and New Zealand. Medsurge was born from the humble beginnings of Kam and Reet, who were motivated by their like-minded passion to help people and make a difference through medicine. Coming from a family of doctors, Kam followed in their footsteps to become a pharmacist with a goal of healing people and benefitting society. Meanwhile, Reet's entrepreneurial spirit was forged through her family background, with many family members engaged in business and technology roles. The duo initially faced challenges getting their business started while working full-time and receiving no bank loans. Today, Medsurge employs 40 staff to service 6,500 hospitals, supplying upwards of 700 medicines. This chapter explores how Kam and Reet grew their start-up into a thriving global business.

DOI: 10.4018/978-1-6684-4986-8.ch007

PASSION WITH PHARMA: FROM A START UP TO A GLOBAL BUSINESS

MEDSURGE

WE VALUE LIFE

Figure 1.

MEDSURGE HEALTHCARE - WE VALUE LIFE

Specialising in procuring hard to source products from anywhere in the world. Rapid response by our high- performance teams, meeting the patients' needs by delivering pharmaceuticals in the most efficient turnaround time possible.

THE COMPANY MEDSURGE

Founded in 2007 by Kam Phulwani • Headquarters in Melbourne, Australia • Department of Health approved facility • Fastest growing company in Australia • ISO 9001:2015 accredited organization • No of employees 40 • Customers 6500 community pharmacies and 1000 hospital pharmacies

This is the humble but passionate story of Medsurge Healthcare which was founded in 2007 by Indian born migrant Kam Phulwani. The Company sources and markets a broad range of specialised, lifesaving and niche medicines to hospital and retail pharmacies across Australia and New Zealand and throughout the Asia Pacific Region. MEDSURGE HEALTHCARE PTY LTD, , is now one of the fastest growing family-owned pharmaceutical companies in Australia supplying specialised lifesaving medicines to healthcare professionals in Australia and New Zealand.

MEET KAM AND REET

Kam and Reet Phulwani both come from the city of lakes - Bhopal, Madhya Pradesh in India.

Kam's father and grandfather were doctors, so from a young age he was surrounded by intellectual talk on subjects ranging from pharmacy, medicines, science, and healing right through to the more philosophical ideals of helping people and doing good for society. After completing his high school, he was desperate to take a Bachelor of Medicine and Bachelor of Surgery (MBBS) degree in India but could not, due to the high costs. Unperturbed, he took a pharmacy degree and immediately loved it. Kam started his career as a qualified pharmacist in 1996.

Reet came from a progressive and modern-thinking family background, with many of her family members engaged in business and entrepreneurial roles. She grew up listening to all the business challenges her parents faced and learned from those conversations. The seed was planted early for what was to become a cherished dream of having a business of her own someday. Her family readily embraced the latest technologies and innovations, and this led to Reet taking information technology as a stream of study. Reet has a Bachelor of Information Systems from her hometown's Bhopal University and, later, a Master's of Information Systems. Kam and Reet met and were married at a young age, falling in love due to their shared values and aspirations.

"Kam's family were always involved in community activities and serving society and patients he also grew up with a culture of giving back to society."

Sharing in Reet's entrepreneurial spirit, Kam also had a passion to have something of his own right from a young age. He applied for and was given a modest grant from the Indian government of INR 25,000 (AUD 461) to set up a business in India.

Husband and wife managed this small business of orthodontic products along with a small lab which conducted testing for Ranbaxy Laboratories, a large pharmaceutical company in India.

Both Kam's and Reet's personal strengths shone through the interview. Kam was passionate about being self-employed with the intention of making a small difference to society and the lives of people. He is a very motivated and passionate man, who is hardworking and sincere and very keen on acquiring knowledge in his field of chemicals and pharmaceuticals due to his love for chemistry and formulation.

From an early age, Reet was a driven woman who wanted to reach the pinnacle in her career. She expressed a desire and dream to go overseas to Australia to pursue her Master's in Information Technology and Kam readily supported her decision. Reet took the initiative and applied for a visa in Australia, and the couple were accepted.

FOUNDER AND CEO KAM PHULWANI

Kam started his career as a qualified Pharmacist in 1996. In 2003 he was made responsible for Pharmaceutical Procurement in a well-known teaching hospital in Melbourne, Australia. In 2007, Kam set up Medsurge Healthcare in Australia as a founder and CEO with vision of **"We Value life"** **.** In just 12 years Medsurge grew from a start-up company to a medium to large enterprise company and created a niche pharmaceutical company with focus on unmet medicine needs. In 2019, Kam acquired major shareholding in an EU-GMP approved Injectable manufacturing site in India. Subsequently the manufacturing site has received US FDA approval in Jan 2020 which has endorsed the quality and industry standards. Kam's vision is to research and develop and manufacture niche and specialised generic injectable medicines not only for ANZ region but for other global markets such as UK, Europe and USA.

Reet, Kam's wife who has a Masters degree in Information Technology, assists Kam in exploring manufacturing options in Australia as well as manages the key part of Indian operation. Reet's plans are to invest time in "Make In India" and built a bridge to bilateral trade connections of India and Australia. Medsurge is an Australian company which will continue to invest in manufacturing in India and connect Victoria with India.

THEIR STORY

Family Background -

Reet comes from a business family background and grew up listening to all the business challenges her parents faced and learning from those conversation and cherishing to have a business of her own someday. While Kam came from a family of doctors where his dad is GP and his granddad was herbal specialist and had an upbringing where he was always exposed to talks on medicines, science, healing, wellness and helping people and doing good for the human health and community. Hence Kam set up a pharmaceutical company like Medsurge with a vision "We Value Life"

Both Reet and Kam believed in two things . First, they had a vision of wanting to do something to contribute to the community and people's lives and for doing that, they felt it was important to be strong themselves and become self-employed. Having their own venture was always on their mind for the greater good of society, they both had this mission of helping people and they both had a mindset where they wanted to do something different and unique and innovative for making a small change to mankind.

It was not about name or fame or money those are all by-products, says Kam and Reet.

They have found a very significant gap in the society that helps save lives and have plugged this hole to help the people in Australia.

Thus, their work experience, education, family background were pillars of strength advancing their passion towards their Medsurge journey. It was a culmination of Reet's knowledge in technology and Kam's passion for pharmaceuticals, leading to the birth of Medsurge. Above all it was the entrepreneurial and giving spirit of the couple to do good for the society which laid down the foundation for Medsurge as Reet mentioned "Kam comes from a family of doctors, and they were always involved in community activities and serving the society and patients and they had both seen this culture of giving back to the society in their families".

For Reet she had a very progressive family who embraced the latest technology and innovations, and this helped her select Information Technology as a stream of study and this background taught her the baby steps of running a business.

Personal Characteristics

Both Kam's and Reet's personal strengths were proven throughout the interview.

Kam was passionate about being self-employed with the intention of making a small difference to society and the lives of people, a very motivated and passionate man, He truly wanted to learn medicines and become doctor in India but could not due to lack of finance then he was convinced by his father (General Practitioner) to obtain a Pharmacy degree instead and loved it and little did he know at that stage that not getting not medicine would be a boon and take him to Australia and become the CEO of a Global Pharmaceutical Company.

Reet was a driven woman who wanted to reach the pinnacle in her career and had a dream of going overseas to pursue her Master's in information technology. She was the one who took the initiative and applied for a Visa for Australia and arrived in Melbourne to pursue her master's in information technology and completed the degree with flying colours and immediately got a job with Telstra after the completion of her degree with a distinction.

Kam experienced the same problems that every migrant faces in Australia, lack of recognition of qualifications from India. He was qualified Pharmacist from India but he was not allowed to work as a Pharmacist in Australia. At this point Kam decided instead of pursuing career as Pharmacist why not develop medicines? To achieve that he needed to learn about Pharmacy, medicines and national healthcare system in Australia.

The links to their country of origin, their family background, business experience, relevant education and good management skills and personal philosophy and most importantly passion assisted them to get started in business slowly and steadily.

Early Days in Australia

Kam and Reet's Australian story began at 7:00pm on Tuesday 23 July 2002, with 18-year-old Reet and 21-year-old Kam landing in Melbourne Airport on a rainy winter's day… with no accommodation booked! It was only the beginning of an adventure the likes of which they could never have imagined.

The couple had mixed feelings about the reality of the challenges that lay ahead, "There was the excitement of arriving in Australia and studying at an Australian university, but also the worry of not having accommodation!" said Reet.

Nevertheless, they managed to get accommodation at a bed and breakfast for AUD 69 a day, which was far too expensive for them to do long term, at that stage. They checked in, and the next stop was Monash University to complete the student registration and get more information on the course as well as seek assistance in finding better priced accommodation.

In the early days in Australia, Reet studied full time and managed two casual jobs – a huge workload for a young person in a new country. Upon arriving in Australia, Kam experienced similar problems to many other new migrants. His pharmacy qualification was not recognised in Australia, so although he had a degree and experience running his own business, he could not secure the pharmacist job he yearned for. Instead, in the early days in Australia he worked a modest job in a small pharmacy to gain some local work experience.

"Those early days were the most difficult," said Kam.

But success did not elude the driven and humble Kam for long. In 2003, he was made responsible for pharmaceutical procurement at a well-known teaching hospital in Melbourne. Meanwhile, Reet worked sincerely and passed her master's with a Distinction. Almost immediately after graduating, she found a professional job with Telstra. She credits her high marks, good English, and presentation skills as critical in finding this job.

Despite early hardships, the next five years passed pleasantly with the couple working hard and slowly progressing in their jobs while saving to kickstart their dreams. Reet and Kam are both grateful that their managers were particularly good and appreciated their respective work. Kam and Reet eventually saved enough money to buy a house, started paying their mortgage and had three beautiful children together - Ronith, Sienna and Kyra. They continued working and progressing in their jobs for 5-8 years and saving all the way for starting their dream business someday. Reet specifically remembers that their managers were very good and appreciated their work which helped . During that period, they bought a house, started paying their mortgage and had kids and made lots of friends and lived a happy life.

One day on the job Kam realised that there were a lot of medicines which were missing in the hospital as he was working for the pharmacy department where he was assigned the work to get these medicines for the overseas suppliers.

The links to their country of origin, their family background, business experience, relevant education, good management skills, personal philosophy and, most importantly, passion assisted them to get started in business slowly and steadily.

Coming to Australia was a great motivation in itself, said Reet and they both were determined that now that we have come to this beautiful country and have this immense opportunity, we will make the most of it and do something to contribute to the society of this country.

The Birth of an Idea

Early on while working in the purchasing/ procurement department of the well-known Melbourne hospital, where he was responsible for sourcing and buying medicines, Kam Phulwani realised that there were often many medicines missing but needed in the hospital due to the profit-driven procurement model. The medicines were often difficult to find in Australia, leaving him to rely on a number of overseas suppliers.

He recalls one particular fateful day when a critical patient was brought to the hospital in an emergency. He needed some injections, which were not available at all in Australia. Kam looked for suppliers all over the world and eventually found a source in a town in Germany. It took three days for the medicine to arrive from Germany – an unacceptable wait for a critical situation.

Fortunately, the patient received his medicine and pulled through, but the struggle to find the required injection to keep this patient alive led to a Eureka moment in Kam's life. He clearly identified a gap in the market. Identifying the market gap led to a business idea in Kam's mind, seeing the niche market which he could tap into.

"There were many lifesaving medicines that were missing and not available in Australia and although the large pharmaceutical companies may have had a big portfolio, they worked on profit basis and hence did not order all medicines until required," said Kam.

"Australia has such a good health care system. How could we not have so many crucial medicines?" mused Kam.

There was a need for someone to get these medicines here in Australia. They were required, and they were lifesaving. Kam had seen patients dying and wanted to give back to society. This was an opportunity to tap into an unmet need and save people's lives. Bringing them from overseas and stocking them, was a financial commitment and obviously the demand and supply situation was not that very promising at that stage. But there was a need for someone to get these medicines here in Australia as they were needed, and they were lifesaving and as they had seen patients dying and Kam had that vision of giving back to the society and this was an opportunity to tap into and also save people's lives.

Moreover, when Australia has such a good health care system how could we not have so many crucial medicines, this gap led to the business idea in Kam's mind and he saw that niche market which he could tap into. Thus, the spirit of saving lives and entrepreneurship led to Kam's brainchild 'Medsurge'

With Reet's knowledge in technology and business, Kam's passion for pharmaceuticals and entrepreneurship, and the couple's shared passion for doing good for society, Medsurge was born. In 2007, Kam registered the company 'Medsurge Healthcare' in Australia as Founder and CEO with a vision of, 'We value life'.

Both Reet and Kam believed in two things. First, they had a vision of wanting to do something to contribute to society and people's lives and for doing that, they felt it was important to be strong themselves and become self-employed. Having their own venture was always on their mind for the greater good of society. They both had this mission of helping people and they both had a mindset where they wanted to do something different, unique, and innovative for making a small change to mankind. Reet said for her it was never about earning a name or fame or money - those are all by-products.

Kam had a passion for chemistry and pharmacy and developing new products to help people and Reet had business skills - thus they combined their skillsets and established Medsurge.

So, Kam decided to register the company in 2007 and laid the foundation for Medsurge.

We did not take any loans from banks for the business, it was always our own savings as we both did not believe in taking big loans and it was difficult to get business loans when you are starting new. We started from a home office and a laptop, still in full time jobs and struggling to build a base for the business working at late in the night".

The starting phase of a business has seen to be difficult with most migrants.

Reet continued in her job to pay the mortgage and meet the household needs while Kam worked on developing the business.

Challenges

Their challenges were basically cash flow and capital requirements, high price or real estate, rents, and finding the clients who would trust them and also finding right partners for business and for support services for the business.

Finding right employees with the appropriate skills was important said, Reet. They now have a very strong team whom they have trained well and look after them as their own family and to them family comes first when it comes to managing their staff. They are proud that they have created employment in the local community.

Capital was also a main concern she said, "That was our challenge on because when you are running a business from little funds, you don't have that much to expand".

But with a lot of hiccups and experiences and through a bumpy ride here and there we managed to take the business forward.

They were initially using third party warehouses and had to slowly develop their own warehouses which was another challenge. Logistics and brand building were big issues because of the nature of the business. " It's such a crucial business and associated with lives and health" said Reet and getting the trust of people and clients was difficult. Breaking into the market was most difficult in this industry as a lot depends on trust and faith. Change of policies and paperwork is also a hassle. The banks were difficult in the early stages but now that we are successful, they are our friends.

MEDSURGE

Headquartered in Melbourne, Australia, Medsurge Healthcare was founded in 2007 and is an Australian Department of Health approved facility and ISO 9001:2015 accredited organisation. Among the fastest growing companies in Australia, it employs 40 staff to service its customers which include some 6,500 pharmacies and 1,000 hospitals, supplying upwards of 700 refrigerated and non-refrigerated medicines.

The Company sources and markets a broad range of specialised, lifesaving and niche medicines to hospital and retail pharmacies across Australia and New Zealand and throughout the Asia Pacific Region. Medsurge is a Therapeutic Goods Australia (TGA) approved pharmaceutical company, supplying specialised lifesaving medicines to healthcare professionals in Australia and New Zealand.

Among its many accolades, Medsurge was awarded 2017 Westpac Business of Tomorrow, AIBC SME of the Year 2019, and 'Ethnic Business Awards' finalist among others. Kam was a finalist in the Executive of the Year awards of CEO Magazine in 2019.

Medsurge recently launched Medicianz Healthcare Australia, a new brand which manufactures products in Europe through its partners and markets in Australia and New Zealand. Medicianz Healthcare Australia follows the vision of building its brand in the Australian healthcare market through its global presence, using strategic alliances, a people focus and innovative technology in the pharmacy world. Both Medsurge Healthcare and Medicianz Healthcare Australia are 100 per cent Australian owned and operated.

The company has built a reputation in the industry through its commitment to quality, compliance, and reliability. The company facility is capable of manufacturing both aseptically filled and terminally sterilised products.

In terms of certifications globally, the Indian site has European Union Good Manufacturing Practice (EU GMP Hungary), Health Canada, The Pharmaceutical Inspection Convention and Pharmaceutical Inspection Co-operation Scheme (PIC/S), National Agency for Food and Drug Administration and Control (NAFDAC), ZAZIBONA, World Health Organization - Good Manufacturing Practices (WHO-GMP), ISO 9001 Qualification for Quality Management System, and in January 2020, the manufacturing site received the United States' Food and Drug Administration's (FDA) approvals which has further endorsed the quality and adherence to industry standards.

Kam's vision is to research, develop and manufacture niche and specialised generic injectable medicines not only for the Australia-New Zealand (ANZ) region, but also for other global markets such as the United Kingdom, Europe, and the United States.

Reet oversees operations in Australia and manages the key parts of Indian operations. Under her supervision, the company has seen 30 per cent growth every year over the years – an astonishing feat for the young migrant couple.

In 2019, they acquired a major shareholding in an EU-GMP approved injectables manufacturing site in India.

Medsurge has grown steadily and seen a rapid increase in their clients as seen below with a lot of hardwork, good management and sincere objectives.

Figure 2.

Figure 3.

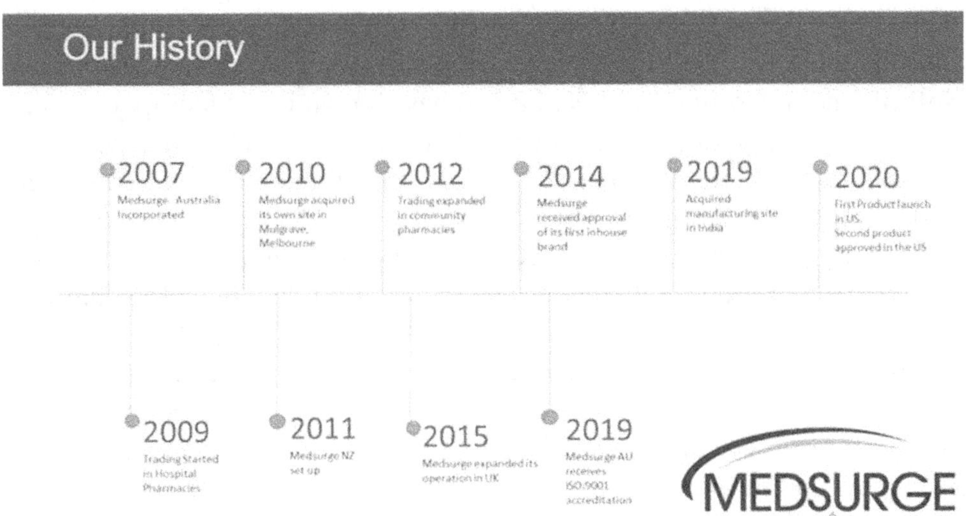

Their current product range provides upwards of 700 refrigerated and non-refrigerated medicines to around 1000 hospital pharmacies and 6500 retail pharmacies. The Company recently started its own brand under the name "MEDICIANZ HEALTHCARE AUSTRALIA". Medicianz manufactures product in Europe through its partners and markets in Australia and New Zealand. Medicianz Healthcare Australia follows the vision of building its Brand in Australian Healthcare market through its global presence, using strategic alliances, been people focus and using innovative technology in pharmacy world. Both 'Medsurge Healthcare' and 'Medicianz Healthcare Australia' are 100% Australian owned and operated.

With a strong commitment to Quality and Compliance, company has built a reputation in the industry for quality and reliability. The facility is capable of manufacturing both aseptically filled and terminally sterilized products. Indian site has EU-GMP (Hungary), Health Canada, PIC/S, NAFDAC, ZAZIBONA, WHO-GMP, ISO 9001 & US-FDA approvals. Medsurge is committed to making a positive impact on the world which our future generations will inherit. They are passionate about working with partners who, believe that operational sustainability and improving the quality of life for all is at the heart of everything we do.

International Expansion

Recently Kam has invested in an Indian manufacturing site which is a Sterile Injectables Company, that manufactures high quality liquid sterile formulations . This facility is an active manufacturing site spread across 5,000 Sqft of land in Hosur, Tamil Naidu and has its own R&D facility on site, it is a US-FDA approved site and currently manufactures pharmaceuticals for markets such as UK, Europe, Australia, Canada and USA and employees 360 employees. Kam mentioned, "In 2019, they engaged in an acquisition in India by purchasing a manufacturing plant in India and that was a very big milestone for our company and employed 360 people and we are now producing we have our own brand and conduct our own R&D. In 2007 they were dealing with 3 products and today they have 900 specialized products in a span of 12 years" . Today Medsurge is not just pharmaceutical trading company but also exporting to a few countries like Middle East, Africa, Singapore and other Asian countries. So, we they are producing a massive range of products. Besides they have also opened an office in UK because they have a similar health system and it was relatively uncomplicated to set up office there and they are doing exceptionally well.

Networks Local and International

Medsurge first built their local networks with hospitals and one client led to another through word of mouth and the trust grew stronger and business evolved. Reet mentioned that besides the local network the international network too was importnat " So first of all, obviously are all suppliers in Europe, so that was our starting point, who connected us with the European suppliers there. That started the building block process".

Leading to the start of an office in the UK, Singapore and then India. .

Secrets to Success and Early Struggles

In just 12 years, Medsurge grew from a start-up to a medium to large sized enterprise pharmaceutical company through fulfilling niche and unmet medicine needs. But it was not all smooth sailing. The starting phase of a business is difficult for most migrants. For Reet and Kam, it was no different.

Reet continued in her job to pay the mortgage and meet the household needs while Kam worked on developing the business.

"We did not take any loans from banks for the business; it was always our own savings as we both did not believe in taking big loans and it was difficult to get business loans when you are starting new anyway. We started from a home office and a laptop, still in full time jobs and struggling to build a base for the business working at late in the night. Capital was our key challenge early on because when you are running a business from little funds, you don't have that much to expand," said Reet.

Bringing critical and needed lifesaving medicines from overseas and stocking them, was a financial commitment and obviously the demand and supply situation was not that very promising at that stage.

"The banks were difficult in the early stages but now that we are successful, they are our friends."

Reet and Kam wish the government and other support services would have had more trust in them at the early stages of setting up of this business as it would have helped them in their struggling days and assisted with developing the business faster.

Another area the couple found difficult was securing the trust of people and clients. Breaking into the market was most difficult, as much depends on trust and faith.

"The early years when we started the business was difficult as people would not trust us. They thought, 'Who are these Indian migrants who want to talk to us about lifesaving medicines? and 'What do they know?!' There is little faith and trust in migrants at that stage," said Reet.

Brand building and trust were big issues because of the nature of the business. "It's such a crucial business and associated with lives and health" said Reet.

Other than money and trust, the other issues faced in the early days were the high price of real estate/ rents, finding clients and the right partners for business as well as finding support services for the business.

In the beginning, Kam used third party warehouses before they could slowly develop their own warehouses.

"With a lot of hiccups along our bumpy ride, we managed to take the business forward," said Reet.

In terms of the secrets to their success, finding the right employees with the appropriate skills was important, and Kam and Reet invested heavily in this area early on. They now have an extraordinarily strong team that they have trained well and look after as if they were their own family. To Kam and Reet, family comes first - and this philosophy applies when it comes to managing their staff too. They are proud that they have created employment in the local community.

Relationships and trust were important too. Medsurge first built their local networks with hospitals and one client led to another through word of mouth and the trust grew stronger and business evolved. Reet mentioned that besides the local network the international network too was important – especially in Europe. Relationships in Europe led to the start of offices in the UK, and then on to Singapore and India. The India acquisition was an important one as 90 per cent of all pharmaceuticals are manufactured in India. Reet appreciated how when all of Germany and UK were shut, they could depend on their India factory to supply the medicines.

Tapping into Indian Government initiatives and country-of-origin knowledge and relationships has also been a secret to the company's success along the way. In line with this, Kam plans to manufacture products in India, following the encouragement of the Indian Government's 'Make in India' initiatives to encourage overseas companies to manufacture in India and make dedicated investments into manufacturing.

"Medsurge is an Australian company and will continue to invest in manufacturing in India and connect Victoria with India," explained Reet.

Recently, Medsurge has invested in an Indian manufacturing site which is a sterile injectables company, that manufactures high quality liquid sterile formulations. This facility is an active manufacturing site spread across 5,000 square feet of land in Hosur, Tamil Naidu and has its own research and development facility on site, it is a US-FDA approved site and currently manufactures pharmaceuticals for markets such as UK, Europe, Australia, Canada and USA and employees 360 employees.

Kam said in 2019 they engaged in an acquisition in India by purchasing a manufacturing plant in India and that was a very big milestone for our company and employed 360 people and we are now producing we have our own brand and conduct our own Research and development. In 2007 they were dealing with 3 products and today they have 900 specialised products in a span of 12 years.

Today, Medsurge is not just involved in supplying medical products from overseas but also exporting to a few countries like Singapore and other Asian countries. So, we they are producing a massive range of products. Besides, they have also opened an office in UK because they have a similar health system and it was relatively uncomplicated to set up office there and they are doing exceptionally well.

Future Plans and Opportunities

Australia is known for its quality in medical products and is trusted around the world because of its strict medical product governing body. "So, when a medicine or medical product is manufactured in Australia it has a lot of respect from the world," says Kam.

As of 2019, global spending on pharmaceuticals topped USD 1.03 trillion. For the United States, the figure was USD 491 billion, for India USD 29 billion, and Australia's share was USD 12.6 billion. By 2023, these figures are expected to grow to USD 1.57 trillion globally, USD 41 billion for India, and USD 16 billion for Australia. Further, pharmaceuticals are Australia's sixth biggest import in terms of value. India is Australia's 13th biggest supplier, selling Australia USD 302 million p.a. Germany is number 4 at USD 1.32 billion and the US is number 2 at USD 1.82 billion.

Needless to say, Kam sees a massive opportunity for this industry in the future.

He expects to expand the Australian business by continuous research and development and hopes to create even more jobs, particularly for Victorians. Expanding bilateral trade between India and Australia is high on his mind.

"With our manufacturing site in India and core operations in Australia we are looking forward to building our strength by finding the right trade-off between global efficiency and local resilience. We are steadily working towards developing a research and development facility in Australia that will create further opportunities for local employment and innovation."

"We have a vision that one day, people will be buying our brand of products all over the world," said Kam.

"We hope to achieve this vision by retaining the manufacturing, research and development and brand building in Australia, generate jobs and promote 'Make in Australia' and build on the knowledge acquired and acquire more knowledge and expand globally through a global network of offices in every country."

"Today, we are in a very good place and feel satisfied with our contribution to society especially when we get emails from hospitals with these beautiful messages saying that, because this medicine came on time because of your service this child was saved, which gives the utmost satisfaction and that we have met our vision of value life and that we keep on going."

"We have created a sense that no life should go. That is the reason we are in this business," Kam said.

NOTE

The information in this chapter is based on a series of interviews with Kam and Reet Phulwani conducted on April 13, 2019.

Chapter 8
Kananjar "Kan" Shivaram Shetty

ABSTRACT

When President Kananjar "Kan" Shivaram Shetty bought the paint business Omega Industries in 2000, little did he know it would grow into a leading global company at the forefront of innovation with commercial and industrial coatings and paintings. At the time, Omega Industries had been operating at a loss of $200,000. However, it was Kan's faith in the business and willingness to learn the secrets of his trade that resulted in Omega Industries substantially expanding their operations through the acquisition with Apco Coatings, securing major contracts with the government and entering new profitable sectors. Today, the company has 200-250 project-based staff across Sydney, Brisbane, Melbourne, Malaysia, UAE, and Texas in the United States and has manufactured 600 different products. This chapter dives into Kan's background, the business challenges he faced, and how he was able to accelerate Omega Industries' growth into a global innovative company.

DOI: 10.4018/978-1-6684-4986-8.ch008

Figure 1.

MANAGING DIRECTOR AT OMEGA PAINTS SYDNEY & BERGER PAINTS SINGAPORE PTE LTD

Omega Projects is an ISO tri-certified commercial & industrial services division of Omega Industries. Specialising in commercial painting and other complimentary services, we have built a prominent position in the industry servicing a myriad of sectors throughout Australia.

Omega Industries is a privately-owned global company. They specialize in commercial and industrial painting and coatings, as well as line-markings and paint manufacturing. With more than three decades of experience, Omega has the experience and know-how to handle all commercial and industrial coating projects.

Omega Industries prides itself on being at the forefront of innovation with coatings and painting. They believe it is vital to give back; they work on research and development while working with universities around the world. It is through these partnerships that they are able to continue to develop, grow, and provide a service that no other company can.

Omega Industries in Riverstone, NSW is a family business and has grown significantly since 2000, when current President Kan Shetty bought the paint business. Today the company has 200-250 project-based staff across locations in Sydney, Brisbane, Melbourne, Malaysia, UAE and Texas in the United States and have created 600 different products. Family values fuel the company culture, yet a number of staff come from diverse backgrounds. Omega has recently launched the Rapid Dry range of paint products in floor coating (FloorKote), pool coating (PoolKote) and road markings (Road Marking). The RapidDry range of products are suited to home application all the way to large scale infrastructure projects. Onsite R&D has taken years to develop an improved epoxy coating that doesn't smell, has faster drying time (to allow same day reapplication) and as well as extending the durability of the product. (Omega Industries, 2022).

MR KANANJAR SHIVARAM SHETTY TRAVELLED FROM MUMBAI TO MUSCAT TO SYDNEY TO SINGAPORE WITH THE STRONG SUPPORT OF HIS WIFE GEETA SHETTY

Mr Kananjar Shivaram Shetty (who goes by 'Kan') was born into a modest farming family in his home country of India. His parents eked out a humble living to support their son and always taught him the value of education in providing a pathway out of poverty. For young Kan, the road to economic freedom was literally a long one; walking to school was a 14-kilometre round trip which he undertook on a daily basis.

In his early schooling, Kan was disciplined and diligent in his studies and quickly excelled in academics. By the time he reached the final and most critical last two years of high school, he achieved Best Student of the Year for two successive years.

College beckoned and so did Mumbai. He said goodbye to his family and made the move to the 'Big Smoke', where he worked long hours during the day and then attended college in the evenings to complete a Bachelor's in Commerce. Upon graduating, he was offered a job with Suhail & Saud Bahwan Group (SSBG), a multinational company in Oman.

"I worked for SSBG for 17 years and learnt a lot from the management including how to run and expand a business. That company started with three employees and later grew to 35,000. Seeing that gradual but exponential growth was inspirational," explained Kan.

In 1985, Shivaram married Geeta Shetty, an educated Indian woman who later worked for a publishing company in Oman called Times of Oman and later Kompass Oman. The couple have two children – Namrata and Ashvat (Ash).

One fateful day, Geeta my wife was flipping through a travel brochure looking for inspiration for their next holiday and she saw a beautiful image of the Sydney Opera House. They decided to go for a visit to Australia.

During their trip, out of sheer curiosity she decided to pay a quick visit to the Sydney branch of Kompass to introduce herself to the Manager. As fate would have it, the Sydney Manager then connected with her Oman Manager, who sang Geeta's praises as an employee. Shortly afterwards, Geeta received a call with an offer of an attractive job at Kompass, Sydney.

They were both surprised, but after discussing the opportunity, they agreed it was a positive step for the couple and she accepted the offer. The young family migrated to Australia in 1997. A holiday and chance meeting had shaped their family destiny!

EARLY STRUGGLES

While Geeta had immediately stepped into secure employment in Australia, for Kan job hunting was stressful and unrewarding. For almost six months, he was unemployed. It was a strange feeling for a highly experienced and educated man who had been reliably employed for 17 years.

To boost his prospects, Geeta suggested he look at doing some local courses. He applied for a bridging course to be a Certified Practising Accountant (CPA). This additional qualification quickly paid off as he was offered a role with IBM, where he worked for a few months before joining another multinational company.

"During my time with the company, I was constantly harassed by my boss. I felt I couldn't continue with the job anymore. To make matters worse, I actually lost my job on my son's ninth birthday," said Kan.

Disheartened by the bad experience and blow to his self-confidence, Kan knew then and there that it was time to start his own business so he would not have to work for anyone else.

"Geeta was working, so we at least had one income and were able to take a risk. That was the core strength I had. It was all I needed to begin."

Kan set about researching to purchase a suitable business the very day he was laid off.

OMEGA INTERNATIONAL COATINGS

He grabbed a copy of The Sydney Morning Herald and saw a classified advertisement for a paint business for sale. Established in 1987, Omega Industries (then known as Omega International Coatings) was a small, light industrial paint manufacturing company in Chipping Norton, NSW. They produced industrial paints, varnishes and thinners - seven products in total.

Kan spoke frankly of his first impressions, "I had no clue [about the paint business]!"

However, he was curious to investigate, and a meeting was arranged. Looking at the company's documentation, Kan drew upon his accounting and business knowledge to analyse the business.

"When I looked at the balance sheet, I saw they had accumulated a loss of $200,000. If you go to any accountant, they'll say, 'It's not a viable business." But I looked at the bank statement and saw it had a continuous balance of $50,000. To me, that was evidence of real customers paying real bills. I said to myself, 'This is it! The business is running.'"

The accounting knowledge was a boon.

"I felt confident that this was a decision I was not going to lose on. I had to step in. I had to do something. People asked me why I was buying a paint business without knowing much about it, but I was confident I could learn."

To secure capital to buy the business, the couple sold Geeta's apartment in Mumbai. In the year 2000, the purchase was finalised.

To reduce expenses in the beginning, Kan did almost everything on his own – from loading bags onto the forklift to pouring paint. It was a back-breaking work coupled with long hours. He only had one employee; a semi-retired paint chemist. There was the added pressure that Geeta was sustaining the family financially. He did not want to fail, especially as their mortgage was being paid from her salary.

"In those days, I would make batches [of paint] during the daytime and sell them in the afternoon. Being able to run everything, from warehousing – one must understand the rigorous process of manufacturing. It's not like other businesses—one has to look after production, lab maintenance, warehousing, invoicing and then finally sales. Every day entailed a series of gargantuan tasks for me."

Sales were slow to pick up. Although he had inherited a few existing buyers of the paint in the handover of the business, the crucial people-to-people relationships and trust were not there yet.

Kan explained, "They were not used to me. A lot of these guys were tradies and knew each other for years and suddenly, I barged in and tried to sell paint—of course, they would have no interest in my product! It was almost impossible to penetrate the mainstream market, but I persevered. It took two years to make one definitive, new sale; an additional sale from what was already there."

Despite these early hardships, he felt a certain sense of peace in being the master of his own destiny at last. He was gradually learning the secrets to his trade. He had his wife's confidence. He had faith in the bank statements. He also had one consistent pillar – the part-time chemist and of course his wife and son Ashwat helped in the business.

Within two years, the company shifted to its own purpose-built factory at Mt Druitt, NSW. Mr. Shetty subsequently acquired Hydrotech Ink, a screen-printing ink company.

GROWTH THROUGH ACQUISITION – APCO COATINGS

After five years of living in Australia, the rewards and healthier profits eventually began to come in and Kan continued to look for more opportunities to grow. In 2002, he learnt about a company called Asian Paints (Apco Coatings), which had a plant in Australia. He contacted them hoping for a subcontract and set up a meeting. During the meeting, he found out that the company was struggling financially, with continuous losses for almost 15 years.

"Asian Paints' owners were ready to just give the business to someone. They had 35 employees and couldn't afford to pay redundancies and supplier liabilities. Therefore, they were highly motivated to sell their operations to pass on liabilities and exit the Australian market. We benefited from incorporating established multinational systems and procedures into our current business operations. This saved us a few decades of time and effort"

Apco proved to be a good, profitable business and resulted in a huge, propitious leap for Kan. Through this acquisition, he secured a lucrative State Government contract, their branded products were more accepted in the market, they received new packaging ideas, new policies, technical assistance and many other things they may have been difficult for a small business to accomplish. But perhaps most fortuitously, they entered the road marking business.

"Back then, there were only a few companies involved in road marking and we were one of the select few. Today, Apco is now the largest producer of road marking paints in Australia," said Kan.

"With Omega International Coatings, we made seven products. With Apco, we had access to 600 products, so expansion and scope increased exponentially."

That translated into solid growth for the company. Throughout all the acquisitions, their major contracts with the government increased their sheer volume.

"When you get volume, you get better supply power. Our cost was reduced. Now, we could compete from different angles and expand our business to different places."

Kan quickly realised that Apco having a presence in both Sydney and Townsville meant incurring expenses unnecessarily. He made the decision to shut the plant in Townsville and consolidate all operations under one roof in Sydney. This decision proved a shrewd one as he was able to reduce costs by 75 per cent.

Although Apco's acquisition was a boon, it was not all plain sailing and Kan admits they were clueless about the product range and its overall management.

"We had to decide what kind of company we wanted to be—do we become a sales company, or delve into operations? Because my background was operations, we removed the sales side of our approach when we took over. We reduced in terms of sales but were still pushing the products out."

GATHERING SPEED

The acquisition ultimately enabled the company (now known as Australian Paint Company) to get a foothold in automotive, decorative and specialty paints.

From a production capacity of 30 tonnes per week in 2015 to 250 tonnes per week in 2020, the organisation has come a long way. They have furthered operations by entering the paint service and applications sector. After acquiring a paint contracting company, Omega Painting in 2011, the group revamped their marketing image under one simple banner 'Omega Industries', thereby creating Australia's first vertically integrated paint company with a 'Supply & Apply' concept.

Today, having solely used and developed the name and trademark Omega Industries, including its variants in Australia, the company is a commercially recognised coatings business. With its Head Office in Sydney, the company manufactures and markets a range of decorative and industrial paint products and application services under its various product brands. Their trump card is their innovation. They have innovated 600 different products and achieved a competitive advantage in the market.

Its operations spread like wildfire across the country. Currently, there are two manufacturing facilities in Australia as well as distribution centres and several regional and area offices.

Omega has recently undertaken several acquisitions. In September 2019, the company acquired Berger Singapore (a subsidiary of Asian Paints). This new acquisition included rights to enter markets in many Southeast Asian countries.

Omega has also ventured into contracting and local integration among other areas, all the while capitalising on their core business.

"With Hydrotech, we didn't have to buy new machinery because the products could be made with what we already had. They supplied us with the screen-printing ink. Any acquisition we do is linked to at least one part of our business. With the painting side of the business slowly emerging, we started using the products to paint the buildings."

Kan and his family prefer acquisitions and takeovers to mergers because it allows the family to maintain control over decision making and eliminate bureaucracy.

"We manage to implement any thought or an idea in a matter of seconds. We don't need to undergo a board meeting to decide. That's not how we do our business."

Kan confesses that the speed of decision making sometimes comes with the risk of forgoing detailed planning, governance and due diligence and hence there is a chance that it may backfire sometimes. He mentions one example when they put $250,000 into a biodiesel plant in Darwin and then the oil prices dropped, meaning a devastating loss for the family business.

"That is also a reason why due diligence is not a bad idea," he said frankly.

CUSTOMER-CENTRIC, PEOPLE AND RELATIONSHIPS-FOCUSSED PHILOSOPHY

Kan attributes their success to a customer-centric, people and relationship-focussed philosophy. They give utmost importance to customer service and customer loyalty is their chief priority.

Kan explains, "If our customers come to us with a complaint, we never argue even if we believe it's not our fault. We say we'll work on improving it - end of story. If a customer asks, 'Can you make it?' We always say 'Yes!' and deliver on that promise. That is why customers keep approaching us and why we are growing. Our customers feel confident in us."

"It's about being accessible. If your phone rings, answer it. If you're one of those people going 'I'll get back to you in two days', you're not going to grow your business. We get a lot of big multinationals' former customers who appreciate that they can call us at 9:00 pm and we will answer."

Kan recalls his early struggles to break into the market as a key driver to his business appreciating customers and maintaining the 'small business touch'.

"Ten years ago, people would not even talk to us and wouldn't buy our paint, so us telling them to find some other place would have been the worst thing to say. We hold our customers in high regard. When a customer negotiates with us, we try to accommodate them. If we are too rigid, we lose - not the customer."

This philosophy extends to Kan's business relationships too.

Kan's son, Ashvat (Ash) Shetty, Director of Omega Industries said, "Our family are good friends with many of our direct competitors. At the end of the day, we are linking with reliable, honest people that we can trust and work with rather than fight against."

"Management skill and negotiation go hand-in-hand. Being able to negotiate and always knowing what you are going to walk out with in a negotiation is key to success in your business. A lot of people negotiate without a plan.

If the deal doesn't go ahead and lead to a fruitful next move or if there is no reward at the end of the lane, it's not worth it."

Focusing on customer relationships means that customer perceptions are also important. This influenced the branding and naming of the company.

"When Asian Paints came to the fold, no one wanted their product. Whether rightly or not, the perception was the word 'Asian' was considered cheap or inferior. So, the actual brand was called Apco (Asian Paints Corporation). They changed their brand. As migrant owners, it was a struggle for us to penetrate the market, especially in Townsville where they're not used to migrants. We had to find gaps in the market for it to work."

Kan's wife Geeta agrees, "It's a crucial lesson for entrepreneurs to know that you may need to adapt your name to the local country."

INTERNATIONAL EXPANSIONS

When the time came to venture into other countries including Vietnam, Fiji, Malaysia, New Zealand and the USA, they ensured they had relationship networks in the new countries or connections with someone already doing business with them in Australia. It would invariably involve somebody working with them or somebody known to them who goes back to that country, which serves as a huge asset for them as they link with others.

"We've got different things to do in different countries. We send some of our products with private labels to Vietnam. We make the products here and send them overseas."

Global or international business can go through institutional constraints. This is evident in the German renewable energy firms that are building new offices in India, Latin America and China, because the German market is now saturated. They are in desperate need to find a partner in India or China and work with them. But small businesses can't always afford joint ventures. They need a local company with local market experience to avoid costly learning errors.

Ash adds, "When I went to the US, I sought out the largest road marking contractor there and contacted them on LinkedIn to discuss a joint venture. Even with the US, if I had a local business partner that helped me, I would have probably saved myself two years. I couldn't get credit. If I had someone who'd taught me and walked me through getting a social security card and all those things, I would have finished everything in a week, but it took me six months to get a lot of things in place."

Kan explains that they are currently renting their plant out to another paint manufacturer and getting them to do all the work – a white labelling strategy. They essentially put labels on the cans for Omega.

Ash explains, "After working here, you kind of realise your missteps—what you wouldn't do again and what you need to skip next time. We would get someone else to do all the groundwork, so that we can just focus on the marketing, the sales and the relationships."

"As of now, we are working for five American multinationals. They don't give you a job unless they have confidence in you. We are the only company in Australia who are the preferred supplier for three State Governments with our supply of road paint."

Kan believes certifications are behind their reputation as preferred supplier.

"You need to get all the ticks for all the standards. That is the reason we got the contract with the State Government. We beat an American multinational. Today, we can proudly say we are the largest producer of road marking paint for the government." Working with the government has gained them a lot a trust in the market.

Today, they have taken over Berger Paints Singapore and Kan is the Managing Director at BERGER PAINTS SINGAPORE PTE LTD.

SECRETS OF SUCCESS

Kan made a point of involving his family and engaging them in the business. There are occasional differences of opinion among the family members, especially with different generations involved. Ash modernises the business while Kan keeps the structure and the old spirit intact.

Ash said, "Since we began, our core values have remained the same. That is why we sustained ourselves in the long run. The business is managed by one family unit, operating in their respective departments. Since everyone is family, they perform their best."

"There is a major difference when we talk about setting up shop in the US versus Australia. In the US, everyone is trying to make it for themselves. In Australia, it's very hard to find labour compared to the US. That doesn't mean that there is a drop in quality and pre-requisites. All the applicants have degrees and they all fit the criteria I was looking for. I'm paying them half the price, but I'm selling the product for the same price. In that regard, the US has advantage over Australia."

Despite this apparent advantage, Ash confesses that he has often thought about leaving the US. He is met with respect when he approaches his Australian customers, courtesy of his father. But in the US, no one wanted to talk to him, since he wasn't a citizen, didn't have the local accent, and was not attuned to the ways of the Americans.

Nevertheless, Ash is grateful that he didn't pack his bags and leave in the face of rejection.

"He has patience. We are a global family business now, but nothing would have been possible if we hadn't stood strong in the face of closed doors." said Kan.

"The US and Australia are vastly different in terms of business culture. The US is a capitalist country where someone is either very rich or marginally poor, whereas Australia holds a very large middle class. Big enterprises kill all kinds of competition," added Kan.

Ash said, "Australia has a culture of co-existence. Many of my father's friends are our main competitors in the market! We all go out for dinner. We exchange raw materials when in need – the concept of a monopoly doesn't exist around here. Due diligence and retaining goodwill of your customers should be the primary absolutes when entering a new market. You need to respect and learn the culture and the ways of the people before making your decisions."

Land is relatively cheap in the US, compared to Australia.

"The Americans place their bets on due diligence. Here, if you spend your time second-guessing, someone else will come and procure the land before you. But over there, you've got plenty of time to decide. You only need to appropriate your marketing strategy that is best suited for them."

Kan says Australia is easier when it comes to banking.

Ash agrees, "I realised how hard it was to get money out of someone in the US. It's far simpler in Australia - I can send $100,000 within seconds. Back there, I have to wait days for a paper cheque and then wait for another two weeks to receive the funds. If it gets lost, I must start again. The banking system in Australia is far ahead of the US."

In terms of future diversification, Omega has ventured into commercial property, especially here in Australia.

"We have a new company called Omega Property Investments. We acquired a few industrial properties and we are renting it to various businesses."

The future certainly looks bright for this close-knit and entrepreneurial family.

NOTE

The information in this chapter is based on a series of interviews with Kananjar 'Kan' Shivaram Shetty conducted on May 7, 2019.

REFERENCES

Omega Industries. (2022). *About Us.* https://omegaind.com.au/corporate/about-us/

Chapter 9
Dhruv Deepak "DD" Saxena

ABSTRACT

Born into modest privilege in Allhabad, India to a university professor, Dhruv Deepak's adaptability, pursuit for excellence, and experience with entrepreneurialism from a young age would catapult him into the CEO and Founder of Riverina Oils & Bio Energy Pty Ltd (ROBE). Riverina Oils has now grown into the largest greenfield agricultural project and refinery plant in Australia. They crush and refine over 200,000 tonnes of oilseeds per year through a state-of-the-art manufacturing facility and produce around 250 tonnes of refined vegetable oil and 350 tonnes of vegetable protein meal per day. For his entrepreneurial accomplishments, Deepak has won many awards including CEO of the Year 2016 – Energy and Resources Category, Asia Pacific Entrepreneur of the Year 2015, and Indian Australian Ambassador of the Year 2014. This chapter explores Deepak's early life, the road to starting his business in Australia, and his future plans for ROBE.

DOI: 10.4018/978-1-6684-4986-8.ch009

Figure 1.

RIVERINA OILS

They crush and refine over 200,000 tonnes of oilseeds per year through a state-of-the-art manufacturing facility, sourcing raw materials from local farms, in order to produce world-class oils and vegetable protein meals. They produce around 250 tonnes of refined vegetable oil and 350 tonnes of vegetable protein meal per day for the poultry, dairy and animal feed industries.

Riverina Oils & Bio Energy Pty Ltd (ROBE) has custom built a state-of-the-art integrated oilseed crushing and refining plant, making the project one of the largest value-added investments in the Agri-Food processing sector in regional Australia in the last 5 years. Our plant is located in Wagga Wagga, NSW, Australia, central to the agricultural hub of the Riverina with world-class logistics and storage facilities with readily available raw material and market access. Their location in the heart of the most productive oilseed growing region in Australia. This has created a cleaner, efficient and stable supply chain well-poised to meet the demandsof the growing US market for Non-GMO ingredients. ***ROBE Australia*** *is proud to be a Non-GMO Project compliant partner. They have set up an efficient supply chain to service a wide variety of customers in the U.S. Their oil is available in bulk shipments. (Riverina Oils, n.d.)*

THE ONLY BROWN FELLOW

Born into modest privilege in Allahabad India, Dhruv Deepak Saxena, known as DD, was the son of a university professor. After completing his early Catholic schooling in India, he moved to New York in 1965, where his father was involved in a chemistry research project at the University of Illinois Urbana-Champaign.

"I was the only brown fellow there who could speak fluent English," laughs DD.

Despite DD's humour, it is evident it was a daunting atmosphere because there was little support back then for immigrants. However, DD's adaptability and desire to excel pushed him forward and he graduated in just two years, becoming the youngest school graduate at the time. The teenaged DD secured admission into five good universities, including Caltech, but the cost of tuition was prohibitively high, and his father had an opportunity to teach at the Indian Institute of Technology, Kanpur India.

His father felt conflicted about depriving his son of the opportunity and confessed as much to his colleague. The colleague kindly offered a direct personal recommendation to IIT for his son. It worked, and DD was accepted as the youngest student in his batch at IIT Kanpur with the chance to rub shoulders with the brightest intellectual geniuses.

"In India back then, there were only three kinds of jobs that had prestige; administration, engineering or medicine. You did what you did to succeed and get a job. The options were fairly limited," explained DD.

DD graduated IIT and started a career in chemical engineering. He continued study at IIM Bangalore, where he met fellow student and fell in love. DD wanted to marry her but her conservative South Indian parents were disapproving of their relationship. DD's gold medal at University were to be the tipping point to win their approval, and DD has now been married to his wife for 40 years.

FORGING A CAREER

After graduating from IIM, DD began a career with Unilever; a company that DD credits with teaching him many life lessons and helping him on his road to success. Unilever demanded huge commitment, with onboard training lasting for 18 months. The salary was 1,200 rupees, or AUD 25.00.

"The company turnover was remarkable when I joined so you must imagine my jubilation when I was hired! Unilever was a great thing for me because I met a most balanced group of people. The seed of entrepreneurialism had been sown in me. The peer group learning made it the best company to work for in terms of systems, discipline, values, culture or even taking some casual time off."

His last assignment in India was with the publicly listed company, where he worked directly for the owners.

"I started five greenfield projects. I was the youngest vice-president in the company. The level of empowerment was addictive and frighteningly liberating."

By the age of 35, he was working for India's fourth largest entrepreneur within a very structured and process-driven corporate organisation.

"I had a lot of experience from quite a young age. It triggered the desire for corporate entrepreneurship in me. I came from a family where nobody had even opened a tea shop! I could never let go of that newfound hunger. My upbringing was always protected, but the challenges I faced working in those companies shaped me the way I am today."

In 1992, DD was given five crores (50 million rupees, or just over AUD1 million) to invest and chose to start a gherkin project in India.

"At that time in India, no one knew what a gherkin was! I had to resort to bank funding, mortgages and offtake agreements through a joint venture. Gherkins have now become the largest container export from India. Since gherkins are hand-picked and value-added, this creates jobs for a million people."

Shortly after the success of the gherkin project, DD and his wife decided to take a leap of faith and leave India to work abroad. They wanted their growing children to be exposed to a cosmopolitan atmosphere. DD was offered a position as CEO for one of the largest South-East Asian groups heading the international operations in Singapore.

It turned out to be a major turning points in DD's life and a catalyst towards him becoming a global leader based in Australia.

FROM SINGAPORE TO AUSTRALIA – UPS AND DOWNS

The move from India to Singapore and eventually to Australia was marked by dizzying highs and worrying lows in the early days, as he became involved in a fertiliser project in Singapore that eventually exposed him to regional Australia.

"During my tenure [with the Singaporean company], I was given a chance to meet Nelson Mandela in person and have supper with him. It also gave me the chance to sit right next to Benazir Bhutto. What more could you have asked for?"

In 2001, DD contracted throat cancer. He had never smoked a cigarette in his life.

"How it got diagnosed was just coincidental. I was having dinner with my wife and I said the food didn't taste the same. I wondered if I had got a boil in my throat. You never know what curveballs life throws at you. I underwent a major surgery and I still have no saliva in one side of the throat. I now realise that even with excessive preparation, it wouldn't have changed the result. The remedial action has to be immediate and effective."

Nevertheless, DD did not slow down and acquired a few million dollars to invest shortly after. He turned his attention to Australia to start something on his own and found himself starting a dairy operation. However, he quickly realised it was going to be tough to operate on this foreign land. Fortunately, he still managed to turn things around and make three times the money back.

"Soon after, we started the first food joint venture between India and Australia from scratch - called UNIBIC biscuits. I was a founding partner, but I had to back out when my father passed away and I couldn't find it in myself to shoulder that responsibility anymore. UNIBIC has become a big brand today."

OIL BUSINESS – IDENTIFYING AND CAPITALISING ON A MARKET GAP

During the early days in getting to know Australia, DD's razor-sharp business acumen led him to identify an opportunity and capitalise on a market gap that was to become, in his own words, his 'magnum opus'.

"Fifteen years ago, a third of India's oils and fat market was tallow – from fish and chips to KFC and McDonald's. I saw an opportunity [in expanding India's oil diet beyond these oils] and I was not willing to let it pass by. There was a shifting market trend in oil consumption. Around 200 plant variants have been put up in India and China in the last decade. I sensed a massive business opportunity amidst avid diversification in the agricultural economy."

DD also realised that there was no state-of-the-art technology to efficiently crush and refine seeds to produce edible oil in Australia. In fact, there was only one integrated plant in Australia, Cargill. He recognised that the major demand in the industry was not retail. In fact, retail amounted to less than a meagre seven per cent. Food manufacturing was the much-needed choice, and DD decided to attack this market gap.

DD set about building a custom-built, state-of-the-art integrated oilseed crushing and refining plant in Wagga Wagga, NSW. He was to become managing director of Riverina Oils & Bio Energy Pty Ltd (ROBE).

He recalls early challenges with raising funds, gaining government approval, and navigating Australia's Goods and Services Tax (GST).

"Nobody understood what we stood for. No Australian bank funded us. There were only a handful of Indian banks that backed us. Truth be told, if there was an Australian bank funding us, our project would have failed. Till date, no Australian has invested a cent, nor any Australian bank affiliated with us. But, look at us now! We exist and thrive despite the government's restrictions."

DD had $160 million in the beginning which went down as initial investment into the Riverina Oils and Bio Energy project (ROBE) – all equity.

"I decided to put up the best refinery factory in the country. Having worked in huge brands like Unilever, I realised the need for product consistency and superiority to maximise the reach of our product. Everything boils down to a efficient design and operations. That is the sole reason for our rapid growth. We are currently in the fourth year of production. We built a plant with 18,000 trucks in operation. We have around 600 tonnes of production and about 42-43 per cent is solely oil."

"We emphasised on differentiating ourselves at quite an early stage, by not having to compete with the big players in the tender business. We created a niche market for ourselves by ensuring that we had the best product quality. For us, the only remaining solution, the clear-cut edge, was a strategised execution to quality."

"This is my ninth greenfield project and Australia is my fourth country. I have worked on multiple projects in Uzbekistan, Egypt and Indonesia. Australia is not only the most difficult, but ten times more difficult to do business in compared to the other nations. As an entrepreneur, you need to understand at quite an early stage that Australia is not a bed of roses!"

GROWTH AND EARLY SUCCESS

"We are the topmost refinery plant in Australia, certainly larger than Cargill and much bigger than GrainCorp. With every fourth glass of milk you drink, the cow has had a canola meal; and with every fourth egg you eat, the chicken has had canola feed sourced from our plant."

His company's reach now extends to every fifth restaurant in Sydney and Melbourne, and every tenth supermarket product. ROBE is the largest greenfield agricultural project whose value-added products top the food manufacturing industries in Australia.

For DD, staying ahead has meant knowing every minute detail of his business from end to end, as well as always keeping abreast of global trends.

"I know every square inch of every equipment. It is a sophisticated plant with 36 kilometres of piping, 42 kilometres of electrical, 18,000 trucks coming in and out."

With global demand shifting towards natural products, they are the only Australian non- genetically modified (GM) certified and non-GM company out of Australia. At present, he has focused resources on exports.

When it comes to growth and expansion, DD's strategy has always been crystal clear.

"We have realised that we are not a trading company and we will not be capitalising on this asset. In large trading companies, they make money originating from your farmers, holding it in the silos and in so many other ways, and they basically try to then trade forward cover hedging and all the rest of it. To them, manufacturing is just a means, but to us, it is very clear. We buy and we sell. So, for us, it is like a manufacturing product."

"We are the only BRC certified double A rated company. There are not many companies in Asia Pacific in any category. So, we already project a phenomenal growth for the company."

In terms of technology, DD believes that their product is superior.

"We produce 600 tonnes of canola every day from 600 million seeds. We extract 99.8 per cent of the oil. Efficient technology is our strength. We extract the oil in the best manner possible."

HUMAN RESOURCES

DD's Unilever days taught him a fundamental lesson – the people are the ones who make a difference in the organisation. At Unilever, directors would be involved in multiple rounds of interviews even for basic role hiring. Money and assets are marginally productive when compared to the right people you can retain. Today, DD believes that his entire team is an extended family to him. He has built goodwill and trust with his employees to sustain his business for the long run.

"I have 34 of the brightest people working for me. If I issue a single advertisement, 500 applications come in. Wagga is a small lovely city where you breathe fresh air. It's only ten minutes' drive to work."

"If you don't have the right people, it won't work. We currently have the best organisation. I have the best traders in the country, I have the best CFO working with me. I have got the best technical team. Many of these guys in India have left their jobs and families behind. They would ask me if the job is safe and fulfilling. I would stare into their eyes and sold a dream to them. A dream that began with me. At the time, I had only commitment and belief and that was enough. It is that unflinching belief and unshakeable faith that has carried us through every obstacle since our inception."

"Recruiting people and getting a good quality organisation – these are the biggest achievements. Acquiring them is one thing, but holding on to them, and making them believe in your vision and motivating them throughout the journey – that will decide the fate of your vision. Nobody of value has left the organisation, and that is a true testament to mine."

ACCOLADES

DD has several outstanding business awards to his credit including CEO of the Year 2016 - Energy and Resources Category; Asia Pacific Entrepreneur of the Year 2015; and Indian Australian Ambassador of the Year 2014.

The ROBE plant is one of the largest value-added investments in the agri-food processing sector in regional Australia in the last five years. The investment brings significant benefits to the regional community, including farmers, transporters, storage, engineering companies, contractors and the entire supply chain industry. The multiplier effect of this investment in Wagga Wagga is significant.

Each day, the factory has the potential to produce over 200 tonnes of high-quality refined vegetable oil for the food industry and 300 tonnes of premium vegetable protein meal each day for the poultry, dairy and animal feed industries. ROBE supplies certified Non-GM canola oil to some of Australia's leading food manufacturers and exports directly or via commercial partners to the USA, New Zealand, India and South-east Asia.

ROBE Foodservice Division pack and supply a variety of culinary oils and specialty blends packed in 20 litre drums to cater for the needs of the Restaurant and Catering markets, all supplied through an extensive network of over 200 distributors.

FUTURE PLANS AND PHILOSOPHY

DD refuses to let go of the momentum that he has created with ROBE. ROBE aims to become a major oilseed processor and exporter, and eventually produce biofuel. DD believes the project will act as a catalyst for further investment in Australia from Asia's emerging giant.

"Our vision is that we will become hopefully an ASX100 company before I hang my boots, which I hope I can delay till the next five or six years. But you never know what may happen."

DD comes back to his plans in India, where he believes product differentiation works to a greater effect than abject fragmentation. He believes that international expansion can only occur with effective backward linkages. He acknowledges that expansive network of food manufacturers acquainted with him would be a great asset to capitalise on.

He wants to dive deeper into food service.

"The American market in food manufacturing comes to a total of 14 million tonnes. In India, it's 20. So, you might know where our current priorities lie."

"I personally believe I work deep with customers. I don't like to fragment. I believe in a lot of products because I think the product differentiation has been one of the key factors for us to succeed, because we are in a commodity business."

Oil and diabetic care products are the current focus in India.

"Our future direction is obviously expansion. I intend to go further downstream. We want to expand and export into the animal feed sector in New Zealand. We already have foundational ties with its dairy sector."

"I can only do business that I understand so I would not do any pharmaceutical business. Romanticising a business is not good. Many people get ideas, but great and revolutionary ideas are not enough to drive the business. What I had may not have been a great idea, but I saw an opportunity and kept working on it. You need to crystallise that opportunity."

"Life is all about execution. Execution, innate knowledge, and talent; and you have a powerful combination. I don't see that I have become successful, because success itself is a process. I don't get carried away because anything can happen at any time."

"Look what a boil turned into!" says DD with a bittersweet smile, referring to his cancer scare.

"I may go but I hope this factory will stay, hopefully for a hundred years. For me, my professional, business and personal life are of considerable substance and significance, but ROBE will be my magnum opus."

He goes out of his way to state that ROBE is not his legacy. DD believes his purpose has always been about creation, and now that he has birthed it, he looks at in utter wonder as his creation breathes life on its own.

NOTE

The information in this chapter is based on a series of interviews with Dhruv Deepak "DD" Saxena conducted between January 1 and 31, 2019.

REFERENCES

Riverina Oils. (n.d.). Retrieved from https://www.riverinaoils.com.au/

Chapter 10
Cristina Talacko

ABSTRACT

Coming from a successful legal background, Cristina Talacko quit her job in Singapore in 1999 to establish her own business, SalDoce Fine Foods, which means "savoury and sweet" in Portuguese, with her husband, Martin Talacko, when she moved to Australia. Christina, who was born in Brazil, missed Brazilian foods and culture back home and struggled to have her legal qualifications recognised in Australia. These initial challenges led Cristina to establish SalDoce Fine Foods in Sydney in 2000, which specialises in manufacturing a Brazilian delicacy called PaÞo de Queijo made with tapioca and cheese. Today, SalDoce Fine Foods supplies more than 30 products to major supermarket chains and independent retailers around the world catering for allergen-sensitive customers, those with diabetes or on reduced sugar diets, vegans and vegetarians, and those who are health conscious. This chapter looks at how Cristina transformed her business into a major national success.

DOI: 10.4018/978-1-6684-4986-8.ch010

Figure 1.

SalDoce Fine Foods is an Australian family-owned company pioneer in manufacturing allergen sensitive and gluten free foods. Since 2000, SalDoce is proud to have introduced many baking mixes to the Australian and other international markets to suit the diet of customers with gluten, dairy and nut intolerance, diabetes and those who wish to control weight or have a healthier diet without compromising taste. Cristina and Martin Talacko founded SalDoce Fine Foods (which means Savoury and Sweet in Portuguese) in Sydney in 2000. Cristina, who was born in Brazil, missed Brazilian foods and its ingredients when she arrived in Australia. She decided to quit her legal career in 1999 and start manufacturing a Brazilian delicacy called Pão de Queijo made with tapioca and cheese. She travelled to Minas Gerais, where Pão de Queijo is originally from, to learn how to manufacture it and to source and transport to Australia the right ingredients and machinery. The cheese breads were a success amongst coeliacs, children and caterers under the Frevos brand.

Cristina and Martin Talacko founded SalDoce Fine Foods (which means Savoury and Sweet in Portuguese) in Sydney in 2000. Cristina, who was born in Brazil, missed Brazilian foods and its ingredients when she arrived in Australia. She decided to quit her legal career in 1999 and start manufacturing a Brazilian delicacy called Pão de Queijo made with tapioca and cheese. She travelled to Minas Gerais, where Pão de Queijo is originally from, to learn how to manufacture it and to source and transport to Australia the right ingredients and machinery. The cheese breads were a success amongst coeliacs, children and caterers under the Frevos brand.

Today, SalDoce Fine Foods supplies more than 30 products to many supermarket chains and independent retailers around the world catering for allergen sensitive customers, those with diabetes or on reduced sugar diets, vegan and vegetarians, and those who are health conscious.

Maria Cristina Dardis Talacko was born in Brazil. Whilst she has always perceived herself as Brazilian, her ancestors – like many Brazilians – were not originally from Brazil. In fact, three of her grandparents were Italian and the other was Spanish. With such multicultural ancestry, being the descendant of generations of migrants before her, perhaps it was written in her destiny to travel the world!

Cristina completed her school in Brazil and went on to be accepted to one of the best universities in São Paulo to study a law degree with the intention of becoming a criminal prosecutor.

Close to the completion of her law degree, she met and fell in love with an Australian, Martin Talacko. The couple married, and in 1990 when Martin was offered a particularly attractive job at ACNielsen in Singapore, the couple moved together. During their time in Singapore, Cristina and Martin had two children, Julia and Peter.

Cristina continued her legal studies in Singapore, attending the University of London (Singapore) to study a Bachelor of Law - Common Law. In 1995, she found work at an Indian legal firm in Singapore.

After seven years living in Singapore, Martin was offered another attractive role as the Regional Business Manager for IAMS Australia. The couple decided the job and the opportunity to move to Martin's homeland of Australia with their young family was too good to pass up.

While she was excited to move to a new country with her family the move to Australia left Cristina feeling very isolated. She had no family or friends for support here. In her Brazilian culture, family relationships are very important, and people traditionally are part of a very close-knit community. Cristina's family were also "a very tight, united family that look after each other, my mother is quite present in my life."

She struggled in the early days.

The other difficulty that Cristina faced was discovering that her Bachelor of Law degree would not meet the standards to practice law here in Australia. She was devastated to learn that she would have to return to study to be able to work here. In fact, this is a problem faced by many fellow migrants to Australia. Despite the blow, she enrolled to complete a Diploma on Corporate Law at Sydney University and began attending evening classes.

After three years of living in Australia, Cristina had finally earned her degree, but this was still not enough to become a lawyer in Australia. Cristina was frustrated and growing desperate to kickstart her career into full drive. She was also homesick for her Brazilian culture after so many years abroad and wanting to reconnect with the people, the lifestyle and especially the food. SalDoce Fine Foods was about to be born.

A NEW BEGINNING

With the support of her husband, Cristina decided to quit her legal career and look at setting up her own business.

"I think a lot of migrants set up a business because of the non-recognition of their qualifications," remarked Cristina.

She is not wrong. A recent study by EY Sweeney research and published by the CGU Migrant Small Business Report found that one third of Australian small businesses are owned by migrants and, of all business owners, just over half of migrant owners have at least a degree as opposed to 38 per cent of non-migrant business owners.

Cristina set her heart upon a business of manufacturing a Brazilian delicacy called Pão de Queijo – a kind of bread made with tapioca and cheese. It was a food she dearly missed, and she was convinced people would love it if they could eat it.

Cristina had to overcome several hurdles to form her business. She didn't have experience in business or a business degree in food, though her husband Martin had studied Marketing during his tertiary study. She also immediately recognised she may face difficulty in converting the cheese bread she baked at home to something that would suit mass production.

Unperturbed, she travelled to the State of Minas Gerais in Brazil, where the cheese bread is originally from, to learn more about it. Here she spent time tapping into her people-to-people relationships in Brazil learning the ins and outs of how to manufacture the cheese bread as well as helpful advice to source and transport the right, bulk ingredients and machinery to Australia.

Cristina and Martin Talacko didn't spend a huge amount of time researching the difficulties of starting a business. Instead they focussed on her cultural links with Brazil and 'gut feelings'. As a result, the business was organically formed, utilising the information she gained from manufacturers who shared their experiences and knowledge in producing the Brazilian cheese bread.

Her contacts in Brazil were happy to provide Cristina with the key machinery that would be required to set up production in Australia, especially once they knew she would not be in direct competition with them. With USD 10,000, she purchased a second-hand machine from Brazil and paid about another USD 10,000 to bring it to Australia. Rather than accessing debt financing from large scale banks, Cristina began her business using personal equity. Cristina explains that this is was due to her "conservative mindset,"

"I always try to do things within my means," she explains.

The initial investments into the machinery required, shipping from Brazil and factory lease in Mascot had to be done slowly to enable the family to build up the business. The couple managed the early operational aspects of setting up a business including renting a factory space and registering the company with Australia business authority with an ABN. Cristina did all the work at the beginning by herself and later with more support from her husband who joined the business part time.

It was the year 2000, and Cristina and Martin had finally founded SalDoce Fine Foods (meaning savoury and sweet in her native Portuguese).

In order to develop beyond their first product, which formed as a result of Cristina's personal experience in baking, Cristina and Martin initially developed breads and pizza bases to expand their lines. The first year was difficult with a lot of trial and error and culminated in investing in flying a Brazilian baker to Australia to provide his expertise and assist in teaching Cristina how to set up this product for production. At this point, they hired food developers and technologists to assist in gradually developing other products to expand their range.

FINDING HER MARKET

Fortunately, SalDoce wasn't competing against another similar product as it was a differentiated and unique product within the Australian market. Although Cristina didn't face a lot of direct competition, she knew she would need considerable investment in market awareness and education to inform potential customers on why they would want to purchase and try her naturally gluten-free product, Frevos.

She set about researching.

Although times have since changed, in the nascent years of her business Cristina found that people suffering from coeliac disease (gluten allergy) or needing to restrict gluten in their diet (perhaps due to an intolerance) really only had the option of eating unappetising gluten-free bread while others eating at their family table enjoyed much more delicious options containing gluten. No tasty gluten free bread existed. During the early 2000s in Australia, the availability of wheat free or gluten free options was limited, essentially only available to health food stores and particularly expensive. Mainstream supermarkets had very limited options for anyone who couldn't purchase normal bread.

In 2003, it was estimated that one in 100 people were diagnosed with coeliac disease. Australia's Coeliac Society estimates that approximately 80 per cent of those suffering from coeliac disease are undiagnosed even with the increasingly better diagnosis over the past decade estimating that the disease likely affects one in 70 Australians.

The presence of food allergies in Australia especially in children is rising, with the most common allergies being cow's milk, eggs and peanuts. Greater numbers of Australians are eliminating certain foods from their diets with wheat and/or gluten and dairy or lactose leading. Whilst gluten allergens aren't as common within Asia, within India the most frequently seen allergies are to cow's milk, peanuts or eggs and amongst young children also wheat intolerances. India and Asia are also showing an increasing appearance of diabetes. In Japan and Korea, anaphylaxis is mostly commonly due to wheat allergies.

The gluten free and allergen market was, and is, growing.

Cristina saw an opportunity to target not just celiac individuals but whole families if she could create the right brand with products that are nice to eat. She determined that the correct target market to start with for Frevos and, eventually, her expanded product range were children and the gluten-free market. She registered Frevos with the Coeliac Association.

The cheese breads were a success amongst those suffering from coeliac disease, children and caterers under the Frevo brand. Today, SalDoce Fine Foods supplies more than 30 products to many supermarket chains and independent retailers around the world catering for allergen sensitive customers, those with diabetes or on reduced sugar diets, vegan and vegetarians, and those who are health conscious.

BUSINESS DEVELOPMENT

In order to become a successful and self-sustaining business, Cristina knew that they needed multiple product lines to allow for market saturation and strong company branding. A single product wouldn't allow the business to grow significantly so SalDoce expanded their range from frozen food into shelf storage range. The key business advantage in this expansion is the cost implications as shelf storage food is significantly cheaper to maintain as transportation and storage is simpler and easier.

Determining and managing the correct time for business expansion is a difficult task as, incorrectly managed, this can result in dire financial situations and potentially the failure of the business. This requires a strong understanding of the market. Cristina understood that the gluten free market was a niche market that had potential for growth as the other products available at that time were tasteless and unhealthy.

The expansion of SalDoce resulted in the 'YesYouCan' brand that encapsulated the full product range of SalDoce, which Cristina perceived have potential for success within Australia. The vision for the company brand is that it 'brings empowerment to people who wish to follow a healthier diet'.

The YesYouCan brand has helped to make gluten-free and allergen free products more widely available for consumers but also a delicious choice for a whole family to enjoy which results in greater sales. YesYouCan is robust brand in Australia selling its own products as well as a private label contract with Woolworths and exporting to over 20 countries worldwide which accounts for 30 per cent of SalDoce's sales.

SalDoce's current product range includes four main ranges, classic baking mix, artisan baking ranges and flours, vegan products and Frevos cheese bites. Within the Classic Baking Mix, there is bread, cake, cupcake, pancake, pizza, falafel and burger mixes and a variety of flours and savoury snacks. The Artisan Baking Ranges are low sugar and high fibre mixes to make cakes, bread, muffins, cookies and pancakes. The company has several vegan products including a variety of flavours of vegan protein shakes and a vegan egg replacement to make home cooking easier. The company's premium artisan flour range includes gram flour, buckwheat, rice, sorghum and white maize flour. All flours in this range are wheat, gluten and dairy-free as well as being non-GMO.

Cristina understood that the correct business organisation structure is key to business development. During the initial development and growth of the company, there wasn't a structure as Cristina was alone and instead focused on planning, researching and learning. She was later joined by Martin once the business had begun in Australia. The organisational structure of the company emerged with organic expansion. As they hired additional staff and delegated work, they formed the company structure. In addition to the permanent team, SalDoce utilises many interns from around the world to expand their team as well as provide opportunities to migrants and individuals looking to get started.

Later, the separation of the manufacturing business for product production and sales, marketing and brand development was key for the success of SalDoce as this ensured that the organisation was able to set up for growth. Cristina found she "couldn't concentrate on the development of the brand and doing the marketing" as the previous organisation structure wasn't set up to provide clear delineation of responsibilities and ownership. One turning point for Cristina was the physical separation of the manufacturing and head office activities, moving the company head office from Mascot where the factory was located to Woolloomooloo, its current location where sales, branding, operations and marketing is now located (Indeed). The production hub of the company eventually moved to Villawood where it is registered as for Halal food production.

PARTNERSHIPS, EXPORTING AND EXPANSION

As part of SalDoce's business expansion they partnered with Woolworths to produce gluten free baking mixes which they "produced for them on their own private label". This private label contract enabled SalDoce's production to utilise economies of scale which meant they had the available revenue to invest in the development of their own brands.

SalDoce is now widely available throughout Australia, being stocked in majority of major food chains in Australia, including all IGA stores, Foodworks, Foodland and individual health food stores. They have nine individual distributors in Australia and 16 online retailers that supply their brands.

The move to begin exporting was a slow and gradual process. The costs of beginning to export are significant; especially registering and accrediting products for export and product their trademark. Cristina and Martin also didn't want to work with locals to import their products.

The first country that they began to export to was Singapore as the couple had lived there for seven years prior to moving to Australia so this was a country in which they understood the market conditions and could adapt to these easily. As they began to export, they found their product was supported by the good international reputation of Australian food as "clean, sustainable, high quality food".

SalDoce Fine Foods now exports to over 20 countries worldwide.

"There have been many important turning points, but I should say reaching international markets was one of them," said Cristina.

Crucial in the early stages of exporting to a new country is understanding the nuances of the local market. The Export Council of Australia, a good resource for Cristina in the early days, recommends you do detailed research into determining the local market, understanding the politics, economics, social and business culture to determine your target market. The details are all key to creating the right organisational structure and many early decisions for exporting including where to base sales and manufacturing, what services to offer, what the correct pricing is and the ideal selling strategy.

Cristina and Martin's export strategy was formed on their experiences selling in Australia and living overseas, based especially on the strong value they have placed on developing their business through forming relationships. Because Cristina and Martin focus so strongly on relationships when determining the correct distributor to work with in a local market, their distributors are closer to sales partners than a traditional overseas distributor relationship.

"I don't like giving my product to a distributor I've never met" said Cristina.

Typically, one of the major disadvantages of working with a distributor is a loss of control over the marketing, branding, pricing and sale of your product. For SalDoce, they manage this potential concern through being very specific about determining the right distributor, tending where possible to work with small family businesses where the YesYouCan brand is central to their portfolio rather than one brand amongst many. They try to understand the needs of the distributor so that they align. Cristina retains some control over the marketing of her products through working together with the distributor on the social media, assisting with marketing and pricing.

To ensure they understood the country and the market before starting to export, they undertook the time and financial investment to spend time visiting the country and becoming involved in a local food show hosted within the country. Their involvement in an international food show locally has been particularly successful as this as often resulted in meeting and forming a relationship with the distributor that they end up using within that country.

Austrade, the NSW Department of Trade and other trade associations have also been important organisations for SalDoce, providing support in understanding local markets and finding the correct distributors in some countries in particular Philippines, New Zealand and Middle East.

Today, SalDoce has been recognised domestically and overseas as a successful innovative company with a strong export arm. SalDoce won the NSW Export Agribusiness Award in 2016 and was nominated in 2015 for the NSW Export Awards Small Business Award. They won the 2017 Ethical Business Award, are featured in the Food Innovation Australia book "Celebrating Australian Food and Agribusiness Innovations" and were awarded the Innovation Award at SIAL Food Exhibition in Shanghai.

Despite their many successes they have faced some challenges within some countries in exporting their product overseas, particularly within China where the wrong distribution partner and incorrect and poor representation of their product required re-starting and re-positioning. In their initial foray into the Philippines, they discovered issues with packaging related to different ingredients being allowed locally than elsewhere in the world which meant their product was not able to make it through customers.

Cristina and Martin undertake significant amounts of research and maintain close relationships with distribution partners. Understanding the necessary branding and packaging focus for each country is very important when exporting as different cultures vary. Exporting to the Middle East required SalDoce to become Halal-certified by the Supreme Islamic Council of Halal Meat in Australia Inc, a widely accepted standard. For any bakery company or manufacturing the operations and cleanliness of their site is a potential issue as there are very strong health and safety guidelines they need to meet. This is even stricter for SalDoce considering their gluten free, halal, nut free operations as their facilities require certification that meet Australian guidelines as well as overseas guidelines.

Registering their product in Philippines and Indonesia was a process that took 18 months. For their brand they need to be accredited as gluten and dairy free as well as halal, these accreditations differ from country to country and the requirements can easily change between countries as to what accreditation is considered equivalent standard. Although issues such as bureaucracy, legislation and brand registration requirements in each country make it difficult, Cristina and Martin continue to focus on exports. Despite these challenges, Cristina believes it is possible to triple their exports.

SALES AND MARKETING

Cristina remains the key decision maker for the marketing of SalDoce as the Director of Marketing and Product Development. The biggest branding changes that SalDoce went through was the creation and the consolidation of the YesYouCan brand the name of the SalDoce business. The evolution of this brand consolidation can be seen through the SalDoce business web page in which the YesYouCan Brand became more integrated and the main branding focus between 2014 and 2015.

SalDoce has a heavy social media presence utilising Facebook, Instagram, Twitter and YouTube. The company's Facebook and Instagram pages were launched in April in 2013 to publicise SalDoce's international activities and expansion, raise product awareness and share examples of baking using their mixes. There are also numerous additional country specific social media pages for the countries that they export to. Cristina helps distributors with social media to ensure that the marketing strategy demonstrates the correct value of the brand and aligns with her vision.

Solid partnerships also drive her sales and marketing efforts. SalDoce's partnership strategy with their distributors globally relies closely on relationships and mutual understand and benefit. Cristina's perception on both business and personal life is that "in every country you go to, it's about context and relationships", an approach she fully adopted in SalDoce Fine Foods.

Cristina has been involved in the Brazil Chamber of Commerce throughout much of her working career in Australia which has provided her with considerable networking opportunities and relationships. Cristina and Martin have also partnered with a Brazilian migrant in Australia to "purchase an organic retail chain of shops called Naked Foods", owning 50 per cent of the business to assist with the capital needed for business expansion. Similar to SalDoce's approach with international expansion, the success of this partnership is focused on the close relationship that they have with their partner in forming business growth ideas and marketing. Naked Foods now has 18 stores throughout NSW, Victoria, ACT and Queensland (Naked Foods).

SalDoce Fine Foods has partnered with several government offices and trade associations in Australia to assist their international expansion. In particular with Austrade who helped SalDoce find their distribution partners in Philippines, New Zealand and other countries as well as NSW Department Trade, NSW Chamber of Commerce and Food Innovation who have been focused in the past five years on promoting NSW and Australia as a food destination and have helped SalDoce access leads in each country, meet distributers and the business visibility during their expansion at Food Fairs and Shows Australia and abroad.

FUTURE PLANS

The future looks bright for Cristina and Martin, with the global gluten-free products market projected to reach $5279 million by 2022, growing at a CAGR of 7.5 per cent from 2016 to 2022 of which the gluten-free bakery products dominates this market.

The process of building SalDoce Fine Foods to become a successful Australian and international business has involved some risks, many challenges, a lot of milestones and considerable amounts of hard work from both Cristina and Martin Talacko.

Cristina's view of the difference between Australia and Brazil is that Australia is a valuable country to grow a business from as it has a stable and reliable economy, political situation and no corruption. As she puts it, "You will see that most of the time you can achieve it, if you work hard."

Cristina plans on focusing on growing their exports of the YesYouCan brand believing that if they focus on this that they can triple this, that there is a lot of growth potential with the joint venture in Naked Foods within Australia and focusing on e-commerce particularly with their Vegan Shakes which is "more of a young product" that can be targeted globally through all markets.

In terms of business growth strategies, the other plan that Cristina has is to expand their product range to include healthy snack ranges that don't require an baking or effect as a global population people are becoming more rushed and "they don't want to put effort into things like that".

Cristina's advice to prospective business owners and migrants looking to establish themselves in Australia is to "immerse yourself in local community and charity" and to give back to these environments as it will always provide more value for you then you put in and is key for increasing your networking reach which has been crucial for Cristina's development and the success of SalDoce for each turning point.

Chapter 11
Lessons Learned:
Outcomes

ABSTRACT

In this chapter, respondents further express their thoughts on other facets of their business – like family, compassion, kindness, giving back to society, the lessons they learned from their parents and their grand parents, as well as their migrant experience of settling in a new country and its impact on their personality.

INTRODUCTION

Additionally, five of the participants discussed the influence of family and family values on future careers . They were very clear about the skills and values that they acquired from their parents. For Pauline (Vietnam), for example, it was "kindness and compassion and a sense of femininity" that she learned from her mother, and Dhruv (India) believed that his father taught him "very strong core values". In addition, for 2 participants, Michelle (China) and Diem (Vietnam), the values that their parents taught them seemed to be particularly important and were at the core of their personal philosophies articulated later in the interview .This was confirmed and revealed that in two transcripts these personal philosophies overlapped with the influence of family and family values on future careers. For Michelle, it was her strong belief in God, as well as the belief that "regardless of which God you believe in, you know, we respect everyone's belief" that she learned from her grandparents

DOI: 10.4018/978-1-6684-4986-8.ch011

and which she later lived by. Diem, who is in a food production business and used to work in her mother's restaurant, appreciated a number of lessons that she learned from several members of her family, and she articulated this influence of family and family values on future career 10 times on different occasions throughout the interview, as demonstrated in the following extracts:

My mother has taught me to do things properly, thoroughly and with all my heart. So whether you are rolling a spring roll or doing a won ton or making fried ice cream you've got to do it like it's the last thing you got to do. So, I think I've learnt from a very young age to do things diligently with all my heart. Doesn't matter if it's a small thing or a big thing.

My father has taught me morals, self-respect, because he's in fashion, so he taught me about being a perfectionist, being attention to detail. About the workmanship. He taught me art, he taught me beautiful and he taught about extremely good manners.

Because my mum said when you work so slow you lose productivity, so she taught me to work efficiently.

So, mum taught me how to multitask, to waitress, to making won tons, to cleaning up the table, to organise bookings, to know how to manage money, cash and to clean up. So mum taught me how to run a business from A to Z, small business restaurant.

So, my business model I've learnt from my grandmother, if you want entire full penetration, you work with the strongest boys. You stay behind them. Let them be the boss and you support them whatever promotions they want, you support them.

My Chinese grandfather taught me an honourable person don't fluctuate their price up and down. Do your costing carefully…

As evident in the above extracts, the influence of Diem's family on her career was both in general values and philosophies that her family taught her and in work-specific skills that she acquired and later found useful when running her business. In Diem's case, therefore, these experiences constitute both the influence of family and family values on future career and the influence of work experience on future career. The latter, was the most frequently discussed aspect of the participants' background that helped them in their future careers. Similar to the influence of their educational background, some participants, including Diem, had the opportunity to directly experience the same or very similar type of work that they would later continue their career in. This was also true, for example, for Pauline, who had "worked in some of the best restaurants in Sydney under the tutelage of some of the best chefs and sommeliers" and who later opened her own restaurant. Others praised the transferable skills that they had gained in their previous work or the general inspiration that it had given them. Both Dhruv (India) and Rustum (India), for example, valued "a lot of exposure" (Dhruv) and "international experience" (Rustum) that they had gained, both of which later helped them expand their own businesses internationally. Diem (Vietnam), although she later started food production business, believed that her previous experience in the cosmetic industry "indirectly taught me marketing" and working in Optus "has taught me the corporate discipline how to run my business".

Apart from discussing their general background and how this background helped them achieve success as migrant entrepreneurs, the participants also discussed a number of other facilitators of success. As previously noted, some of these facilitators were their direct responses to factors they believe contributed to their development and success and some were inferred from the participants' general discussions of the process of starting their business.

The most commonly discussed facilitator was determination, motivation and resilience which were discussed by all interviewees and. Joseph (Lebanon), who eventually developed the world's first agency specializing in multicultural marketing, showed this determination, motivation and resilience from the very beginning when he arrived as a migrant who did not speak English at all. A year and a half later, however, he enrolled in Sydney University and even though "it was hell, because imagine trying to catch up with the lecturers and all the words" he managed to obtain his Bachelor of Arts degree. When discussing the main traits that he believed contributed to his success, he explained that

Joseph mentioned that the most important thing is resilience and perseverance. Because it's very easy, we all dream, and then you try to make your dream a reality, of course you encounter immediately obstacles, handicaps, so a lot of percentage of people would give up. But people who succeed don't give up, right, you keep going.

Although all participants had encountered initial difficulties and obstacles (discussed in the following section), their determination, motivation and resilience helped them overcome these obstacles. Cristina (Brazil), for example, when she started her business producing and selling Brazilian food, after renting a factory "started working in the factory myself, and managing the equipment, and trying to fix things" because she did not have any employees. Later, when marketing her products, which were not familiar to her target audience, she "started baking it, putting it in the car, and going to the school canteens all over the place, to introduce them to the canteens".

Diem (Vietnam) also believed that being resilient and determined is crucial, and, as she explained

I'm not lucky. I spent nine years eating rice and soy sauce I'm not lucky, I've worked really hard, It hasn't been smooth for me, I make a lot of mistakes, I fall over, I improvise, but like I said I do take risk, I'm fearless…

Dhruv (India) also believed his determination, motivation and resilience to be the main factors that helped him succeed. In early days, as noted above, he succeeded at the university despite being "the only brown fellow" there, and his determination later surfaced when starting and running his oil business. He summarized the determinants of his success as follows:

All I had was commitment and belief that this would happen (…) You have to have total conviction. This project was not built on money, it was built on perseverance, it was built on commitment (…) If somebody is not made of stuff that I am made [of], you would have had five heart attacks and died three times.

For Rustum (India), determination, motivation and resilience is also mainly about being able to overcome difficulties, and he explained that "you do get 90 rejections and things fail all the time [but] you've got to be able to think of the remaining ten things that are going to succeed and ignore the 90 that fail".

Another facilitator of success that was frequently discussed and which, arguably, enabled the participants to show the determination and resilience discussed above were dedication and passion . Not only did the participants' stories, in themselves, undoubtedly reflected a great amount of passion, such as Marina's (Italy) account of her and her husband's decision to sell their house in order to purchase the building in which their company would operate, they directly spoke about dedication and passion on several occasions. Joseph (Lebanon), for example, when describing his general belief about what he does, explained that "to me, it's like a drug, every year you take a dose of it, because when you see success of it, you think Wow". Michelle (China) explained that "we are passionate. We love what we do" and "we really put in 120 percent into everything we do", and Dhruv (India) believed that "without passion you can't do anything. If you're not passionate, forget doing anything".

Compassion and being good with people was also a frequently discussed topic. The belief shared by 7 participants was that, in general, "the more you give, the more you receive" (Joseph, Lebanon). This theme was mainly about caring for customers and employees, as demonstrated in the following extract:

If I have a worker where I pay him well, I think he's amazing, I endorse him, I teach him more, I build him to be a leader in a multinational company leader, why wouldn't he want to work for me? Why would he want to leave?

Because I treat him like a family member. He can be open to me (…) I have to appreciate their work and I have to treat them like gold.

Diem (Vietnam)

Diem, in fact, seemed to be extremely compassionate towards her employees, and, as previously noted, this was something she had learned from her mother. She also explained that as an employer "you have to worry about their family at home. If they've got a family problem you can't solve all the problems, but at least you can give them reassurance that their job is safe". She also treats her restaurant customers similarly, as she explains in the following extract:

I remember even the mums that come to my restaurant they have the Laksa for $15, I have to give them two extra bowls for their kids. I give them extra water, doesn't matter. My mum said Yim there's some customers you make more, some you just have to give for free, because you can't make money with everyone. You have to have a heart.

Others who commented on compassion and being good with people also mostly discussed being honest and loyal towards their customers and treating their employees well ("we care about the person. We care about out team. We care about every single person that we connect with" – Michelle, China).

Another facilitator of success that was frequently mentioned, although this time it referred to specific actions rather than personality traits, was doing research.. This, along with understanding your target audience , enabled the participants to gain understanding of the market and the customers' needs and, as a result, successfully sell their products. For Cristina (Brazil), in turn, travelling to Brazil and doing research on the local producer's practices helped her learn her trade and understand how to develop her food company from scratch:

So, I bought a ticket to Brazil, and went to Brazil by myself, and I decided to do research on that product. So, I visited factories in Brazil that were making tonnes of this product, and exporting, and selling them to bakeries. They gave me a lot of information on how to do it at factory-style production.

Similarly, for Michelle (China), doing research prior to starting her outdoor furniture business involved visiting "every single international furniture fair so we knew what was coming", as well as studying "every single customer" and "every single retailer, what they were charging, what they were pricing, what the retail prices were". As noted above, doing research frequently overlapped with understanding your target audience, and in this case, it involved studying either the local market or the market abroad where the participants planned to expand to. As Joseph (Lebanon) explained, "right from the beginning, (…) if you want to be effective in your communication, you have to understand the culture and the language of your target audience". He later provided the following account of how crucial doing research and understanding your target audience prove to be in his work as a multicultural marketer:

They used to have a product called QuickEze, which is for heartburn and indigestion. But it wasn't selling at all in all the western suburbs. And they said to me "Can you find out why?". So, I did the research, I found out that they see it placed amongst all other confectionary, they don't read, they take it, they put it in their mouth – spit it out. I said "Well, you can't put it there, because they take it as a lolly, and it doesn't taste nice". "What do we do?". So, I said "Produce small brochures". And I started distributing them in all these western suburb shops, pharmacy and so on. And I explained to the people what it is. And immediately the sales went up.

Doing research and understanding your target audience also involved listening to the customers and "constantly monitoring" (Cristina, Brazil) social media activity to explore their needs. Ashwat (India), in turn, described how hiring a local veteran in the US branch of the company benefited him:

I hired one guy, and he was a – one thing I learnt was in Texas they're very focused on the army people. So out of all the 80 resumes I saw one guy who was in the army. So I hired the vet, and he gets appointments like that, because they're very respectful to veterans and things like that, and this guy's bringing all the sales in, and then I built my team underneath him. So, I can sit here and be upset with the world that no one's giving me an appointment, or see what do they like? Local people like veterans, they like all these things, so I got some of them.

This, to some extent, links to Cristina's (Brazil) belief that finding a "partner that has a lot of knowledge in the market" can be beneficial. Joseph (Lebanon), when explaining that translating product names and slogans directly from one language to another can affect sales "because sometimes the words can be misleading, can be offensive", also commented that "you have to understand your target audience" and "you have to use people from within that community to create that message".

This, in turn, relates to another facilitator of success, namely forming collaborations and partnerships . For Dhruv (India), "without strategic partnerships you can't do it", and when reflecting on what he would have done differently if he was to start his business again, Rustum (India) explained that "I would be more active earlier on to bring in some partners and some other investors". Ashwat (India) also raised the same concern, and explained:

Even with the US, if I had a business partner that helped me, I would have probably saved myself two years. I mean, I had to learn things, I couldn't get credit, I couldn't do all these things. If I had someone who'd taught me, walked me through getting a social security card and all these things, I would have finished everything in a week. But it took me six months to get a lot of things in place.

Forming partnerships could also be less formal and involved surrounding yourself with knowledgeable and skilful people. This usually involved either strategic partnerships with "a person who can mentor me, that I can look up and learn something from him or her" (Diem, Vietnam) or hiring specialists with relevant skills and knowledge. With regard to the latter, it is common for the participants to hire such specialists, and the benefits of doing so are evident in the following example extracts:

I loved the food business and I knew that the way to get there faster was to surround myself with people smarter than myself (…) So while we can do it now I employ people who are much smarter than me who can do it much better than I can. So [unclear 33:47] for example she can do stuff in 10 minutes that would literally take me probably two days. I don't play where my weaknesses are. I don't play there. It doesn't fire me. I play where my strengths are.

Pauline (Vietnam)

So it took a good year, trying to improve that recipe, getting it right, getting it to work on the machine. Everything wasn't going quite well, so I thought, "Okay, I need help from an expert from Brazil. I need to bring a baker here for a few months, to teach me how to do everything in this factory. We invested in bringing someone here; he came with his wife. He was just a small business operator from Brazil who was happy to come and be paid for a few months to teach me what to do here.

Cristina (Brazil)

It appeared from the interviews that another facilitator of success for the migrant entrepreneurs are having a clear brand identity and self-positioning, which also links to understanding the market and the competitors. Those who commented on these topics seemed to be very aware not only of the current state of the market and potential gaps in it but also, most importantly, of what makes their brand distinctive and how they fill that gap. For some, to realise this kind of brand identity took longer, but when they did, it resulted in clear goals and, as a result, expansion of their business. Michelle (China) explained, for example, that it took her and her husband one year after they started their outdoor furniture company to "understand where we fit ourselves in". Defining a clear brand identity and self-positioning themselves within the market appeared to be an important facilitator, and it is easy to notice that all those who commented do not have problems with self-positioning themselves and their business in very few sentences:

It's a Vietnamese restaurant, the most awarded Vietnamese restaurant in the world.

Pauline (Vietnam)

We can proudly say we are the largest producer of liquid paint for the government.

Shivram (India)

We differentiated ourselves by having not to compete with the big guys in the tender business. We differentiated by having the best product quality. We differentiated by having the best factory.

Dhruv (India)

We became building our name as an allergen-free type of company that produces in Australia (…) We sell nuts, we sell beautiful honeys, and vegetable oils, and we sell flowers, cereals, we sell beautiful products in a very sustainable, environmental-friendly shop.

Cristina (Brazil)

As noted above, having a clear understanding of a brand identity also relates to being able to position oneself within the market, for which understanding the market and the competitors is crucial. Diem (Vietnam), for example, explained that she had "learnt one thing from my dad, don't disrupt the big boys. Why do you think I don't touch adult food in Australia? Because the adult food is owned by four major companies". Therefore, rather than competing with these companies in the adult food category, she aims to be "the champion of the kids' meals (…) in Australia", "because no one's done it before". Rustum (India) also elaborated on this topic, and the following extract demonstrates how developing brand identity and being aware of the competition relate to each other:

From the beginning we knew we were a technology company and we wanted to be number one. So, we weren't just developing a technology. You can say "I want to set up a business" and you can start a coffee shop (…) but to expand that business is difficult, because there are so many other people who also make coffee. So, for us, we had to say we want to be a technology company, so we have to come up with a technology that is unique…

Rustum's account demonstrates that offering a "unique" product helps an entrepreneur to position him/herself in the market and develop a clear and recognizable brand identity. Not surprisingly, therefore, being creative and innovative was another facilitator of success as an entrepreneur. Diem (Vietnam), whose junior food business won an international food award in

London, explained that when Steve Jobs invented the iPad or the computer, was there are product like that? Just because it's new, it's innovative, it's unique. It fills the gap of the market (...) I'm very, very positive my brand junior foodies Coco & Lucas works is because no one's done it before.

She also believed that "if you're a small medium business like mine and you're not innovative, you're not thinking two steps ahead, you're behind". Similar views were expressed by the restaurant owner Pauline (Vietnam), who believed that "doing something that is taking the traditional and changing it all up" is essential, and that "innovation is (...) pushing humanity forward". It is clear, therefore, that being innovative and creative is what set these small business owners apart from the competition and, coupled with them understanding the market and the competitors and having a clear brand identity and self-positioning, it enabled them to succeed.

Another facilitator that emerged is being proactive. The participants believed that if "you want to influence, you want to make change, go ahead and do it" (Joseph, Lebanon), and although the code was applied to accounts which directly described this kind of attitude as a facilitator of success, arguably this proactive attitude is evident in most of the participants' whole life stories. Arguably, it is this unique proactive attitude with which the migrant entrepreneurs feel that "we can do it in a heartbeat because we decided [to]" (Pauline, Vietnam), coupled with the previously discussed passion, determination and resilience, that enabled some of the participants to "always convert a problem into an opportunity" (Ashwat, India). This unique skill of turning challenges into advantages was discussed by 6 interviewees, who not only demonstrated great amounts of resilience when coming across an obstacle but were often able to draw conclusions from these challenges and adjust their further course of action to their advantage.

Planning and setting up goals was another important skill and it mostly referred to planning the budget and developing a business plan, as well as deciding on milestones for each year that the business operates. This, as Cristina (Brazil) explained, enables one to "see where you're going to be in 10 years, if you work towards". This was also related to the previously discussed brand identity and planning to achieve certain goals, such as Diem's (Vietnam) previously mentioned plan to become "the champion of the kids' meals, wellbeing and health".

Networking, unlike the previously discussed surrounding yourself with knowledgeable and skilful people and forming collaborations and partnerships, referred to less formal, and not necessarily strictly business-related, communication. It involved reaching out to, and forming bonds with, the local communities and making friends, and for Cristina (Brazil), for example, making "long-term relationships with Australians (…) helped me feel like I'm part of Australia too". Although this is not always directly related to running a business, it certainly contributes to the overall emotional well-being which undoubtedly is important to achieve any success. Moreover, in some cases casual communication did, in fact, eventually influence the future success, such as in Joseph's (Lebanon) case, where a random conversation with strangers turned out to be crucial in one of his future work assignments:

I was sitting in the Hilton Café in Sydney, sometime in the late '80s. And there was hardly any tourists coming to Australia at that time. No tourists, only migrants. And two people were sitting across the table from me, and they were speaking in Arabic, with a Gulf dialect. Out of courtesy, I got up, I greeted them, and they told me one's from Bahrain, one's from the UAE. So, I invited them, afterwards took them around, showed them, the next day came, took them coffee and they were extremely happy, they gave me their cards. When Lifesavers wanted me to go, I didn't have anybody there. I remembered these two gentlemen (…) So I called the people, the Bahraini, he said "Come here". I went there. I said, "I want to go to UAE", he said "Oh, my sister in law married to somebody", I went, so from one country to the other, I built, and it worked for people to take me at least there. Where from? If I didn't get up at the Hilton Café and spoke to those people, I don't think I would have been able to offer to do it.

Surprisingly, specialised knowledge of how to run a business was only discussed by 3 participants. Ashwat (India), for example, believed that his accounting background was essential for his success, and Druv (India) believed that "unless you are capable you can't manage anything". Diem (Vietnam), in turn, commented that "you have to have corporate discipline, administration, how to run a corporate business, like corporate discipline, (…) infrastructure".

Other facilitators include positive attitude, which for some is "everything" (Cristina, Brazil), and willingness to take risks. Two participants believed that familiarity with the industry is important ("I can only do business that I understand" – Dhruv, India), and one argued that you can only start a business if you have enough financial backup. Finally, Pauline (Vietnam) explained that willingness to learn and develop is what constantly helps her improve and become "the next best version of myself". She is "addicted to learning" and, as previously noted, she likes to surround herself with knowledgeable people because "now I have the strength, the control, the knowledge and the mentors to constantly move into my next best self and so who you see today, hand on my heart, you will not see this person next year".

Challenges

Among the discussed challenges that the entrepreneurs face, the most mentioned was finding and retaining employees . The participants raised concerns about finding skilful employees, "people that had knowledge in that product" (Cristina, Brazil), as well as motivating these employees, because "getting them is one thing, holding onto them, making them believe in you, motivating them [is another]" (Dhruv, India). Additionally, two participants raised concerns about the challenges of finding employees as a small company owner, because "we can't give them all the perks that you get in the big companies" (Rustum, India). Another challenge was heavy workload , and this referred in particular to early stages of running the business, in which the entrepreneurs often had to spend long hours at work. Cristina (Brazil) who, as noted above, struggled to find knowledgeable and skilful employees, initially worked in her factory by herself, "managing the equipment, and trying to fix things", before she managed to bring an expert from her home country. Ashwat (India) also raised concerns about "being able to run everything", where "you're looking after production, you're looking after lab, warehousing, then invoicing, then sales…". As discussed later, this heavy workload also affects the entrepreneurs' work-life balance.

Institutional and legislative challenges refer to various obstacles that the participants faced with regard to restrictions from the government. Marina (Italy), for example, who specialises in interior design, was not allowed to place overhead signs on her building, and not allowed to paint the interior anything but eggshell white. She managed, however, to turn challenges into advantages by putting up fake walls in different colours. Pauline (Vietnam) also raised concerns about various "conditions and policies" that make it difficult to run a business in Australia, and Dhruv (India) believed that "everybody who wants to be an entrepreneur has to be quite clear that Australia is not a bed of roses" because of problems with support from the government and banks.

This leads to another three challenges that were related to each other, namely financial problems, lack of support from the banks and the government and lack of public understanding and awareness . 4 interviewees shared Dhruv's (India) belief that, when starting a business, "the first challenge [is] to raise funds". For some, this was also a problem in light of the lack of support from the banks and the government. Rustum (India) believed that the "government strategy as a whole" is "inadequate" with regard to supporting entrepreneurs. Only three interview participants reported getting support from the government , while 8 discussed investing personal money when starting their business. When discussing the lack of support from the banks and the government, three participants explained that it is difficult to obtain funding from banks because of the lack of public understanding and awareness:

The technology was all so new (…) So, it was very difficult to raise any funding for it.

Rustum (India)

The biggest issue for us was that nobody understood. So, no Australia bank banked with us. That is the first teething problem. They didn't want to know us.

Dhruv (India)

Innovation for me is pushing humanity forward and so it's a different base and the government aren't going to pay for that.

Pauline (Vietnam)

For two participants, the lack of public understanding and awareness also surfaced in later stages, when trying to sell the products when the business already operated. Rustum (India) explained that artificial intelligence "seemed like magic" to his customers, who "would say okay let me try it out, and that's about all they did". Cristina (Brazil), in turn, who tried to sell Brazilian food in Australia, also faced initial difficulties because "it's a product that nobody knew". With her proactive attitude, however, she managed to overcome this obstacle and she "had to educate everybody on how this Brazilian cheese bread is delicious, and healthy, and how to bake it, and serve children, and all of that".

When discussing industry-specific challenges,Pauline (restaurant) raised concerns that in general, restaurants do not generate much profit, June (real estate) explained that it is difficult to find buyers and reliable tenants, and Ashwat (paint) discussed safety issues related to safety of "a highly explosive environment" of their factory.

3 participants discussed lack of specialised knowledge on running a business. Cristina (Brazil) did not know how to "change from baking at home to mass production in a factory", and June generally struggled with how to run her business on a day to day basis, including trust accounting, communicating with the customers and monitoring payrolls. Ashwad (India), in turn, "didn't have any idea of this new product range, there was definitely issues within managing those people, then we had to decide what kind of company we

wanted to be, did we want to be this sales company, or this operations kind of company?". Branding and marketing , were also discussed, and these participants initially faced problems with getting recognized in the market, particularly Cristina and Rustum who, as previously noted, offered products of which there was no understanding and awareness among the public.

2 participants faced problems with finding partners and suppliers . Marina (Italy) struggled with finding suppliers to produce small batches of her product, as most suppliers would only manufacture a minimum of 10000 units. She also felt that it was difficult to find manufacturers who could be trusted, and she reported unreliable suppliers who did not make deadlines, which, she felt, affected her relationship with the customers who had to wait as a result. Ashwad (India), in turn, found it difficult to be trusted by the circle of "guys and tradies (…) [who] knew each other for years". 2 interviewees also faced market-specific challenges. June generally believed that selling in the Australian market was challenging, and Cristina faced difficulties with foreign markets because of varying requirements in terms of food packaging.

Feeling alienated and being on your own was a challenge that two of the participants faced. Ashwad (India) reflected:

No one wanted to talk to me. I had the same situation, like it was another, like a migrant, I wasn't a local person, I didn't have the accent, I didn't give them that trust that they're used to having, that was it, it was like going back to how my father started. And from going from having an established business when I left where I didn't have to go through that, it was another shock, going "I'm back to zero again"

For Cristina (Brazil), in turn, this sense of alienation and being left on her own related to both not having friends and being "with absolutely no family" and to her qualifications not being recognized .As she explained, her law qualification obtained in the UK was not recognized, and this "doesn't really help even the system itself, because I would have added a lot of knowledge with my international law and experience. So, the system didn't work for me, in that sense, and I was very demotivated".

Finally, 2 participants mentioned lack of equipment, space or resources . Cristina, as previously noted, did not have equipment to produce food, and Rustum (India) "discovered that when you get technology from a university type environment, it doesn't necessarily work in practice".

Personal philosophies and work-life balance

Eight participants discussed their personal philosophies during the interview. Although not all of them directly attributed their success to these philosophies, and this is why they were not categorised as facilitators of success, it does seem that having a strong set of beliefs and principles which they believed and followed helped them recognize and maintain their brand identity, as well as define their general approach to running their business. For three participants, these philosophies were linked to religion and spirituality, as in the case of Marina (Italy) who strongly believes in Karma and, therefore, always ensures that everything she does is honest and "by the book". Michelle (China), in turn, is highly religious as a result of early exposure to her Christian father and her grandmother who strongly believed in Buddha. She explained that "I always believed in Buddhism and I always believed in Christianity", and her religious nature seemed to be reflected in her approach to facing difficulties:

What we do is, regardless of what we experience in our life, it's something we should experience, whether it is good or whether it is bad (…) You have to go through hardship. Every good result at the end is all the hard work and it's all the hardship…

It is possible that her belief that each obstacle one faces is "something we should experience", which results from her religious nature, may have contributed to her determination, motivation and resilience which, as previously noted, was the most mentioned facilitator of success. Arguably, such approach to difficulties may have also contributed to her turning challenges into advantages, which is something Michelle also discussed in her interview. Michelle also extensively discussed compassion and being good with people during the interview, and this, again, may have resulted from her strong personal philosophies resulting from her being religious. She extensively discussed her approach of being kind to her clients and employees, and explained that

When they are down, you try to encourage them, help them up (…) It is the life, you know, it's the time that God lets you up is giving you the ability to help others. It's not really at that time to let them know you are good. Of course, you can let them know that you are good, but the key is to be able to help more people.

Pauline (Vietnam), on the other hand, explained that although she is highly spiritual, and her life is "all about spiritual entrepreneurship", "it has nothing to do with religion". She explained that his has to do with the previously discussed willingness to learn and develop, and about meeting her "next best self". It seems, therefore, that in this case, again, her personal philosophies do, in fact, seem to contribute to her success.

Other participants' philosophies did not necessarily relate to their religion or spirituality, but rather to their overall beliefs and principles with regard to how to run their business, such as Aswad's believe "one rule we've always had [is] never borrow money". For Joseph (Lebanon), in turn, the principle that he applies to his business is "I treat my business like my family, and I treat my family like my business". This, as he explained, means not taking unnecessary risks with either his family or his business, and spending "enough time with your family" and enough with the business. Dhruv's (India) philosophy was also related to the work-family relationship, and he explains that his wife understands that "I've been in demanding job all my life" and, therefore, "we never talk work at home".

This links to the issue of work-life balance that 7 participants discussed . As noted above, Joseph believes that one should "spend enough time with the family, not all your time and neglect your family" because "if you fail in your family, you fail in your business". He mentioned, however, initial difficulties and heavy workload which resulted in him working all nights and referred to it as a "price you pay" for being an entrepreneur. Several other participants reported similar problems. Cristina (Brazil), as previously noted, also had to work in the factory and spend most of her time there at the beginning, and Michelle (China) talks to her children to explain to them why she is so busy. As a result, "they know what we're busy doing and what we're really working for". Ashwat and Geeta (India) believe that "the negatives of business life" are that "we have nothing else in our life" and "we just work". Ashwat further explained that this affects their family, as even during family gatherings the conversation is dominated by his business conversations with Geeta:

Ashwat: And my sister, she's a doctor, she's in that healthcare industry, she's actually pretty good because she doesn't interrupt us, but she just sits there, and she's been sitting here for two hours not even talking, we haven't even talked to us.

Geeta: She just sits there, when she visits us, she works in a hospital in Newcastle, so when she visits us, and then I feel "Oh, God, she's come to visit us and here we're talking business" [unclear 00:55:08].

Ashwat: And then she'll tell us a story about the hospital and we're waiting for her to shut up so we can talk business again, that is how intense it is to be in business, it just does not leave you, its your baby.

Geeta: Even when go out – we rarely go on holiday together, but if we go, there again we sit up in a corner and talk business.

For Rustum (India), maintaining a healthy work-life balance is also challenging, and he explained that "when you run a business, it becomes a 24-hour job", which can be particularly challenging if one has young children:

when you run a business, it becomes a 24-hour job, which means you can't take a holiday, because even on Christmas Day a customer in the Middle East, who doesn't celebrate Christmas, will call you in the middle of the night. It takes a toll on your personal life, you can't easily take holidays when you feel like it. You don't get four weeks of holidays ever. You're lucky if you can take two days here at that. So, in that sense, it poses a very high personal toll on you, in terms of your family life. I think if I was trying to do this when my kids were very small, it would have had a very negative impact. Again, I'm lucky that I started when the kids were finishing school.

NOTE

The information in this chapter is based on a series of interviews with all 10 respondents throughout 2019.

Chapter 12
Conclusion:
Research Outcomes

ABSTRACT

Extant literature on immigrant family businesses (IFBs) refers to the vital role of embeddedness in their success. Yet, little is known about how embeddedness evolves from family to global and how it helps IFBs to establish themselves in a host country, survive the related challenges, and thrive in the international market. By drawing on the lived experience of 25 highly successful family business entrepreneurs in Australia, the authors develop an integrated process model and discover a four-phase chronology of IFBs' success toward global expansion: arriving, establishing, expanding, and thriving. Further, this model links these transitory phases to the IFBs' embeddedness that evolves from family to local, host-country, and global.

How do IFBs establish themselves as highly successful in the global market? How do they survive the related challenges in the host country, and what drivers help them to expand and thrive in the local, national, and international markets over time? We address this critical lack of knowledge by drawing from the lived experiences of 25 highly successful Australian IFBs. Respondents are immigrant family entrepreneurs who arrived in Australia with their families and have been operating in a multicultural environment where several ethnic communities have been well settled over the last decades[1]. Our data analysis reveals a chronology of four phases: arriving, establishing, expanding, and thriving. In particular, our process model explains how IFBs accrue network

DOI: 10.4018/978-1-6684-4986-8.ch012

benefits from different forms of embeddedness (family, local, host country, and global), and it highlights the related drivers and barriers along the four transitioning phases.

Existing literature on immigrant family businesses (IFBs), defined as organizations established and owned by immigrant families in a host country (Adendorff & Halkias, 2014; Tata & Prasad, 2015; Villares-Varela, 2017), is replete with studies on successes and challenges relating to their migration and integration (e.g., Azmat & Fujimoto, 2016; Barrett & Vershinina, 2017; Bird & Wennberg, 2016; Bonjour & Kraler, 2015; Collins, 2020; Dana, 2007b; Tata & Prasad, 2015). IFBs play a significant role in the host country's economy by creating employment (Jones et al., 2018) and increasing growth opportunities through the products and services offered. Yet, they are also unique and complex organizations due to the intertwined roles of the family and business systems once established in the new host country (Barrett & Vershinina, 2017; Dabić et al., 2020; Nazareno, Zhou, & You, 2019; Ram, 1997). A large and growing body of literature references the role of embeddedness, defined as "being embedded in a network of … social relations and family ties" (Kloosterman, 2010: 26), as an important driver of IFBs' success (Anderson, Dodd, & Jack, 2012; Beckers & Blumberg, 2013; Moyo, 2014; Ram, Jones, & Villares-Varela, 2017; Wigren-Kristofersen et al., 2019). Embeddedness has facilitated IFBs' success in many countries in Europe (Jones, Ram, Edwards, Kiselinchev, & Muchenje, 2014; Ward & Jenkins, 1984), as well as in the United States (US) (Bonacich, 1987; Hopp & Martin, 2017; Light, 1972; Waldinger, 1984; Wang & Altinay, 2012; Zahra, 2020) and Australia (Azmat & Fujimoto, 2016; Chavan & Taksa, 2017; Collins & Collins, 1995; Szkudlarek & Wu, 2018).

While family embeddedness recognizes the intertwined nature of the family and business systems and the role of the "family" in entrepreneurial decision-making and outcomes (e.g., Aldrich & Cliff, 2003; Cruz, Hamilton, & Jack, 2012), the social context dimension of mixed embeddedness focuses on the extent to which firms are connected to other actors via linkages of a social network (local, host country, global) to achieve economic gains (Kloosterman, Van Der Leun, & Rath, 1999; Uzzi & Gillespie, 2002). In particular, research shows that family embeddedness plays a vital role, especially in the start-up phase, given that IFBs rely on family bonds for support and unique advantages that are made available by distinctive family networks and resources (Bird & Wennberg, 2016; Dana, Gurau, Light, & Muhammad, 2020; Iacovou, Benbasat, & Dexter, 1995; Tata & Prasad, 2015; Verduijn & Essers, 2013). For instance, informal family labor and access to loans from family members to start and expand businesses make it possible for family immigrants to establish their enterprises in a new country (Bird & Wennberg, 2016; Dana et al., 2020; Iacovou et al., 1995; Sanders & Nee, 1996; Sirmon & Hitt, 2003). Despite a wealth of studies that have investigated immigrant entrepreneurship from an embeddedness perspective (Constant, Kahanec, & Zimmermann, 2009; Edelman, Brush, Manolova, & Greene, 2010; Kloosterman et al., 1999; Millar & Choi, 2008), we know relatively little about the process of how different forms of embeddedness affect IFB entrepreneurship, as well as the factors that enable IFBs to thrive and expand into global enterprises beyond the country of migration over time. Existing IFB literature mainly focuses on why embeddedness is crucial for migration management. However, the literature has not explored how different embeddedness forms evolve within the social context and how this evolution may help IFBs succeed in the host country and beyond it into the global market. This neglect is critical because a clear framework explaining this process can help IFBs to plan and implement successful strategies in the host country. Without this insight, not only does the IFB literature remain deficient, but so does our understanding of how research institutions and governments can support IFBs to flourish and contribute further to the economy of the host country, especially in nations where immigrant entrepreneurs are prevalent.

How do IFBs establish themselves as highly successful in the global market? How do they survive the related challenges in the host country, and what drivers help them to expand and thrive in the local, national, and international markets over time? We address this critical lack of knowledge by drawing from the lived experiences of 25 highly successful Australian IFBs. Respondents are immigrant family entrepreneurs who arrived in Australia with their families and have been operating in a multicultural environment where several ethnic communities have been well settled over the last decades[2]. Our data analysis reveals a chronology of four phases: arriving, establishing, expanding, and thriving. In particular, our process model explains how IFBs accrue network benefits from different forms of embeddedness (family, local, host country, and global), and it highlights the related drivers and barriers along the four transitioning phases. All IFBs examined as part of the present study are located in Sydney, New South Wales (NSW), which provides a valuable setting for our work given that NSW has experienced the largest influx of immigrants in Australia since a mass migration policy was introduced after World War II. According to data from the Australian Bureau of Statistics (ABS), overseas migration in 2019 resulted in a net increase in Australia's population of 239,600 people, with NSW, and in particular Sydney, consistently recording the largest intake of all Australian states and territories (86,200 people) (ABS, 2019; Simon-Davies, 2018). In addition, family businesses have long been the backbone of the Australian economy, constituting more than 70% of all Australian businesses (Graves & Thomas, 2004; KPMG Enterprise, 2018). In particular, IFBs represent one-third of the 2.1 million small businesses in Australia and about 11% of the country's gross domestic product (GDP) (ASBFEO, 2016). Yet, research on IFBs in Australia has been sparse (Chavan & Taksa, 2017; Collins, 2003, 2011, 2012), and little attention has been paid to IFBs in public policy and academia (ASBFEO, 2016; Corporations, Services, & O'Neill, 2013).

Our research offers important insights and discoveries in relation to immigrant entrepreneurship and IFB research through a process model that extends the application of embeddedness and how it evolves to explain IFBs' success in Australia. First, we address what Anderson et al. (2012) referred to as fragmented entrepreneurship theorizing and the dichotomous nature of entrepreneurial scholarship (Tatli, Vassilopoulou, Özbilgin, Forson, & Slutskaya, 2014) by offering an IFB model linking *family*, *local*, *host country* and *global* embeddedness to the phases of *arriving*, *establishing*, *expanding*, and *thriving*. In particular, family embeddedness denotes the network benefits derived from family ties (Aldrich & Cliff, 2003); local embeddedness signifies the local network benefits resulting from co-ethnic acquaintances (i.e., immigrants from their own and other countries/ethnic backgrounds (Jones et al., 2014; Szkudlarek & Wu, 2018); host country embeddedness represents the network benefits derived from familiarity with the host country's business environment (Constant, Shachmurove, & Zimmermann, 2007; You & Zhou, 2019); and global embeddedness represents the network benefits derived from international networks (Duan, Kotey, & Sandhu, 2020; Useche, Miguelez, & Lissoni, 2019; Zolin & Schlosser, 2013). In this regard, our study focuses on embedded networks (Bisignano & El-Anis, 2019), which extend beyond the IFBs' own immigrant families to include other ethnic groups in the host country, mainstream locals in the host country, and international actors outside the host country. As such, our research work and related findings offer important discoveries on how IFBs develop and the key roles played by embeddedness which evolves over time while the IFBs transition across different phases aim to achieve global expansion (see Figure 2). Second, our study reveals that while the *strength* of family embeddedness is critical over time, its *scope* is limited as IFBs form larger, more extensive networks to facilitate the establishment, expansion, and thriving of successful global businesses (see Figure 3). Our argument dovetails with the notions that businesses from different and distinct cultures can thrive within the same micro-context (Ado, Chrysostome, & Su, 2016; Chand & Ghorbani, 2011; Poirine, Dropsy, & Gay, 2017; Tata & Prasad, 2015), and that family embeddedness for IFBs involves not only high levels of family support in the host country, but also family links with the country of origin and across countries, which have the potential to facilitate IFBs' global success when interacting with other forms of embeddedness over time.

THEORETICAL BACKGROUND

Immigrant Entrepreneurship

The increasing rate of immigration alongside globalization over recent decades has spurred scholarly interest in immigrant entrepreneurship across numerous fields, including anthropology, economics, psychology, sociology, and public policy (Bailetti, 2018; Barrett & Vershinina, 2017; Brzozowski, 2017; Contreras-Sweet, 2015; Dabić et al., 2020; Dana, 2007a; Jones, Ram, & Edwards, 2006; Nazareno et al., 2019; Ram et al., 2017). Existing literature views immigrant entrepreneurship as a dynamic process that is influenced and shaped by complex interactions between macro-, meso-, and micro-level factors (Crawley & Hagen-Zanker, 2019). Existing studies have focused on immigrant entrepreneurs' lack of or unrecognized skills and qualifications, including language capacity in the host nation and limited employment opportunities (Volery, 2007; Waldinger, Aldrich, & Ward, 1990). Literature suggests that due to a lack of resources, many immigrants migrate and establish their business with their family in a host country where their ethnic community is already well developed (Chavan & Taksa, 2017; Jones et al., 2018; Jones et al., 2014). As such, their family and social networks become key drivers to facilitate the establishment of niche ethnic businesses[3] (Griffin-EL & Olabisi, 2018; Kloosterman, 2010; Rath, 2000; Rath, 2002; Villadsen & Wulff, 2018; Volery, 2007; Waldinger et al., 1990). Scholars have identified that such entrepreneurs are often dependent on their family for labor and start-up capital (Sanders & Nee, 1996). These entrepreneurs typically serve low-end markets in which they mainly compete on price by offering cheap goods and services while also creating jobs in urban areas where unemployment tends to be substantial (Chrysostome, 2010; Kloosterman & Rath, 2003; Kloosterman, 2010; Rath, 2000; Rath, 2002; Waldinger et al., 1990). Demetry

(2017) provided significant insights into the importance of the transitionary nature of entrepreneurship. Of particular value for the approach taken in this manuscript is her argument that entrepreneurship involves "a succession of activities carried out across time, culminating in business creation" (Demetry, 2017: 204). It is this emergent perspective that forms the basis of our process model. To generate entrepreneurial ideas, immigrant entrepreneurs count on networks and resources in both the host and home countries (Bolívar-Cruz, Batista-Canino, & Hormiga, 2014; Evansluong & Ramírez-Pasillas, 2019; Kloosterman, 2010). In particular, family networks and resources often help entrepreneurs build and connect with multiple network types to create and develop their businesses (Evansluong, 2016).

Today, in contrast to previous decades, not all immigrant entrepreneurs seek to solely provide self-employment for survival when starting a business. There are many different types of immigrant entrepreneurs, some of whom are highly educated and successfully exploit innovative ideas (Kushnirovich, Heilbrunn, & Davidovich, 2018). Immigrant entrepreneurs tend to provide vital goods and services to both business and household customers in the host country. They increasingly embrace knowledge-intensive activities and intricate global webs of interdependence (Kloosterman, Mamadouh, & Terhorst, 2018). According to some scholars, immigrant entrepreneurs are fostering the emergence of new spatial forms of social cohesion (Simon, 1997; Tarrius & Péraldi, 1995) by opening up trade links through networks to their home countries (Chavan & Taksa, 2017) and transnational networks of culturally distinct immigrant entrepreneurs (Faist, 1997; Guarnizo, 1996; Kloosterman et al., 1999; Portes, 1995; Wallace, 1997). However, entrepreneurship literature has been criticized for overlooking the socially and culturally embedded nature of immigrant entrepreneurial activities (De Clercq & Voronov, 2009; Moghaddam, Aidov, DuVal, & Azarpanah, 2017; Szkudlarek & Wu, 2018; Thornton, Ribeiro-Soriano, & Urbano, 2011), and for promoting an overly deterministic view of disadvantaged immigrant entrepreneurs whereby co-ethnic social networks are seen as their only business resource (Jones et al., 2014).

In contrast, this study focuses on highly successful IFB entrepreneurs who have relied on their families and multiple embedded networks to establish and enable their business to expand and thrive in the host country and ultimately in the international market. Our findings support the evolving nature of embeddedness, which has helped transform IFBs into transnational businesses, linking together their country of origin and country of settlement, and even beyond to international networks for global expansion.

Embeddedness and Immigrant Family Businesses

Embeddedness is a vital concept in network research that was first introduced by Granovetter (1973, 1983, 1985), who claimed that economic judgment must always be embedded within social relationships, and that this perception is often overlooked (Uzzi, 1997). Accordingly, the literature on embeddedness has investigated the process by which individuals' social relations shape economic action, and how ties with other actors facilitate the mobilization of resources (Granovetter, 1985; Uzzi, 1996). Put differently, it describes the overlap between social ties and economic ties (Cuypers, Ertug, Cantwell, Zaheer, & Kilduff, 2020; Kilduff & Brass, 2010; Waldinger et al., 1990).

In particular, the concept of mixed embeddedness has been employed by various scholars to emphasize the multiple contexts in which immigrants are embedded and how this influences their entrepreneurial opportunities through access to a variety of resources and markets (Beckers & Blumberg, 2013; Kloosterman, 2010; Szkudlarek & Wu, 2018). Mixed embeddedness focuses attention on the "interplay between the social, economic and institutional contexts" (Kloosterman et al., 1999: 257; Ram et al., 2017), suggesting that, besides the home-country culture, immigrants can be affected by their positioning within a given meso-organizational and macro-national context (Kloosterman & Rath, 2001). While we recognize the significance of economic, regulatory, and institutional contexts for mixed embeddedness (Kloosterman et al., 1999: 257, 262–263), we also note that the "concept remains fuzzy, difficult to operationalise and to verify empirically" (Bisignano & El-Anis, 2019: 990). Accordingly, the present study focuses on the social context dimension of mixed embeddedness emerging from the constellation of networks with other actors in local, host country, and global landscapes (Kloosterman et al., 1999; Uzzi & Gillespie, 2002).

Another important and related stream of research has focused on family embeddedness, arguing that family and economic activities are "inextricability intertwined" (Aldrich & Cliff, 2003: 573). The family household represents a closely knit small group of embedded members (Lancaster, 1975) that play a key role "in venture creation (i.e., opportunity recognition, the launch decision, resource mobilization, and the implementation of founding strategies, processes, and structures" (Aldrich & Cliff, 2003: 57; Cruz et al., 2012; Zahra, 2003). This perspective highlights the vital role of family ties and support in venture creation (e.g., Arregle, Miller, Hitt, & Beamish, 2013; Criaco, Sieger, Wennberg, Chirico, & Minola, 2017; Pittino, Chirico,

Henssen, & Broekaert, 2020; Pittino, Martínez, Chirico, & Galván, 2018), especially for immigrant entrepreneurs, which in the start-up phase usually lacks other forms of networks in the host country (e.g., Azmat & Fujimoto, 2016; Dabić et al., 2020; Evansluong & Ramírez-Pasillas, 2019; Evansluong, 2016; Tata & Prasad, 2015). For instance, adopting a family business perspective, Azmat and Fujimoto (2016) found that for Indian migrant women entrepreneurs and their partners in Australia, entrepreneurship is a complex phenomenon influenced by their being an Indian, a woman and a new Australian, all of which interact and influence their family dynamics and entrepreneurial experience. Similarly, Tata and Prasad (2015) focused on a sample of immigrant family business owners from the Midwest US and revealed that, in particular, family ties help them obtain network benefits and improve business performance. In a sample of Swedish IFBs, Evansluong and Ramírez-Pasillas (2019) found that family support is the key to creating entrepreneurial business opportunities in the host country. The key contention is that family embeddedness offers valuable unique advantages (Aldrich & Cliff, 2003; Sirmon & Hitt, 2003), "such as access to information, networks, knowledge, and support, and tangible resources consisting of financial capital and unpaid family labor" (Bird & Wennberg, 2016: 687).

However, little is known regarding how different forms of embeddedness affect highly successful immigrant family entrepreneurs and their expansion over time. Our study seeks to address this gap by drawing on the family embeddedness (Aldrich & Cliff, 2003; Criaco et al., 2017) and social context dimensions of mixed embeddedness (Kloosterman et al., 1999; Uzzi & Gillespie, 2002). In particular, we examine how family embeddedness is leveraged and interacts with co-ethnic local (local embeddedness), mainstream host country (host country embeddedness) and international (global embeddedness) networks to influence IFBs' success as transitional companies.

METHODOLOGY

Business management scholarship has increasingly adopted process models to understand the mechanisms that facilitate change in organizations[4] (Burgelman, 1983; Corley & Gioia, 2004; Langley, 1999; Nag, Corley, & Gioia, 2007). According to Van de Ven (1992), a process model illustrates the sequence of events, describes how things change over time and clarifies how they lead to an outcome—in our case, IFBs' success in Australia and beyond. A large body of strategy and management literature uses different process theories to understand change (e.g., life cycle for regulatory change; dialectics for conflictive change; teleology for planned change; and evolution for competitive change) (Van De Ven, 2011). The evolution theory applies when firms competing for scarce resources develop different ways of being innovative and succeed in a given market (Van De Ven, 2011). Our empirics follow an evolutionary view whereby firms learn, adapt, and acquire novel variations in their strategy, structure, policies, procedures, technology, or culture at different times through their life span (Langley, 1999; Van de Ven & Poole, 1995).

According to Van de Ven (1992), a process model comprises three essential components: a) *a set of starting conditions*, which in our case is "a family immigrating to Australia while establishing a new business;" b) *a functional endpoint*, which in our case is "thriving in the international market;" and c) *an emergent process of change*, which in our study relates to how an IFB evolves as it is established in Australia, becomes embedded in multiple networks, and subsequently internationalizes. Researchers have identified several elements that play a vital role in developing a process model (Langley, 1999; Mohr, 1982; Van de Ven, 1992). One significant feature is that a firm-level change along the process is not fixed but contains an emergent element that involves phase transitions as a response or adaptation to change (Van de Ven, 1992). We inductively discover the pattern of transition between the phases of the IFBs' success through the embeddedness lens, which, according to many studies, plays a vital role in IFB's success (Aldrich & Cliff, 2003; Azmat & Fujimoto, 2016; Barrett & Vershinina, 2017; Collins, 2012, 2020; Dana, 2007a). In the present study, a phase transition denotes a transformation between two qualitatively different states of an IFB's embeddedness in a system. The premise is that a phase transition is driven by some change within input variables (drivers and barriers). Barriers inhibit the transition into the next level of embeddedness and hence success in the host country and beyond. Thus, barriers break down the process by creating inertia, which prevents the change from unfolding as expected. In contrast, drivers motivate firms to diagnose and overcome barriers, thus propelling the transition. This basic insight guides our theorization about how IFBs' embeddedness evolves across different stages of success, as well as our approach to tracing the underlying pattern to a cohesive process model.

Research Design

While we recognize that immigrating to Australia, establishing in the local market, and achieving global expansion take a long time, a full longitudinal study was beyond our available resources. Instead, we adopted a processual approach (Burgelman, 1983; Gehman et al., 2018; Pettigrew, 1979). More specifically, we began with a biographical narrative interpretive method (BNIM) to collect qualitative data through interviews (Corbally & O'Neill, 2014; Ganzin, Islam, & Suddaby, 2020; Wengraf, 2011). Second, following the recommendations of multiple scholars (Corley & Gioia, 2004; Gehman et al., 2018; Gioia, Corley, & Hamilton, 2013; Langley, 1999), and in line with research adopting a narrative approach (e.g. Ganzin et al., 2020), we analyzed the data using a grounded theory–based methodology, which draws on the experiences and mental maps of those who lived the change process. For this purpose, we interviewed successful IFB entrepreneurs about "specific factual events that happened in the past" (Gehman et al., 2018). The BNIM largely accepts that oral biographies (stories) are illustrative of interviewees' personal and sociocultural projections (Corbally & O'Neill, 2014; Ganzin et al., 2020; Wengraf, 2011). This method pursues subjective representations of past narratives, prompting the interviewee to navigate an uninterrupted web of reconstructed anecdotes, including those that may be extraneous. It is this focus on historically situated subjectivity that makes BNIM more suitable for process data (Corbally & O'Neill, 2014; Wengraf, 2011).

Data

The multi-source data used in this study comprised: (a) 70 in-depth interviews with 25 entrepreneurs from IFBs in Australia; (b) archival and documentary sources including newspaper and magazine articles, ledgers, transaction records, press releases, websites, and phone conversations; and (c) observations during the time spent with the respondents in informal meetings and social interactions that supplemented the interviews. The interviews were our main data source; archival data and observations were used as supplementary sources for triangulation and to gain additional perspectives (Jick, 1979; Miles & Huberman, 1994).

Interviews

The interviews were conducted during 2018 and 2019. Participants were invited via email to take part in face-to-face interviews at their company. The interview protocol adhered to an open narrative structure with uninterrupted, active listening by the interviewer (Corbally & O'Neill, 2014; Pabian & Vandebosch, 2021). At the start, an overarching open-ended question was posed to elicit a narrative. This single-question (SQUIN) practice acts as a tactful mechanism to project a general, broad-scope response inviting interviewees to seize control of constructing their personal narrative (Corbally & O'Neill, 2014; Pabian & Vandebosch, 2021). We asked respondents to provide an account of their lives and businesses in order to gather background information on their lived experiences and the evolution of their entrepreneurial journeys, and to generate a narrative description of their cases (Ganzin et al., 2020; Miles & Huberman, 1994). We also gathered information on what has remained the same for them, what has changed throughout their tenure, how they currently understand these changes, and how this relates to their transition from struggling to integrating, to establishing their business, and to achieving success in Australia. Interpretation by the researchers began within the interview process, and observations commenced while maintaining the position of active listener (Bolton & Dewatripont, 2005: 15).

Following the SQUIN, closed-ended prompts (specific to an incident narrative) were posed in the interviewee's own words to elucidate further descriptions (Corbally & O'Neill, 2014). We asked probing questions about particular incidents that emerged from the initial stories and that had significance to the overall research question. This session produced accounts of specific incidents in the past and narratives that summarized the interviewees' attitudes, views of the world, and the orientations that they believed had enabled the change. The interviews (lasting 1.5/2 hours on average) were audio-recorded with the participants' consent and were later transcribed (Bell & Bryman, 2007). The interview recordings were listened to by at least two (and sometimes three or four) members of the research team to check for consistency of elucidation and to ensure the internal reliability of the study. After each interview, a debrief meeting was arranged to discuss the observations, analyze the situation, and finetune the questions for the next interview.

Sample

Two initial interviews with the founder/proprietor of the IFBs were helpful in developing the interview guide and identifying initial respondents. In the first instance, we selected highly successful IFB entrepreneurs from the Australian Ethnic Business Awards nominees using a purposive sampling technique (Gartner & Birley, 2002; Pratt, 2009). We identified highly successful family entrepreneurs based on their firm's revenue for the last three years (more than $2 million), three-year growth percentages (more than 7% yearly), operations lasting more than 10 years, and governance structure (family owned with a 100% family share). We divided these indicators into two major categories: (a) survival indicators (Kalleberg & Leicht, 1991), such as the age of the business and its profitability, and (b) growth indicators. Profitability refers to the fact that the costs of doing business are covered by its income, with a substantial surplus. Growth indicators refer to increases in elements such as sales, market share, net profit, and number of employees, as well as return on investment, return on sales, return on assets, and return on cash flow (Keats & Hitt, 1988; Muse, Rutherford, Oswald, & Raymond, 2005). We gathered this information from the popular press on business success and related performance measures, which identifies a wide range of indicators to measure the performance of small businesses such as those owned by immigrant entrepreneurs.

Initial broad sampling became more selective as the conceptual categories started emerging (Strauss & Corbin, 1998). Sampling and data collection ceased after data saturation was reached—that is, when the codes, categories, dimensions, and relationships between them were well-developed—and no new information was found (Glaser & Strauss, 1967; Strauss & Corbin, 1998). On the demographic side, our interviewees were age-diverse, had held a variety of jobs, were from different educational backgrounds, and had work experience in diverse industries. The breakdown of the interview participants is presented in Table 1.

Table 1. List of interview participants

Case Study	Gender	Origin	Years in Business	Industry	Education/ Profession	Number of Interviews	Secondary Data
1.	Husband & wife	India	25	Technology	Engineer	2	Webpage and Facebook
2.	Female	Brazil	15	Food	Lawyer	3	Publications
3.	Female	Vietnam	14	Food	HSC	3	Brochures and webpage
4.	Female	Vietnam	20	Restaurant	Graduate	3	Site visit, family lunch at restaurant, and observation
5.	Male	Lebanon	50	Marketing	Graduate	4*	Webpage
6.	Husband & wife	India	25	Paint manufacturing	Accountant and airline	2	Brochures and webpage
7.	Male	India	25	Oil	Engineer	2	Webpages and newspapers
8.	Female	China	15	Outdoor furniture	Graduate	2	Webpage
9.	Sisters	Germany	25	Real estate	Graduate	5*	Facebook
10.	Female	Italy	30	Architectural hardware	Graduate	2	Brochures
11.	Male	Lebanon	50	Real estate	Graduate	2	Facebook and webpage
12.	Male	Greece	35	Construction	Graduate	3	Facebook and webpage
13.	Husband & wife	Italy	25	Wine	Graduates	3	Phone call
14.	Male	Korea	18	Service industry	TAFE	5*	Brochures
15.	Husband & wife	Scotland	30	Shipping	Graduates	2	Observation
16.	Male	Italy	40	Hotel industry	Graduates	3	Lunch with family and phone calls
17.	Brother & sister	China	16	Property developer	Graduate and postgraduate	4*	Brochures, site visit, and observation
18.	Male	India	20	Technology	Postgraduate	2	Facebook and webpage
19.	Husband & wife	Greece	15	Wine	Graduates	2	Brochures, site visit, and observation
20.	Male	Vietnam	20	Seafood	HSC and TAFE	4*	Facebook and webpage
21.	Female	Sri Lanka	16	Architecture	Postgraduate	2	Facebook, webpage, and brochures

Continued on following page

Table 1. Continued

Case Study	Gender	Origin	Years in Business	Industry	Education/ Profession	Number of Interviews	Secondary Data
22.	Husband & wife	China	20	Hire business	Graduates	2	Facebook, webpage, site visit, and observation
23.	Female	Middle East	22	Resort	Graduates	3	Site visit and observation
24.	Husband & wife	Germany	19	Kitchens	HSC and TAFE	3	Facebook, webpage, and observation
25.	Husband & wife	Turkey	30	Dry cleaning	HSC and graduate	3	Facebook
Note: All participants held an important management role for the success of the IFBs; hence, they provided in-depth comments on their firm's success. The * sign indicates member check interviews.							

DATA ANALYSIS AND RESULTS

As we collected the data, we inductively analyzed them, following the constant comparison technique specified for grounded theory (Dacin, Munir, & Tracey, 2010; Glaser & Strauss, 1967; Lincoln & Guba, 1985; Strauss & Corbin, 1998). Adhering closely to the guidelines of multiple scholars (e.g., Burgelman, 1983; Corley & Gioia, 2004; Gioia et al., 2013; Nag et al., 2007), our analytic strategy embraced an established procedure to assemble first-order codes, second-order themes, and dimensions for building a data structure (Strauss & Corbin, 1998). This procedure involved four steps. First, all interview transcriptions were uploaded into NVivo software to code the patterns as they emerged during the data collection. A line-by-line micro-analysis of the transcripts (Strauss & Corbin, 1998) using NVivo helped to identify important concepts, which formed our *first-order codes*. These initial codes were used as precursors to analyze all of the remaining transcripts, and new codes were added to the list as they emerged. We retained the language used by the participants and assigned additional codes with the agreement of the research team. After engaging in discussions, comparing coded documents, and reaching an agreement, the research team finalized a total of 308 first-order codes that represented remarks about entrepreneurial activities, factors, elements, and attitudes that were viewed as contributing to the entrepreneurial success of IFBs in Australia.

Second, we searched for codes across the interviews and clustered them into meaningful abstract *higher-order nodes*. Triangulating interview data, observations, and archival information helped us to refine and categorize the higher-order nodes into a set of *first-order categories*. Examples included: "Hardships of unemployment and unrecognized qualifications" and "Lacking capital or bank loans." The third step was a recursive process. We moved iteratively through the first-order categories to identify interrelationships (Dacin et al., 2010; Glaser & Strauss, 1967), which we collapsed into theoretically distinct *second-order themes* (Eisenhardt, 1989). For example, categories "Hardships of unemployment and unrecognized qualifications" and "Lacking capital or bank loans" were collapsed into a theme labelled "Immigrant disadvantages."

Finally, we delved deeply into our qualitative data and the existing literature in an ongoing manner to expand our emergent model. This enabled us to sort second-order themes into *overarching dimensions*, which in turn helped us to theorize the embeddedness of IFBs in Australia. Overall, a total of 308 first-order codes were grouped under 112 higher-order nodes that were collapsed into 18 first-order categories, refined into 13 second-order themes, and ultimately sorted into five aggregate dimensions that underpinned our theorizing.

The final data structure exhibiting the categories, themes, and aggregate dimensions is presented in Figure 1. Following this, Table 2 contains illustrative quotes evoking the overarching dimensions and the second-order themes.

Concept Mapping

The data structure presented in Figure 1 forms the basis of our process model. However, multiple scholars (e.g., Gehman et al., 2018; Gioia et al., 2013) argue that a data structure depicts a static picture of an inevitably dynamic phenomenon; therefore, analyses must penetrate the dynamic relationship among the emerging concepts in order to convert the static picture into a motion picture (i.e., a process). In this vein, researchers recommend "concept mapping," which helps visualize concepts and their relationships with each other (Buckley & Waring, 2013; Ligita, Nurjannah, Wicking, Harvey, & Francis, 2020). Indeed, a visual illustration of process data supports the development and verification of theoretical ideas and allows the presentation of large quantities of information in relatively little space (Langley, 1999). Accordingly, we used concept mapping to graphically represent the dynamic process model (Ligita et al., 2020). Our concept map, corroborated by "member checks" by interviewees, is presented in Figure 2.

Figure 1. Data analysis structure

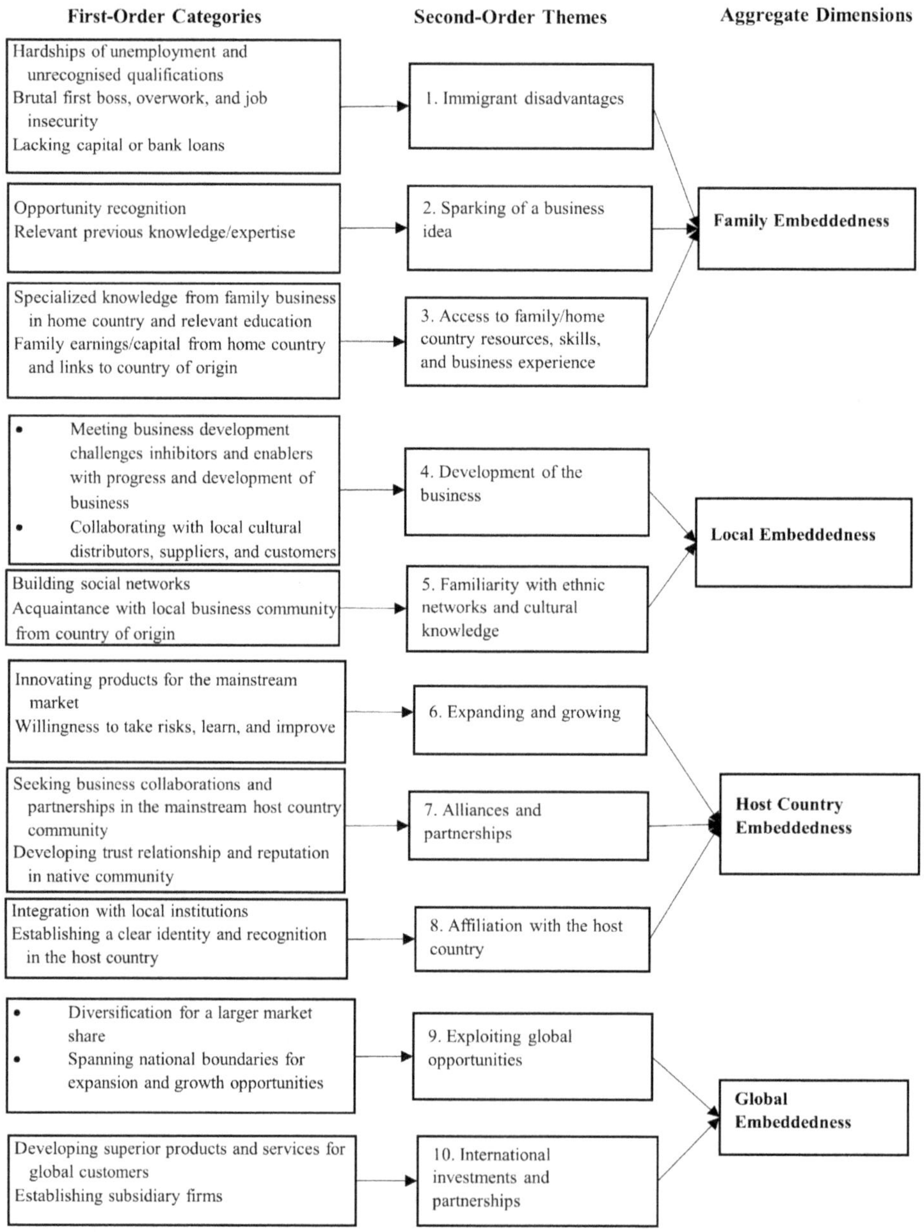

Table 2. List of overarching dimensions, themes, and illustrative quotes

DIMENSION *Second-Order theme:* **First Order categories**	**Illustrative Quotes from Interviews**
FAMILY EMBEDDEDNESS /ARRIVING ***1. Immigrant disadvantages*** A. Hardships of unemployment and unrecognized qualifications B. Brutal first boss, overwork, and job insecurity C. Lacking capital or bank loans	A1:"Non-recognition of qualifications is a big issue ... I'm not the only [victim] ... It's demotivating, and it doesn't really help even the system itself. I would have added a lot of knowledge with my international law and experience. But they're not going to approve my degree ... So, the system didn't work for me, in that sense, and I was very demotivated ... and frustrated." **(Case 2)** A2:"It was all trial and error and a learning process. No one wanted to believe in artificial intelligence in those early years.I had my family's support, which gave me the strength. My wife was earning and that is what kept me going. My family from home helped me with some capital too." **(Case 18)** A3:"We migrated to Australia in 1970, we had the two little kids with us. At that time, it was hard to find a job. Almost six months I was not employed." **(Case 6)** A4:"The reply that I got from everywhere was 'Sorry, your qualifications do not match, and you do not have local experience." **(Case 6)** A5:"Although I worked as an accountant with a large firm in the Middle East, I failed to get any employment. Then my wife said, 'you better study.' I got into the bridging course of CPA." **(Case 6)** A6:"One day I saw some classified ad in *The Sydney Morning Herald*, and I contacted the person. It was a paint business. I had no clue. So, I started working in the factory myself, and managing the equipment and trying to fix things. Lots of headaches, and really wasn't qualified to do it, but I decided we'll do it somehow. I mean, I physically manufactured—doing labor work for the first time in my life and ended up physically lifting bags, in the forklift, pouring paint."**(Case 6)** B1:"I joined [XXX], I worked there for a few months, then after I joined another multinational company [XXX]. There my boss was constantly harassing me. I couldn't continue the job anymore. I lost my job on my son's birthday. Then I decided okay, now I'm not going to work for somebody, I'll start my own business." **(Case 6)** B2:"The jobs that I got was on contract, I was an engineer by profession so I enrolled in a course to further my education and told my boss I had to leave a bit early to attend my classes and he was in a rage and did not like it was time to think of a business." **(Case 12)** C1:"The biggest issue for us was that no Australia bank was ready to work with us. That was the first teething problem. They [banks and investors] did not want to know us. No Australian invested a single cent even till today. Though everybody invites me for the board dinners, I am known, but I am just telling you this is reality on the ground okay." **(Case 7)** C2:"To start off with, we couldn't raise any funding, because, as I said, people didn't even believe what we were doing, they thought we were selling magic. Artificial intelligence in those days was not considered a recognized technology. Today, because people like Google talk about it, now, suddenly it's become very mundane, and everybody does it. **(Case 1)** C3:"Raising capital was a major problem. We had to scrounge and invest everything we could invest, and we borrowed to invest and so on. So, for both my wife and I we had to put money in our own money from home and it was very difficult". **(Case 1)**

Continued on following page

Table 2. Continued

DIMENSION *Second-Order theme:* **First Order categories**	**Illustrative Quotes from Interviews**
2. Sparking of a business idea D. Opportunity recognition E. Relevant previous knowledge/ expertise	D1:"I felt like, okay, well, how many more years am I going to invest in studying law? I'm going to look for something that I can do. I'll set up a business. And I think that's what a lot of immigrants do, because their qualifications are so hard to be recognized. So, what I decided to do was to set up a business in which I would be able to reconcile my role as a mother, because I had very young children, with my time flexibility, and all of that." **(Case 2)** D2:"After a stressful five months of not getting work I started working for my uncle in his stall selling fish at the fish market, I did not like it, then my uncle send me to restaurants to deliver fish, I liked that job, saved money bought a van and started my own fish distributing business, this is how I started. My uncle's help and knowledge helped me and today I have a million-dollar business where my retired retired uncle is the business strategist." **(Case 20)** E1: "The first thing I thought about, because really other than law, I had no other interests; but for many years I'd been baking at home these little Brazilian cheese bread, which is the only thing that would make me feel close to Brazil. Whenever I miss Brazil, I bake it at home; this little cheese puff that I grew up eating in Brazil, was a cultural skill and everybody loved it, every time I served it, families and children loved it; and I said to my husband, 'Well, I might just set up a business baking this Brazilian bread, and see what happens.' I now have an empire of unique food." **(Case 2)** E2: "On seeing the account books of the business, I realized that the business was making money. I was an accountant with 10 years in an accounting role and that knowledge gave me the confidence that I can do this and run this business." **(Case 6)**
3. Access to family/home country resources, skills, and business experience F. Specialized knowledge from family business in home country and relevant education G. Family earnings, capital from home country, and links to country of origin	F1: "It's quite simple because we had to have something to do. The only thing we knew was trading from our family business at home. We started the trading of the outdoor furniture. My husband did the trading of the outdoor furniture 30 years ago, so he is the first generation of outdoor furniture in China. This experience from home helped us develop this Australian business with so many partners." **(Case 8)** F2: "We had contacts and links at home … our brothers and sisters helped. So, at that time we knew all the business contacts back 20 years ago, pretty much we knew every single good key factory and they knew us as well. We set up a company with our first Furniture Fair in the year 2002. We sold nearly nothing." **(Case 8)** G1:"The gherkin, small little cucumber. Nobody had heard of that in India. So, my brother gave me five crores, and that was a lot of money in 1991-92. India is today the largest producer of gherkin. I mean, if you asked me what the biggest contribution has been when I go into my grave, it would be creating jobs for one million people in India. Gherkin is today imported from India the largest—not anybody knew of gherkin, so we put in our money and we had a joint venture. We really had to put in 120% into everything we did. We do lots of things that our competitors never do. The problem-solving, the relationship-building, understanding the culture helped building this business. If it were not for my brother's help, this would not be a global business supplying gherkin to the world." **(Case 7)** G2:"We received this big export order from Malaysia for 750 bottles of wine and it had to be done in a week and we were going through a cash crunch and my wife's brother in our country lent us the money in three days and the entire family helped in meeting this big order." **(Case 19)**

Continued on following page

Table 2. Continued

DIMENSION *Second-Order theme:* **First Order categories**	**Illustrative Quotes from Interviews**
LOCAL EMBEDDEDNESS /ESTABLISHNG ***4. Development of the business*** H. Meeting business development challenges: co-ethnic networks I. Collaborating with local distributors, suppliers and customers through family and friends	H1:"It makes it harder and harder to stay in business because the wage costs are so high and all these different rules and regulations and all we want to do is stay in business, create an amazing life for our team members because I'm not the only person in it. You put an ad in the paper. The only ones who are interested in working are the immigrants or the ones on tourist visas. I have to depend on the local ethnic people from my community as my product and business is Vietnamese and culturally coded and I need a lot of Vietnamese raw materials and food and a lot of Vietnamese cooking skills and talent. But as a reputable business we want to do things right and nothing is made easy for us. The government is making it more and more difficult each day to hire and bring workers from overseas. But the government constantly makes it so hard for us now to sponsor, to have people from overseas." **(Case 4)** H2:"The bank doesn't help us much. It's really hard for the bank. Pretty much the bank will lend us money while we give them a property. So, the bank is not really helping much. I think we should really give more help to the small businesses, especially the immigrants, you know, the way it works and all that. But to do business here in Australia is tough. It's really tough. The salaries are really expensive here. The salaries are more expensive than America. The rent for commercial property is a huge burden too. I got funding from my engineering college mates who trusted me and from the local people from my community residing in Sydney." **(Case 8)** H3:"The second lesson learnt was the labor cost in Australia and that I would obviously try to not put up so much capital-intensive projects, because this cost is very high. So, let me give you an example. The whole of equipment in my factory cost me $30 million, only. The piping cost me $700,000, to put up those pipes and my pipes are 36 kilometers long. I mean, electrical wiring, it's a huge factory. You know how much it cost me to put those pipes and electrical? $8 million. The materials aren't worth even $2 million. So, this is what the whole thing is, the labor costs in Australia are too high." **(Case 7)** I1: "During that period, I wanted to be close to Brazil, so I got very involved with the Brazil Chamber of Commerce, and also because I was importing products from Brazil; some raw materials to make the cheese breads. I wanted to assist Brazilians who come here, like me, who had no idea what they could be doing here, because basically they couldn't get their degrees recognized … yeah. So, I got involved with the chamber as a member, and then as a director, and then I became the president, and I was president for 10 years. So, I did a lot of assisting Brazilians and companies that come here, or Australians that want to do business with Brazil. I build a number of international business networks due to this engagement." **(Case 2)** I2: "Finally, after lots of presentations to different retailers, [XXX] decided to put this Brazilian cookie that I had learned to make from my home country in the freezer and on the shelf. Today I export to more than five countries. So, we developed packaging and put it on the shelf. But it wasn't very easy, because we only had one product, and all the other brands in the freezers at [XXX]. They have hundreds of products, and we're this little new product, hiding behind the door, that people have to open to see it. Very difficult to brand it and market it. So, there was a real need from my perspective that we can't just rely on this one product so we started talking to locals and understanding the need in the market for gluten-free food." **(Case 2)**

Continued on following page

Table 2. Continued

DIMENSION *Second-Order theme:* **First Order categories**	**Illustrative Quotes from Interviews**
5. Familiarity with ethnic networks and cultural knowledge J. Building social networks K. Acquaintance with local business community	J1: "The Korean neighbor took me to this Korean business network, and they gave me funding from a chit fund, which I had to return back in 10 months with no interest payment but 5% of profits that I make in 10 months, that helped me buy the van and start providing distribution of Korean food." **(Case 7)** J2: "I found out that many Indian friends owned post offices and travel agencies, and I talked to one of them and asked for help although I was an engineer and interested in an IT tech business, they gave me a lot of help with getting initial funding from top Indian businesses who were happy to partner in my business." **(Case 18)** K1:"But one thing that's really good, all our managers in the branches, they want to be partners of our store. So, we're kind of selling a small percentage of our store to our team who are all from our ethic background from my country. Our distributors also are all from China. So, we now have three managers: one is the warehouse manager, one is the account manager, and one is a new partner for a different percentage at a different store, you know. They may have 5%, they may have 10%, it's a set rate for them and they knew that. Our system is really open so everybody will know what the sales are of every store. Speaking the same language and understanding the culture helps us understand them and it is also a way of giving back to our community. We have helped many people from our community become distributors and with providing logistics services." **(Case 8)** K2:"So, if they are the accountant, they know my figures even better than I do and then they're looking at that and they really like it. So, we've got three managers and now they have another one and he is talking to me for partnerships. So, we aim to sell 49% of the store. We will always hold 51%. Franchising is not our direction. We do not believe in franchising. But we believe in partnership, especially if they are our team. We love it. They become like partners. They put the money in, they share the profit. It is the best. But not all staff like it. But the ones that want to do it, they normally care, and they normally work harder, they treat it as their own store, and they have 5% or 10%. It's their store. We always give them more profit share. So, our structure is like we hold 51% of that share but we share the 51% of the profit. So, we hold 49% of the profit. They've got more profit than we do. So pretty much it can be 5%, it can be 10%, it can be whatever they believe they can afford to invest in the store. So, the same thing in other branches, our team all have a share there. We find that is really good." **(Case 8)**

Continued on following page

Table 2. Continued

DIMENSION *Second-Order theme:* **First Order categories**	**Illustrative Quotes from Interviews**
HOST COUNTRY EMBEDDEDNESS /EXPANDING ***6. Expanding and growth*** L. Innovating products for the mainstream market M. Willingness to take risks, learn, and grow	L1: "Since then, we developed the XYZ brand, which we started doing shelf-stable products, because freezer was very difficult and expensive. So, then we decided to set up our own brand, XYZ, and we wanted to empower people who had food allergies to be able to eat like any other person, without being ostracized, and without having to eat products that were tasteless, bad texture, or whatever. So, we wanted to first of all offer the best taste, the best food experience, even though it was gluten free. So, this was my premise. People with allergies, they should be able to eat and enjoy the foods that we enjoy." **(Case 2)** L2: "I actually solve an allergen problem, gluten and lactose free. My products are all biodegradable. All my packaging—I'm the first person to have a biodegradable packaging in 92 years. So that's a very expensive statement, because if you use a black tray, it's 12 cents. If you use a biodegradable tray like mine, it's 28 cents. So, I lost $200,000, because that cost more—150% more than a normal tray people use." **(Case 3)** L3: "And I look at the social media and see that it has paid off as my food products are very trendy, because these days kids age 12 they have social media, they have Instagram. So, on the packaging you can't patronize the junior foodies, because they're cool, they're arty. There is a junior foodie's movement. So, I tap into that. And I look at balance convenience. So, balance means my food is made up of the highest meat content to comparable products. So, it's got double the meat content—mine is anywhere between 18–30% meat content, which is the most expensive raw material in any meat. Most comparable products only got 8–12%. And I look at the demographic growth of the age group, there's a 12% growth. And there is 4% of people who have allergen problems, but 25% of people eat gluten- or lactose-free for lifestyle. I understand the local needs and cater to them through innovative products." **(Case 3)** M1:"Come with an open mind. Come with a hard-working mindset, too. Attitude is everything. So, I don't want to change my ethics and my authenticity. I don't let people bully me once I've done my homework. So that's how I work. I'm very strong-headed of what I stand for. We work hard and take risk, and we know the success will follow. Our little store at [X] suburb, how much do you think that we can sell? We asked an agent and then he picked out some average sales per square meter and he said, 'Yeah, if you can do something like 600,000 sales from that store a year, it would be good.' Then I said to him, 'No, no. We can sell for more than that.' I said that to him, but I was taking a risk holding on. I said, 'I can sell over a million.' Then one year after, we sold just over a million and then in my email, I said, 'I told you I can sell …' So, I think we sold about a million and ten thousand dollars or something like that, that is the kind of risk we have to take in business because cash is king in any business." **(Case 8)** M2:"I started baking it, putting it in the car, and started going to the school canteens all over the place, to introduce them to the canteens, and say, 'This is a gluten-free product. It's baked; it's fat free. It's got calcium and cheese, it's very good for your children, and they will love it.' So, I started doing demonstrations at canteens, and then we got it registered with the coeliac association as a gluten-free product. That's how I built that little niche market of gluten free. And 20 years ago, it was very hard, because not much awareness of what gluten-free was, and people with coeliac disease might be suffering from it, but they wouldn't know about it. So, diagnosis was bad. You have language barriers. If you put all your effort into mingling and belonging, it will happen. And as an immigrant here, I found comfort in meeting resilience. Innovating is hard in Australia. The support is not there." **(Case 3)**

Continued on following page

Table 2. Continued

DIMENSION *Second-Order theme:* **First Order categories**	**Illustrative Quotes from Interviews**
7. Alliances and partnerships N. Seeking collaboration and partnerships in the mainstream host country community O. Developing trust relationship and reputation in native community	N1:"We have developed a special product, so again it's a strategic partnership with an Australian firm. We have partnered with DDD. DDD is the largest plantation company. It is a British company, but they're the largest plantation company in the world, which helped to sell to the mainstream market in Australia and the USA and UK. This happened because my wife's brother helped with his friend's network who works in that firm as a top manager." **(Case 7)** N2:"Well, I don't know any secrets, but without strategic partnerships you can't do it. I'm a great believer of strategic partnership and we are selling a range of product through our collaborations to the native community in Australia and also overseas to USA and Japan. The main thing that we found with going to these different countries is we've had networks or someone who's doing business with us here. So, they're already in that country. So, it's very easy for them too … But essentially, it's trust-based. With Malaysia, a prime example, my father's good friends with GG, he does manufacturing, and his nephew is in Malaysia, and we linked up with his nephew." **(Case 12)** O1:"If you know them and their background, and your family or friend has introduced you to them, you know they're not going to stab you in the back with money or anything like that. It's just good honest people that you can trust. **(Case 12)** O2: "…Doing business overseas with people that you and your family know and they speak your language and understand your culture was very helpful to take your business international. It's the reputation and the long-term family network that helps." **(Case 12)** O3: "As you know so many Indians are in the technology business in Sydney and there are large Indian Tech firms operating in Sydney, the local Indian network is a great asset as all the primary information for getting contract was obtained from them thus setting up my business in IT was smooth because of the local community network." **(Case 18)**

Continued on following page

Table 2. Continued

DIMENSION *Second-Order theme:* **First Order categories**	**Illustrative Quotes from Interviews**
8. Affiliation with the host country P. Integration with local institutions Q. Establishing a clear identity and recognition in the host country.	P1: "In 2007 we were building our factory; we didn't have much business. I approached XYZ Paints. They had a plant in Australia. They were running in a loss for almost 15 years. I called them, 'Do you have any work for me?', I could subcontract the job from them. They said, 'We don't have any job to give it to you, but we have other opportunities, are you interested?' I said, 'I'm always open for all opportunities.' They said, 'We are in the process of diversifying our business, are you interested in buying our business?' I said, 'Yes, I can think of it.' We ended up buying the business, and that was a good boost because they had all the, what do you call, branding done in Australia, and they had spent a lot of money on development of the products, so it was very handy. That helped us to grow our business. And we got into the road marking business. There are only a few companies who were doing it, and we were one of them at that time. And today we are the largest producer of road marking paint in Australia. But that was essentially the growth. Then with acquiring them we got some contracts with the government, and then we increased our volume. When you get volume, then you get better supply power. Then our costs reduced; now we can compete in different angles and different places. As of now, we are working for five American multinationals, and they don't give you a job unless they have the confidence in you, and we are the only company in Australia who are the preferred supplier for three state governments for supplying their liquid paint." **(Case 6)** P2: "I think on the positive side, one of the things that has worked for us is the fact that from the beginning we knew we were a technology company and we wanted to be number one company serving everyone in Australia and not just immigrants or the ethnic community. So, we weren't just developing a technology. You can say, 'I want to set up a business,' and you can start a coffee shop and you'll make some money, and probably make more money than we made in the first year. But, then to expand that business it's difficult because there are so many other people who also make coffee. So, for us, we had to say we want to be a technology company, so we have to come up with a technology that is unique and so unique that even today, after 17 years, even with all the big guys like Google and so on coming into the market, we can still say we are ahead of all of them. All the big local companies like IBM and Cisco and so on still continue to use us as partners today." **(Case 18)** Q1:"One advice I have, too, which I've done, is if you immerse yourself in local community and charity, and you start giving back, you'll be surprised that in those circles, you get a lot of support as well, back. I love being involved in not-for-profits and charities and NGOs, because often people who get involved in those things, they're quite helpful. They're quite giving. These are good things. So even though we have businesses, and we're business-focused, don't have to be too greedy, only focus on business. Give to community, when you have time, because that will really make you an established person in the community. **(Case 1)** Q2: "…we started off in the security space with our technology, but today, our technology is not used just for security globally; it's used in hospitals for dementia patients or geriatric patients, and it's used for banks for IT fraud. It's used in shopping malls for finding lost children. It's used for so many different areas, and there are probably more areas that we can dream of that we haven't even got into yet. Wherever there's imaging, for instance, in medicine. If you think of in medicine there are lots of imagines like brain scans, x-rays and so on." **(Case 1)** Q3 " Although we have many resorts now in four countries, it was important to adapt the model to each country and we have collaborated with Australian staff and local people to understand their needs and choices and align our model to the host country. Our Australian friends and other stakeholders in our business, our distributors and our local manager assisted us in this." **(Case 23)**

Continued on following page

Table 2. Continued

DIMENSION *Second-Order theme:* **First Order categories**	**Illustrative Quotes from Interviews**
GLOBAL EMBEDDEDNESS /THRIVING ***9. Exploiting global opportunities*** R. Diversification for a larger market share S. Spanning national boundaries for expansion and growth opportunities	R1: "Now we are number one Australia's refinery, bigger than [XXX] Corp. We are not biggest crusher because they are multiple. Would be the biggest refined product. That's point one. The second is to give you a perspective of the impact we have. So, every fourth glass of milk you drink, the cows had a canola meal. Every fourth egg you eat, the chicken has had canola. Every fourth chicken you eat, right. Every fifth restaurant in Sydney and Melbourne that you go to, every 10 supermarket product. So that has been the impact. So, it's a huge multiplied effect." **(Case12)** R2: "The market is saying we want to move towards natural products, and we are the only Australian non-GM certified and non-GM company out of Australia, and only second in the world and United States. The other is GP, which is a $300 billion company. So that means that we can put up three factories probably over time, because we've hit upon the most interesting thing, and we are Australia's second largest exporter of liquid products into the United States." **(Case 12)** S1: "We've also launched in India, but India is again the largest retail market. Let me tell you, India's retail market is bigger than US, Canada, whole of Americas, Japan, all of Europe, combined together multiplied by five. The Indian market is 20 million tons. Sunflower oil need is two and a half million tons and more." **(Case 7)** S2 " We now have purchased the popular plant company in Singapore XXX and have a pain plant in Brisbane and have purchased several sick paint plants in the USA which my son is managing. The USA business was possible as I have two borther in laws living in the USA for a long time and the Singapore opportunity came from a previous employee who moved to this Sinagapore paint company.We have now diversified into the automobile accessories and parts retail business in Sydney." **(Case 6)**

Continued on following page

Table 2. Continued

DIMENSION *Second-Order theme:* **First Order categories**	**Illustrative Quotes from Interviews**
10. International investments and partnerships T. Developing superior products and services for global customers U. Establishing subsidiary firms	T1: "Today, we operate in 47 countries around the world. We are everywhere, and Australia is probably only about 2% of our revenue base. We have legal entities in five other countries. We have people in probably 12 countries or something like that. It's more like a one-man office in a place like Bahrain, where we don't have a legal entity, but we put one guy there and we say you just get out for us. Then we have resellers and distributors in about 50 or 60 countries. …So, when the team here goes to sleep, somebody in Singapore is awake and take on the next calls, and then the next team is in Dubai and so on. We set ourselves up to work internationally right from the beginning. And managing different cultures, I learned when I was in Japan and I said to them 'do this.' They'd all say, 'yes sir,' and then three months later nothing was done. But that was the culture; they'd all say 'yes.' So, you learn how to manage the different cultures and so on. …We have our patents covering the US, Europe, Japan and so on. It's a very important lesson for new entrepreneurs to know that you need to adapt your name to the country too." **(Case 1)** T2: "When we started, we were a mom-and-pop business selling architectural hardware in batches. Little did we know that one day we would be exporting to China in millions and providing our products to several high skyscrapers in China, and we are really humbled." **(Case 10)** U1:"What really worked for us: in most countries, we started with a small market. The first country we started exporting to was Singapore. It was a comfortable market for us because we lived there for seven years, so we knew the market and had relationships there…. So, Singapore was an easy entry; it was quite easy to do business with them. They're fast, reliable, it was easy. Then there's challenges with other countries because we wanted to be in many other places. So, Indonesia was very challenging; took a very long time to have everything registered and organized. They are extremely painful with all the ingredients system and registration, and we had to redesign and adapt the product. The bureaucracy, it's costly. Some countries are very difficult. But what really worked for us in those countries is, I believe really in relationships, so I don't like giving my product to a distributor that I've never met. A lot of businesses do that." **(Case 21)** U2:"Now we have a firm in subsidiary in the USA that does contract work for US large paint firms, we recently bought a large paint manufacturer in Singapore. Besides that, we have two facilities in Brisbane and two in Sydney." **(Case 6)** U3:"I spoke to my classmate from engineering days who was settled in Singapore, and when I told him I was struggling to get a job in Sydney, he said 'just export Australian wine to me.' Singapore had many buyers and that is what I started doing. From unemployed, I became an exporter with an international business in two years of arriving in Australia." **(Case 13)**

Figure 2. Process model of IFBs' success toward global expansion

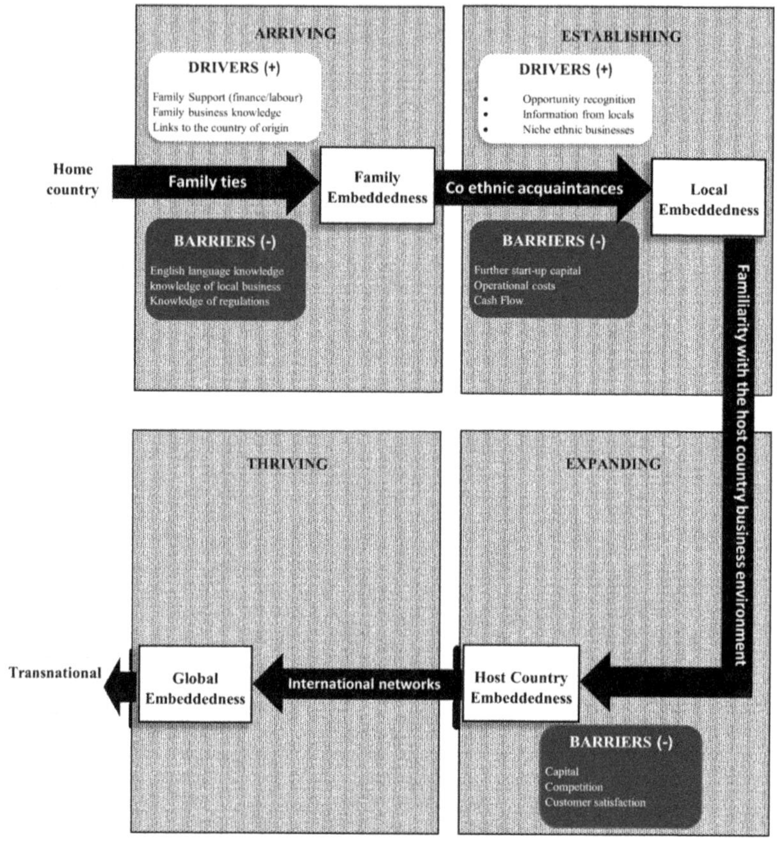

Inter-Rater Coding Reliability

To ensure rigor (Miles & Huberman, 1994), inter-rater reliability seeks to establish that the interpretation of the data is credible. Inter-rater reliability exists when there is concordance among raters in interpreting and coding the data. In NVivo, we achieved this by measuring the kappa coefficient for each coded interview segment (Cohen, 1960). A value of 1.0 was used to indicate perfect consistency between the coders, and 0.0 implied no commonality at all (Judge & Douglas, 2013). The closer the kappa coefficient to 1.0, the more reliable the data analysis. In this study, Cohen's kappa for the three raters was .92, a value higher than the inter-rater reliability threshold of .75 (Anand & Watson, 2004), which indicates a reliable coding effort.

Validity of Interpretation

Our repeat interviews comprised five member checks to ensure the trustworthiness of our interpretations—that is, the emergent process model's sketch was taken back to the site and subjected to the scrutiny of the interview participants (Lincoln & Guba, 1985). The aim was to verify that the interpretive scheme was "sensible to, and affirmed by, those living the phenomena of interest" (Nag et al., 2007: 829). Member checks helped us achieve three goals: fine-tuning, participants' concordance, and deriving a process model more grounded in the qualitative data. Indeed, member checks is an important validation technique in qualitative research (Dacin et al., 2010; Lincoln & Guba, 1985; Nag et al., 2007). The interviews provided explicit self-theories, stories of continuity and change, and insights from incident reporting, arguments, and descriptions (Ganzin et al., 2020). These interviews and member checks, combined with secondary data and the interpretive process, paved the way for theory building—one that is unaffected by the imposition of a grand meta-narrative by researchers and is simply navigated through the lens of the interviewee's first-hand experience (Dacin et al., 2010; Nag et al., 2007; Wengraf, 2011).

FINDINGS AND PROPOSITIONS

The model depicted in Figure 2 details the process model of IFBs' success in regard to global expansion from settlement in the host country via four consecutive phases of arriving, establishing, expanding, and thriving. The ensuing family, local, host country, and global embeddedness types trigger drivers that help IFBs address potential barriers emerging in each phase of development. Below, we detail our findings and propositions in relation to each phase and the related embeddedness type attached to each phase to drive IFBs' success in the host country and internationally. In support of each proposition, in addition to the quotes reported below, we also offer some more illustrative quotes from interviews in Table 2.[5]

Arriving Phase

The members of the IFBs who were interviewed indicated that they faced multiple disadvantages/barriers upon arrival in Australia, such as a lack of knowledge of local businesses and regulations; non-supportive banks; and a lack of government support. Indeed, immigrants usually encounter difficulties in the new (host) country because of inequities and societal exclusion, which results in prejudice in the labor market and isolation from the local community (Griffin-EL & Olabisi, 2018). However, the presence of strong family ties through family members and close family friends in Australia, as well as links with the family in the home country, allows them to rely on what the literature refers to as "family embeddedness" (Aldrich & Cliff, 2003). We found that IFBs gain access to key information and resources (e.g., knowledge on (family) business matters in Australia, and family support in Australia and from the country of origin) to overcome the barriers they encounter while triggering new business opportunities. In fact, IFBs do not usually possess all of the relevant resources to start a new business in the host country; thus, they often rely on family ties as a significant channel to gather information and receive support (Arregle et al., 2015). As Case 16 mentioned, "*I came to Australia not to work but because my friend [a close friend of my family] moved here and two of my uncles lived here and one of my family friends in Italy said he will give me finance to set up an Italian restaurant in Australia for him ... My family has hotels in Italy and so that is what I knew best so moved to Australia to set up the hotel*" (see Table 1).

Family embeddedness helps immigrants to tap into unique benefits such as information, resource mobilization, and access to financial and other productive resources (Habbershon, Williams, & MacMillan, 2003; Khayesi & George, 2011). The benefits developed through being embedded in the family assists in recognizing new business opportunities (Chiesi, 2014). Case 16 added, "*I did not get a job on my own on arrival, my uncle hired me in his restaurant in Melbourne and taught me everything and introduced me to all the suppliers and labor providers and financiers, and then the opportunity came up to buy this old restaurant and renew it in Sydney, which I have been running for the last 16 years.*" Similarly, Case 20 mentioned, "*I helped my mum's brother soon after I arrived, who was settled in Sydney for 10 years, to deliver fresh fish to shops in the suburbs. He taught me this business, and then in three years I bought my own van to deliver fish and after some years I bought a fishing trawler and the business expanded ... so having my family, and trust between us, helped me to establish quickly in finding contacts and getting information and starting my own business*." These quotes illustrate the overriding significance of family embeddedness for most immigrants undertaking their migration journey, which provides one of the most significant resources—notably, trust—and also a sense of community in the host country to facilitate collective action toward business creation (Aldrich & Cliff, 2003; Cruz et al., 2012; Jack & Anderson, 2002). Formally:

Proposition 1: Family embeddedness through strong family ties facilitates the startup of an IFB after arriving in the host country.

Establishing Phase

While family embeddedness facilitates initial access to vital resources, it may be insufficient to establish the business in the host country effectively without the support of other key members and networks (Uzzi, 1997). Being embedded in the local market is crucial because it ties IFBs to the local environment (Dacin, Beal, & Ventresca, 1999). Our findings suggest that family embeddedness and the related family network enabled the IFBs to become acquainted with local co-ethnic immigrants—that is, local immigrants from their own and other country/ethnic backgrounds (Jones et al., 2014; Szkudlarek & Wu, 2018)—thereby leading to local embeddedness.

We observed that during the establishing phase, these acquaintances helped the IFBs to be and feel part of the local immigrant community. This led them to further engage in and drive business opportunity identification/recognition and set up niche ethnic businesses while mitigating potential barriers during this phase of development (e.g., cash flow; see Figure 2). For example, Case 10 explained: "*Attending meetings at the Italian Business Chamber of Commerce and meeting other local Italian family businesses [some of them linked with our family] was helpful as one of the gentlemen there introduced us to an Italian builder who became our very first large buyer for kitchen handles and today, we have regular large orders from him for the high-rise complexes he builds. Besides, he has also helped us by introducing us to his Chinese partner, which started us off on exports ... We worked with his team to customize designs that their business needed*." Case 2 further supported the value of local coethnic relations: "*Working actively with the Brazilian Chamber of Commerce enabled me to meet many local Brazilian entrepreneurs, as well as other immigrant entrepreneurs who had expanded their business to other countries, and talking to them gave me direction on how to establish my business … Singapore, where I took my business, was through one such contact I made at the Chamber of Commerce.*"

Thus, the IFBs were able to leverage their family ties and build acquaintances with local co-immigrants (Evansluong & Ramírez-Pasillas, 2019). By involving local co-immigrants of various ethnicities, they were able to adapt their products and services and cater to a wider market. As Vissak and Zhang (2014) noted, immigrant entrepreneurs are bicultural and cognitively more comfortable in taking a non-linear approach. Our work highlights the power of the co-immigrant community in assisting IFBs in the business development process. In formal terms, we propose that:

Proposition 2: The IFB's acquaintance with the local business environment promotes local embeddedness with co-ethnic immigrants, which helps the family business to become established in the host country.

Expansion Phase

Mere acquaintance with the local business community may not provide sufficient traction to expand in the host country unless the IFB becomes familiar with the business environment. However, our case studies show that the network benefits originating from family and local embeddedness provide an initial basis through which IFBs expand in the host country. Case 24 supported this by saying that "*the kitchen needs of the Australian public is different from that of German families as such initially our products were not catching market share but our Australian local neighbors [some of them related with our family] gave us some ideas on what works in Australia, and we proceeded with appointing a local kitchen designer [well networked with multiple players in the national territory], and adapted our products, and this helped us increase our market share in the kitchen industry in Australia.*" Knowledge sharing with host country stakeholders such as business partners increases familiarity with the host business environment, leading to knowledge accumulation and knowledge spillovers flowing into IFBs. The resulting host country's embeddedness with mainstream Australian locals facilitates innovation and the development of customized products suitable for the host market. Li et al. (2018) endorsed this by explaining how immigrants develop new business activities in the host country by engaging with the host community through knowledge spillovers.

For instance, Case 2 explained that after arriving in Australia and establishing themselves locally in Sydney, it took them some time to expand across Australia. Starting from establishing the original family and local ties, a lot of knowledge was subsequently built, shared and acquired over time from multiple key stakeholders in the country, which led to the IFB's success. This respondent reported that, "*We are pioneer in manufacturing allergen sensitive and gluten-free foods specifically produced for the local Australian market [it all started in Sydney with our family and the local community]. Since 2000 we have introduced many baking mixes to the Australian (and other international markets) to suit the diet of customers with gluten, dairy and nut intolerance, diabetes, and those who wish to control weight or have a healthier diet without compromising taste. This started as a Brazilian delicacy called Pao de Queijo made with tapioca and cheese. I travelled to Minas Gerais where I originally come from to source and transport the ingredients and machinery to Australia. Today these cheese breads are very popular among coeliacs and children, and they are also exported to many countries ... Establishing contacts and sharing knowledge with key stakeholders in Australia was key.*" Similar quotes in our case studies reveal that IFBs are resource-dependent. They address their dependence by networking with those who possess the needed resources (see Table 2). Accordingly, IFBs continually need to expand their network to "survive" and expand in the host country. In addition to relying on their families and local networks, IFBs tend to progressively partner with stakeholders in the larger country community (cf. host country embeddedness) to accumulate further knowledge. Being part of a broader network helps them mitigate the potential barriers to expansion, such as providing customer satisfaction and competing with other businesses. Thus, we propose:

Proposition 3: The IFB's familiarity with the host country business environment promotes host country embeddedness, which helps the family business to expand in the host country.

Thriving Phase

Expanding in the host country by developing new products for the local market opens the door to internationalization. New opportunities emerge for IFBs in the international market, enabling them to span boundaries and build what is termed "global embeddedness" with international stakeholders. Yet, while family embeddedness, local embeddedness, and host country embeddedness continue to play essential roles in IFBs' success, global embeddedness becomes the path to establish a transnational business. In the light of Jack and Anderson's (2002) model, it is conceivable that by being boundary spanners embedded in multiple countries' social structures, it is easier for an IFB to recognize what is required and accessible in the various markets. This knowledge enables immigrant family entrepreneurs to (re)configure their existing relationship structure and develop new ties across countries, thus capturing maximum value from the local, ethnic, and cross-country family and non-family ties. Case 6 points out that, "*Besides purchasing two sick paint manufacturing firms in the USA through family contacts in the USA, which is managed by our son, we recently bought over XXX Paints Ltd and its entire stake in Singapore, and that was a tip off from our partners in Singapore.*" In a similar vein, Case 1 stated that, "*We are pioneers in video analytics with almost two decades of commercial experience - since 2001. The family company has recently extended its already comprehensive analytics capability to provide an artificial intelligence–based multi-sensory analytics platform that includes sound and smell, as well as video, to better replicate human reasoning. These technologies have been implemented by commercial and government users in 60+ countries around the world ... partnerships with international players [some family related] helped to expand quicker.*"

In particular, IFBs have a multitude of networks that are linked by family and non-family ties crossing national boundaries (Boyd, 1989; Castles, 2002). These transnational communities expand the possibility for trade between home, host, and other countries because cross-border social networks and networks established in the host country increase their access to information that is otherwise unavailable or costly to obtain (Useche et al., 2019). As Case 7 explained, "*We manufacture oil with Australian Canola, and because most Australian canola is GM-free, the plant's GM-free oil attracts a premium, especially in the United States, where the non-GM market for foods such as mayonnaise and potato chips is growing rapidly. This has increased our global business for the GM-free oil. We export directly [or via family and non-family related partners] to the USA, New Zealand, India, and South-East Asia.*" Our empirics also show how, by retaining family ties specifically with their country of origin, IFBs can mitigate significant barriers to internationalization, such as the costs involved in setting up in a foreign country (Riddle, Hrivnak, & Nielsen, 2010). For instance, Case 18R reported that, "*I was involved in developing mining software for one of my clients in Sydney and understood that the Indian mining sector would benefit from this software for mapping the environmental impacts and safety. My brother-in-law runs a software company in India that could customize this software for Indian mining needs.*

Partnering with this family company enabled me to export this software to India. Today I export the same software to five countries across the world."

In summary, the IFBs' strong international networks across countries and with the country of origin (cf. global embeddedness) (Useche et al., 2019) enabled them to develop their global businesses, thereby becoming boundary spanners and transnational entrepreneurs after settling in their host country (Evansluong, Ramírez Pasillas, Discua Cruz, Elo, & Vershinina, 2019; Fouron & Schiller, 2001; Park & Waldinger, 2017). Thus, we propose:

Proposition 4: The IFB's international networks in the global market promote global embeddedness, which helps the family business to thrive as a transnational business.

DISCUSSION

The present study offers important insights and makes discoveries for existing immigrant entrepreneurship and IFB research on how IFBs can achieve global expansion. Our work details how different forms of embeddedness evolve over time and can potentially help IFBs from arrival to expansion in the host country and beyond. First, our data, based on the lived experiences of 25 IFBs and the resulting process model of IFBs' success toward global expansion (Figure 2), contributes to the immigrant entrepreneurship literature. It reveals a chronology of four phases—*arriving*, *establishing*, *expanding*, and *thriving*. Each phase has its own drivers and barriers that are linked respectively to different embeddedness forms (*family, local, host country, and global*) to address IFBs' business needs in regard to global expansion. Important discoveries emerge from the process model on how IFBs progress over time in pursuing entrepreneurial opportunities in and beyond their host country, as well as the important role of different embeddedness types in enabling IFBs' transition into the subsequent phases.

Second, we contribute to the literature on IFBs by showing that family embeddedness helps build resources that support the firm's competitive advantage by coupling it with other important local, host country, and global networks. More specifically, family embeddedness is leveraged and evolves into a multi-network of local, host country, and global embeddedness forms that help businesses create new resources and opportunities in the local and global markets. Interestingly, we observed that strong networks—in particular, links with family members in the country of origin, as well as across countries—enable some IFBs to internationalize more rapidly and achieve a higher likelihood of success in terms of global expansion. As such, our work helps to expand our understanding of the mechanisms underlying the family resources–embeddedness–performance link, while underlining that family embeddedness is key, but is not sufficient *alone*, to propel international success.

Third, our findings support the evolving nature of embeddedness where IFBs act as boundary spanners, blending local and international resources to create value. As depicted in Figure 3, our work enabled us to derive an "IFB embeddedness matrix" based on the strength and scope of different embeddedness types across four phases. The matrix shows that while family embeddedness remains strong, its scope shrinks over time. Our findings and related logic provide a contrast to, and therefore extend, family firm literature that has focused on the key and often exclusive role of "strong" family ties to propel (immigrant) family business success over time and across generations (see, e.g., Arregle et al., 2015; Chirico & Salvato, 2016; Mustafa & Chen, 2010). In fact, our work reveals that as the business grows, although the family ties' strength and benefits remain a perennial source throughout all of the phases, other forms of embeddedness with a broader scope (yet, with a relatively lesser strength) emerge to help the IFBs' transition into the local, host, and global markets. This finding and the related IFB embeddedness matrix represent a key discovery connected to the present study, which extends existing prevalent logic in the family business literature.

Figure 3. The IFBs' embeddedness matrix

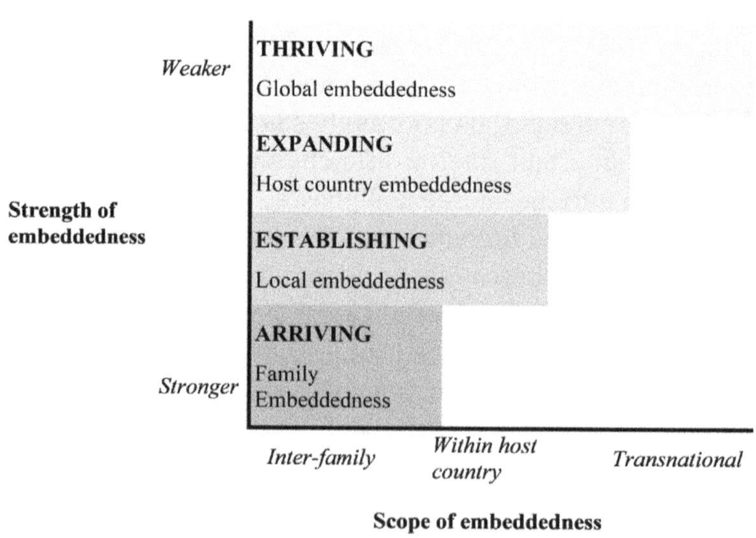

Fourth, the context for this study is important (Welter, 2011; Zahra, Wright, & Abdelgawad, 2014). Similar to other countries, Australia has fallen into a deep recession due to COVID-19 and the stringent measures adopted by the government, which are the focus of intense debate in Australia. For example, state and territory border closures had an unprecedented catastrophic effect on Australian businesses and entrepreneurial activities (Australian Bureau of Statistics, 2020). Interestingly, IFBs are the Australian economy's backbone and significantly contribute to its GDP and employment (ASBFEO, 2016). Unfortunately, research on IFBs, as well as Australian Government programs to help them survive and grow, is relatively limited (Corporations et al., 2013), making the insights of this study especially important during such a crisis. For instance, a 2013 report from the Australian Government Senate (Corporations et al., 2013) indicated that "although family owned and operated commercial enterprises are an established and enduring feature of the Australian economy [most of them founded by immigrants], they have been overlooked by Australian governments," suggesting that more resources should be channeled to IFBs to enhance their prosperity over time. However, little progress has been made in this direction. Overall, IFBs are growing around the world and are particularly important for the economies of countries that heavily rely on them, such as Australia. Therefore, strong support is needed to help immigrant entrepreneurs generate more wealth for themselves and their host country. It is important to note that although rates of entrepreneurship are higher among foreign-born populations in many developed countries (Naudé, Siegel, & Marchand, 2017), their success is variable (Neville, Orser, Riding, & Jung, 2014). Accordingly, government policies need to address this divergence (Collins, 2008). Overall, it is vital for Australia and many other nations to develop a more sustainable migrant entrepreneurship support and management agenda to increase IFBs' contributions to GDP, employment, and entrepreneurial activities (Sherrell, 2015). The different drivers and barriers in each of the models depicted in Figure 2 may offer important insights to help governments in this direction.

Limitations and Future Research Directions

The first limitation of our empirical study relates to data constraints; our data are biased toward highly successful IFBs. However, the focus was important to develop a process model of successful IFBs in Australia. The second limitation relates to the sole focus on the metropolitan city of Sydney.

Although this city has attracted the highest number of immigrants in the past, in recent decades other cities in Australia, as well as regional cities, have started attracting more immigrants. In addition, while the research could be replicated in other parts of Australia or in other countries characterized by high immigrant populations, the results may vary because the environment may not be as conducive to entrepreneurship as in Sydney. Future research could use a much larger sample and a mixed methodology approach. In addition, a comparative study of IFBs from different ethnic groups could add to our understanding of the business experiences of specific groups. Distinct institutional and cultural environments, especially in developing countries (Wood, 2003), and their effect on the various embeddedness forms identified could also benefit from further exploration (Batjargal et al., 2013).

This study's measurement of business performance using revenue for the last three years (in millions of dollars) and the three-year growth percentage could also be a limitation because different outcomes could have emerged through the use of other measures of success, such as profitability or return on assets or investment (Naudé et al., 2017), or even nonfinancial measures of success (Chirico, Gómez-Mejia, Hellerstedt, Withers, & Nordqvist, 2020). Further empirical studies should be conducted in Australia and other countries to investigate the potentially positive, as well as negative (Hack-Polay, Igwe, & Madichie, 2020), effects of different embeddedness forms on multiple IFBs' financial and nonfinancial outcomes. Future research should also compare successful and unsuccessful IFBs and their potential related paths toward success or failure. Additionally, as with many qualitative studies, the narrative approach has certain limitations. As Gartner (2007: 619) noted, "the narrative approach recognises that a story is never the whole story since any story is embedded in a context." Yet, following the guidelines offered by Langley (1999) and Gioia et al. (2013), we are confident that the multiple steps we undertook allowed us to minimize biases and the related limitations.

Some other facets of IFBs that emerged from this research and could be explored further are the implications for next-generation family members, whether born in the home or host country (Tata & Prasad, 2015; Wang & Poutziouris, 2010). Research converges on the importance of family embeddedness in successor selection; yet, limited knowledge exists on what specific dynamics may occur when the owning family has established a business and thus the family succession takes place in a country different than the one of origin (Cabrera-Suárez, De Saá-Pérez, & García-Almeida, 2001; Steier, 2001). Finally, different approaches to measuring embeddedness could provide a fruitful area of investigation (Dahl & Sorenson, 2012: 1063) for research on IFBs. The influence of embeddedness on the realization of non-financial goals such as work–life balance and giving back to the home country and target communities is also a prospective area for future research. Overall, we believe that more studies on IFB processes and development can further inform entrepreneurship literature and IFBs' success. In particular, it is important to examine how the different levels of education and prior experience of IFBs' family members may affect the way they develop and manage multiple networks.

In summary, the present study developed an integrated process model for understanding how an IFB achieves global expansion. In so doing, our study responds to calls for more micro-processual approaches (Wang & Warn, 2018) to *discover* what IFB entrepreneurs do, or should do, to be successful as transnational entrepreneurs.

REFERENCES

Adendorff, C., & Halkias, D. (2014). Leveraging ethnic entrepreneurship, culture and family dynamics to enhance good governance and sustainability in the immigrant family business. *Journal of Developmental Entrepreneurship*, *19*(2), 1450008. doi:10.1142/S1084946714500083

Ado, A., Chrysostome, E., & Su, Z. (2016). Examining adaptation strategies of sub-Saharan African immigrant entrepreneurs in China: The case of Guangdong. *Journal of Developmental Entrepreneurship*, *21*(4), 1650027. doi:10.1142/S1084946716500278

Aldrich, H. E., & Cliff, J. E. (2003). The pervasive effects of family on entrepreneurship: Toward a family embeddedness perspective. *Journal of Business Venturing*, *18*(5), 573–596. doi:10.1016/S0883-9026(03)00011-9

Anand, N., & Watson, M. R. (2004). Tournament rituals in the evolution of fields: The case of the Grammy Awards. *Academy of Management Journal*, *47*(1), 59–80.

Anderson, A. R., Dodd, S. D., & Jack, S. L. (2012). Entrepreneurship as connecting: Some implications for theorising and practice. *Management Decision*, *50*(5), 958–971. doi:10.1108/00251741211227708

Arregle, J. L., Batjargal, B., Hitt, M. A., Webb, J. W., Miller, T., & Tsui, A. S. (2015). Family ties in entrepreneurs' social networks and new venture growth. *Entrepreneurship Theory and Practice*, *39*(2), 313–344. doi:10.1111/etap.12044

Arregle, J. L., Miller, T. L., Hitt, M. A., & Beamish, P. W. (2013). Do regions matter? An integrated institutional and semiglobalization perspective on the internationalization of MNEs. *Strategic Management Journal*, *34*(8), 910–934. doi:10.1002mj.2051

ASBFEO. (2020). *Australian Small Business and Family Enterprise Ombudsman. Inquiry into small business loans*. ASBFEO.

Australian Bureau of Statistics (ABS). (2020a). ABS measures COVID-19 impacts. Author.

Australian Bureau of Statistics (ABS). (2019). *Australian Bureau of Statistics - Business indicators*. https://www.abs.gov.au/statistics/economy/business-indicators

Australian Bureau of Statistics (ABS). (2020b). *Australian Bureau of Statistics - Measures COVID-19 impacts*. https://www.abs.gov.au

Azmat, F., & Fujimoto, Y. (2016). Family embeddedness and entrepreneurship experience: A study of Indian migrant women entrepreneurs in Australia. *Entrepreneurship and Regional Development*, *28*(9–10), 630–656.

Bailetti, E. (2018). Transnational entrepreneurship: Distinctive features and a new definition. *Technology Innovation Management Review*, *8*(9), 28–38. doi:10.22215/timreview/1184

Barrett, R., & Vershinina, N. (2017). Intersectionality of ethnic and entrepreneurial identities: A study of post-war Polish entrepreneurs in an English city. *Journal of Small Business Management*, *55*(3), 430–443. doi:10.1111/jsbm.12246

Batjargal, B., Hitt, M. A., Tsui, A. S., Arregle, J.-L., Webb, J. W., & Miller, T. L. (2013). Institutional polycentrism, entrepreneurs' social networks, and new venture growth. *Academy of Management Journal*, *56*(4), 1024–1049. doi:10.5465/amj.2010.0095

Beckers, P., & Blumberg, B. F. (2013). Immigrant entrepreneurship on the move: A longitudinal analysis of first-and second-generation immigrant entrepreneurship in the Netherlands. *Entrepreneurship and Regional Development*, *25*(7-8), 654–691. doi:10.1080/08985626.2013.808270

Bell, E., & Bryman, A. (2007). The ethics of management research: An exploratory content analysis. *British Journal of Management*, *18*(1), 63–77. doi:10.1111/j.1467-8551.2006.00487.x

Bird, M., & Wennberg, K. (2016). Why family matters: The impact of family resources on immigrant entrepreneurs' exit from entrepreneurship. *Journal of Business Venturing*, *31*(6), 687–704. doi:10.1016/j.jbusvent.2016.09.002

Bisignano, A. P., & El-Anis, I. (2019). Making sense of mixed-embeddedness in migrant informal enterprising. *International Journal of Entrepreneurial Behaviour & Research*, *25*(5), 974–995. doi:10.1108/IJEBR-03-2018-0114

Bolívar-Cruz, A., Batista-Canino, R. M., & Hormiga, E. (2014). Differences in the perception and exploitation of entrepreneurial opportunities by immigrants. *Journal of Business Venturing Insights*, *1*, 31–36. doi:10.1016/j.jbvi.2014.09.005

Bolton, P., & Dewatripont, M. (2005). *Contract theory*. MIT Press.

Bonacich, E. (1987). "Making it" in America: A social evaluation of the ethics of immigrant entrepreneurship. *Sociological Perspectives*, *30*(4), 446–466. doi:10.2307/1389213

Bonjour, S., & Kraler, A. (2015). Introduction: Family migration as an integration issue? Policy perspectives and academic insights. *Journal of Family Issues*, *36*(11), 1407–1432. doi:10.1177/0192513X14557490

Boyd, M. (1989). Family and personal networks in international migration: Recent developments and new agendas. *The International Migration Review*, *23*(3), 638–670. doi:10.1177/019791838902300313 PMID:12282798

Brzozowski, J. (2017). Immigrant entrepreneurship and economic adaptation: A critical analysis. *Entrepreneurial Business and Economics Review*, *5*(2), 159–176. doi:10.15678/EBER.2017.050209

Buckley, C. A., & Waring, M. J. (2013). Using diagrams to support the research process: Examples from grounded theory. *Qualitative Research*, *13*(2), 148–172. doi:10.1177/1468794112472280

Burgelman, R. A. (1983). A model of the interaction of strategic behavior, corporate context, and the concept of strategy. *Academy of Management Review*, *8*(1), 61–70. doi:10.2307/257168

Cabrera-Suárez, K., De Saá-Pérez, P., & García-Almeida, D. (2001). The succession process from a resource-and knowledge-based view of the family firm. *Family Business Review*, *14*(1), 37–48. doi:10.1111/j.1741-6248.2001.00037.x

Castles, S. (2002). Migration and community formation under conditions of globalization. *The International Migration Review*, *36*(4), 1143–1168. doi:10.1111/j.1747-7379.2002.tb00121.x

Chand, M., & Ghorbani, M. (2011). National culture, networks and ethnic entrepreneurship: A comparison of the Indian and Chinese immigrants in the US. *International Business Review*, *20*(6), 593–606. doi:10.1016/j.ibusrev.2011.02.009

Chavan, M., & Taksa, L. (2017). Shifts in intergenerational mobility of Indian immigrant entrepreneurs. *International Migration (Geneva, Switzerland)*, *55*(1), 99–127. doi:10.1111/imig.12303

Chiesi, A. M. (2014). Interpersonal Networking and Business Resilience: How Immigrants in Small Business Face the Crisis in Italy. *European Sociological Review*, *30*(4), 457–469. doi:10.1093/esr/jcu052

Chirico, F., Gómez-Mejia, L. R., Hellerstedt, K., Withers, M., & Nordqvist, M. (2020). To merge, sell, or liquidate? Socioemotional wealth, family control, and the choice of business exit. *Journal of Management*, *46*(8), 1342–1379. doi:10.1177/0149206318818723

Chirico, F., & Salvato, C. (2016). Knowledge internalization and product development in family firms: When relational and affective factors matter. *Entrepreneurship Theory and Practice*, *40*(1), 201–229. doi:10.1111/etap.12114

Chrysostome, E. (2010). The success factors of necessity immigrant entrepreneurs: In search of a model. *Thunderbird International Business Review*, *52*(2), 137–152. doi:10.1002/tie.20320

Cohen, J. (1960). A coefficient of agreement for nominal scales. *Educational and Psychological Measurement*, *20*(1), 37–46. doi:10.1177/001316446002000104

Collins, J. (1995). Literacy and literacies. *Annual Review of Anthropology, 24*(1), 75–93. doi:10.1146/annurev.an.24.100195.000451

Collins, J. (2003). Australia: cosmopolitan capitalists down under. In R. Kloosterman & J. Rath (Eds.), *Immigrant Entrepreneurs: Venturing Abroad in the Age of Globalization* (pp. 61–78). Berg. doi:10.5040/9781350151468.ch-004

Collins, J. (2008). Globalisation, immigration and the second long post-war boom in Australia. *Journal of Australian Political Economy*, *61*, 244–266.

Collins, J. (2011). The governance of immigration in Australia. In N. Phillips (Ed.), *Migration in the Global Political Economy*. Lynne Reinner. doi:10.1515/9781626370050-012

Collins, J. (2012). Integration and inclusion of immigrants in Australia. In International perspectives: Integration and inclusion. Queen's Policy Studies/ Metro Project.

Collins, J. (2020). Immigrant Entrepreneurship in Sydney: Australia's Leading Global City. In *Immigrant Entrepreneurship in Cities* (pp. 47–65). Springer.

Collins, J., & Collins, J. (1995). *A shop full of dreams: Ethnic small business in Australia*. Pluto Press.

Constant, A., Shachmurove, Y., & Zimmermann, K. F. (2007). What makes an entrepreneur and does it pay? Native men, Turks, and other migrants in Germany. *International Migration (Geneva, Switzerland)*, *45*(4), 71–100. doi:10.1111/j.1468-2435.2007.00420.x

Constant, A. F., Kahanec, M., & Zimmermann, K. F. (2009). Attitudes towards immigrants, other integration barriers, and their veracity. *International Journal of Manpower*, *30*(1/2), 5–14. doi:10.1108/01437720910948357

Contreras-Sweet, M. (2015). *Immigrant entrepreneurs help fuel record growth streak*. https://www.sba.gov/blogs/immigrant-entrepreneurs-help-fuel-record-growth-streak

Corbally, M., & O'Neill, C. (2014). An introduction to the biographical narrative interpretive method. *Nurse Researcher*, *21*(5), 34–39. doi:10.7748/nr.21.5.34.e1237 PMID:24877909

Corley, K. G., & Gioia, D. A. (2004). Identity ambiguity and change in the wake of a corporate spin-off. *Administrative Science Quarterly*, *49*(2), 173–208. doi:10.2307/4131471

Corporations, A. P. J. C. o., Services, F., & O'Neill, D. (2013). *Family businesses in Australia—Different and significant: Why they shouldn't be overlooked*. Commonwealth of Australia.

Crawley, H., & Hagen-Zanker, J. (2019). Deciding where to go: Policies, people and perceptions shaping destination preferences. *International Migration (Geneva, Switzerland)*, *57*(1), 20–35.

Criaco, G., Sieger, P., Wennberg, K., Chirico, F., & Minola, T. (2017). Parents' performance in entrepreneurship as a "double-edged sword" for the intergenerational transmission of entrepreneurship. *Small Business Economics*, *49*(4), 841–864. doi:10.100711187-017-9854-x

Cruz, A. D., Hamilton, E., & Jack, S. L. (2012). Understanding entrepreneurial cultures in family businesses: A study of family entrepreneurial teams in Honduras. *Journal of Family Business Strategy*, *3*(3), 147–161. doi:10.1016/j.jfbs.2012.05.002

Cuypers, I. R., Ertug, G., Cantwell, J., Zaheer, A., & Kilduff, M. (2020). *Making connections: Social networks in international business*. Springer.

Dabić, M., Vlačić, B., Paul, J., Dana, L.-P., Sahasranamam, S., & Glinka, B. (2020). Immigrant entrepreneurship: A review and research agenda. *Journal of Business Research*, *113*, 25–38. doi:10.1016/j.jbusres.2020.03.013

Dacin, M. T., Beal, B. D., & Ventresca, M. J. (1999). The embeddedness of organizations: Dialogue & directions. *Journal of Management*, *25*(3), 317–356. doi:10.1177/014920639902500304

Dacin, M. T., Munir, K., & Tracey, P. (2010). Formal dining at Cambridge colleges: Linking ritual performance and institutional maintenance. *Academy of Management Journal*, *53*(6), 1393–1418. doi:10.5465/amj.2010.57318388

Dahl, M. S., & Sorenson, O. (2012). Home sweet home: Entrepreneurs' location choices and the performance of their ventures. *Management Science*, *58*(6), 1059–1071. doi:10.1287/mnsc.1110.1476

Dana, L.-P. (2007a). *International handbook of research on indigenous entrepreneurship*. Edward Elgar Publishing. doi:10.4337/9781781952641

Dana, L.-P. (2007b). *Handbook of research on ethnic minority entrepreneurship: A co-evolutionary view on resource management*. Edward Elgar Publishing. doi:10.4337/9781847209962

Dana, L.-P., Gurau, C., Light, I., & Muhammad, N. (2020). Family, community, and ethnic capital as entrepreneurial resources: Toward an integrated model. *Journal of Small Business Management, 58*(5), 1003–1029. doi:10.1111/jsbm.12507

De Clercq, D., & Voronov, M. (2009). Toward a practice perspective of entrepreneurship: Entrepreneurial legitimacy as habitus. *International Small Business Journal, 27*(4), 395–419. doi:10.1177/0266242609334971

Demetry, D. (2017). Pop-up to professional: Emerging entrepreneurial identity and evolving vocabularies of motive. *Academy of Management Discoveries, 3*(2), 187–207. doi:10.5465/amd.2015.0152

Duan, C., Kotey, B., & Sandhu, K. (2020). Digital entrepreneurship for immigrants: Motivations, strategies, ecosystems, and performance. In K. Sandhu (Ed.), *Leadership, Management, and Adoption Techniques for Digital Service Innovation* (pp. 162–181). IGI Global. doi:10.4018/978-1-7998-2799-3.ch009

Edelman, L. F., Brush, C. G., Manolova, T. S., & Greene, P. G. (2010). Start-up motivations and growth intentions of minority nascent entrepreneurs. *Journal of Small Business Management, 48*(2), 174–196. doi:10.1111/j.1540-627X.2010.00291.x

Eisenhardt, K. M. (1989). Building theories from case study research. *Academy of Management Review, 14*(4), 532–550. doi:10.2307/258557

Evansluong, Q., & Ramírez-Pasillas, M. (2019). The role of family social capital in immigrants' entrepreneurial opportunity creation processes. *International Journal of Entrepreneurship and Small Business, 36*(1–2), 164–188. doi:10.1504/IJESB.2019.096973

Evansluong, Q., Ramírez Pasillas, M., Discua Cruz, A., Elo, M., & Vershinina, N. (2019). Migrant entrepreneurship beyond place and space: A call to explore the roles of family across borders and contexts. *Journal of Enterprising Communities: People and Places in the Global Economy*.

Evansluong, Q. V. (2016). *Opportunity creation as a mixed embedding process. A study of immigrant entrepreneurs in Sweden* [PhD thesis]. JIBS.

Faist, T. (1997). Migration in contemporary Europe: European integration, economic liberalization, and protection. In *European integration in social and historical perspective 1850 to the Present*. PUB - Publikationen an der Universität Bielefeld.

Fouron, G., & Schiller, N. G. (2001). All in the family: Gender, transnational migration, and the nation-state. *Identities (Yverdon)*, *7*(4), 539–582. doi:10.1080/1070289X.2001.9962678

Ganzin, M., Islam, G., & Suddaby, R. (2020). Spirituality and entrepreneurship: The role of magical thinking in future-oriented sensemaking. *Organization Studies*, *41*(1), 77–102. doi:10.1177/0170840618819035

Gartner, W. B. (2007). Entrepreneurial narrative and a science of the imagination. *Journal of Business Venturing*, *22*(5), 613–627. doi:10.1016/j.jbusvent.2006.10.003

Gartner, W. B., & Birley, S. (2002). *Introduction to the special issue on qualitative methods in entrepreneurship research*. Elsevier. doi:10.1016/S0883-9026(01)00077-5

Gehman, J., Glaser, V. L., Eisenhardt, K. M., Gioia, D., Langley, A., & Corley, K. G. (2018). Finding theory–method fit: A comparison of three qualitative approaches to theory building. *Journal of Management Inquiry*, *27*(3), 284–300. doi:10.1177/1056492617706029

Gioia, D. A., Corley, K. G., & Hamilton, A. L. (2013). Seeking qualitative rigor in inductive research: Notes on the Gioia methodology. *Organizational Research Methods*, *16*(1), 15–31. doi:10.1177/1094428112452151

Glaser, B., & Strauss, A. (1967). *The discovery of grounded theory*. Aldine.

Granovetter, M. (1973). The strength of weak ties. *American Journal of Sociology*, *78*(6), 1360–1380. doi:10.1086/225469

Granovetter, M. (1983). The strength of weak ties: A network theory revisited. *Sociological Theory*, *1*, 201–233. doi:10.2307/202051

Granovetter, M. (1985). Economic action and social structure: The problem of embeddedness. *American Journal of Sociology*, *91*(3), 481–510. doi:10.1086/228311

Graves, C., & Thomas, J. (2004). Internationalisation of the family business: A longitudinal perspective. *International Journal of Globalisation and Small Business*, *1*(1), 7–27. doi:10.1504/IJGSB.2004.005615

Griffin-EL, E. W., & Olabisi, J. (2018). Breaking boundaries: Exploring the process of intersective market activity of immigrant entrepreneurship in the context of high economic inequality. *Journal of Management Studies*, *55*(3), 457–485. doi:10.1111/joms.12327

Guarnizo, L. E. (1996). "Going home": Class, gender, and household transformation among Dominican return migrants. *Center for Migration Studies Special Issues, 13*(4), 13–60.

Habbershon, T. G., Williams, M., & MacMillan, I. C. (2003). A unified systems perspective of family firm performance. *Journal of Business Venturing*, *18*(4), 451–465. doi:10.1016/S0883-9026(03)00053-3

Hack-Polay, D., Igwe, P. A., & Madichie, N. O. (2020). The role of institutional and family embeddedness in the failure of sub-Saharan African migrant family businesses. *International Journal of Entrepreneurship and Innovation*, *14*(4), 289–299. doi:10.1177/1465750320909732

Hopp, C., & Martin, J. (2017). Does entrepreneurship pay for women and immigrants? A 30 year assessment of the socio-economic impact of entrepreneurial activity in Germany. *Entrepreneurship and Regional Development*, *29*(5–6), 517–543. doi:10.1080/08985626.2017.1299224

Iacovou, C. L., Benbasat, I., & Dexter, A. S. (1995). Electronic data interchange and small organizations: Adoption and impact of technology. *Management Information Systems Quarterly*, *19*(4), 465–485. doi:10.2307/249629

Jack, S. L., & Anderson, A. R. (2002). The effects of embeddedness on the entrepreneurial process. *Journal of Business Venturing*, *17*(5), 467–487. doi:10.1016/S0883-9026(01)00076-3

Jick, T. D. (1979). Mixing qualitative and quantitative methods: Triangulation in action. *Administrative Science Quarterly*, *24*(4), 602–611. doi:10.2307/2392366

Jones, P., Maas, G., Dobson, S., Newbery, R., Agyapong, D., & Matlay, H. (2018). Entrepreneurship in Africa, part 2: Entrepreneurial education and eco-systems. *Journal of Small Business and Enterprise Development*, *25*(4), 550–553. doi:10.1108/JSBED-08-2018-400

Jones, T., Ram, M., & Edwards, P. (2006). Ethnic minority business and the employment of illegal immigrants. *Entrepreneurship and Regional Development, 18*(2), 133–150. doi:10.1080/08985620500531865

Jones, T., Ram, M., Edwards, P., Kiselinchev, A., & Muchenje, L. (2014). Mixed embeddedness and new migrant enterprise in the UK. *Entrepreneurship and Regional Development, 26*(5–6), 500–520. doi:10.1080/08985626.2014.950697

Judge, W. Q., & Douglas, T. J. (2013). Entrepreneurship as a leap of faith. *Journal of Management, Spirituality & Religion, 10*(1), 37–65. doi:10.1080/14766086.2012.758047

Kalleberg, A. L., & Leicht, K. T. (1991). Gender and organizational performance: Determinants of small business survival and success. *Academy of Management Journal, 34*(1), 136–161.

Keats, B. W., & Hitt, M. A. (1988). A causal model of linkages among environmental dimensions, macro organizational characteristics, and performance. *Academy of Management Journal, 31*(3), 570–598.

Khayesi, J. N., & George, G. (2011). When does the socio-cultural context matter? Communal orientation and entrepreneurs' resource accumulation efforts in Africa. *Journal of Occupational and Organizational Psychology, 84*(3), 471–492. doi:10.1111/j.2044-8325.2011.02029.x

Kilduff, M., & Brass, D. J. (2010). Organizational social network research: Core ideas and key debates. *The Academy of Management Annals, 4*(1), 317–357. doi:10.5465/19416520.2010.494827

Kloosterman, R., & Rath, J. (2001). Immigrant entrepreneurs in advanced economies: Mixed embeddedness further explored. *Journal of Ethnic and Migration Studies, 27*(2), 189–201. doi:10.1080/13691830020041561

Kloosterman, R., & Rath, J. (2003). *Immigrant entrepreneurs: Venturing abroad in the age of globalization*. Berg. doi:10.5040/9781350151468

Kloosterman, R., Van Der Leun, J., & Rath, J. (1999). Mixed embeddedness: (In)formal economic activities and immigrant businesses in the Netherlands. *International Journal of Urban and Regional Research, 23*(2), 252–266. doi:10.1111/1468-2427.00194

Kloosterman, R. C. (2010). Matching opportunities with resources: A framework for analysing (migrant) entrepreneurship from a mixed embeddedness perspective. *Entrepreneurship and Regional Development*, *22*(1), 25–45. doi:10.1080/08985620903220488

Kloosterman, R. C., Mamadouh, V., & Terhorst, P. (2018). *Introducing geographies of globalization: genealogies of the concept, existing views on globalization inside and outside geography. In Handbook on the geographies of globalization*. Edward Elgar Publishing. doi:10.4337/9781785363849

KPMG Enterprise. (2018). *Family business: The balance for success*. https://assets.kpmg/content/dam/kpmg/nz/pdf/June/family-business.pdf

Kushnirovich, N., Heilbrunn, S., & Davidovich, L. (2018). Diversity of entrepreneurial perceptions: Immigrants vs. native population. *European Management Review*, *15*(3), 341–355. doi:10.1111/emre.12105

Lancaster, K. (1975). The theory of household behavior: Some foundations. *Annals of Economic and Social Measurement*, *4*(1), 5–21.

Langley, A. (1999). Strategies for theorizing from process data. *Academy of Management Review*, *24*(4), 691–710. doi:10.5465/amr.1999.2553248

Li, C. G., Isidor, R., Dau, L. A., & Kabst, R. (2018). The more the merrier? Immigrant share and entrepreneurial activities. *Entrepreneurship Theory and Practice*, *42*(5), 698–733. doi:10.1177/1042258718795344

Light, E. (1972). *Ethnic enterprise in America*. California University Press. doi:10.1525/9780520322882

Ligita, T., Nurjannah, I., Wicking, K., Harvey, N., & Francis, K. (2020). From textual to visual: The use of concept mapping as an analytical tool in a grounded theory study. *Qualitative Research*.

Lincoln, Y. G., & Guba, E. (1985). *Naturalistic inquiry*. Sage Publications. doi:10.1016/0147-1767(85)90062-8

Miles, M. B., & Huberman, A. M. (1994). *Qualitative data analysis: An expanded sourcebook*. Sage Publications.

Millar, C. C., & Choi, C. J. (2008). Worker identity, the liability of foreignness, the exclusion of local managers and unionism: A conceptual analysis. *Journal of Organizational Change Management*, *21*(4), 460–470. doi:10.1108/09534810810884858

Moghaddam, K., Aidov, A., DuVal, C., & Azarpanah, S. (2017). High-growth entrepreneurial firm funding: A qualitative study of native-born and immigrant entrepreneurs. *Venture Capital*, *19*(1–2), 75–94. doi:10.1080/13691066.2016.1256295

Mohr, L. B. (1982). *Explaining organizational behavior*. Jossey-Bass.

Moyo, I. (2014). A case study of black African immigrant entrepreneurship in inner city Johannesburg using the mixed embeddedness approach. *Journal of Immigrant & Refugee Studies*, *12*(3), 250–273. doi:10.1080/15562948.2013.830172

Muse, L. A., Rutherford, M. W., Oswald, S. L., & Raymond, J. E. (2005). Commitment to employees: Does it help or hinder small business performance? *Small Business Economics*, *24*(2), 97–111. doi:10.100711187-003-3098-7

Mustafa, M., & Chen, S. (2010). The strength of family networks in transnational immigrant entrepreneurship. *Thunderbird International Business Review*, *52*(2), 97–106. doi:10.1002/tie.20317

Nag, R., Corley, K. G., & Gioia, D. A. (2007). The intersection of organizational identity, knowledge, and practice: Attempting strategic change via knowledge grafting. *Academy of Management Journal*, *50*(4), 821–847. doi:10.5465/amj.2007.26279173

Naudé, W., Siegel, M., & Marchand, K. (2017). Migration, entrepreneurship and development: Critical questions. *IZA Journal of Migration*, *6*(1), 1–16. doi:10.118640176-016-0077-8

Nazareno, J., Zhou, M., & You, T. (2019). Global dynamics of immigrant entrepreneurship: Changing trends, ethnonational variations, and reconceptualizations. *International Journal of Entrepreneurial Behaviour & Research*, *25*(5), 780–800. doi:10.1108/IJEBR-03-2018-0141

Neville, F., Orser, B., Riding, A., & Jung, O. (2014). Do young firms owned by recent immigrants outperform other young firms? *Journal of Business Venturing*, *29*(1), 55–71. doi:10.1016/j.jbusvent.2012.10.005

Pabian, S., & Vandebosch, H. (2021). Perceived long-term outcomes of early traditional and cyberbullying victimization among emerging adults. *Journal of Youth Studies*, *24*(1), 91–109. doi:10.1080/13676261.2019.1695764

Park, S. S., & Waldinger, R. D. (2017). Bridging the territorial divide: Immigrants' cross-border communication and the spatial dynamics of their kin networks. *Journal of Ethnic and Migration Studies*, *43*(1), 18–40. doi:10.1080/1369183X.2016.1211003 PMID:32952437

Pettigrew, A. M. (1979). On studying organizational cultures. *Administrative Science Quarterly*, *24*(4), 570–581. doi:10.2307/2392363

Pittino, D., Chirico, F., Henssen, B., & Broekaert, W. (2020). Does increased generational involvement foster business growth? The moderating roles of family involvement in ownership and management. *European Management Review*, *17*(3), 785–801. doi:10.1111/emre.12366

Pittino, D., Martínez, A. B., Chirico, F., & Galván, R. S. (2018). Psychological ownership, knowledge sharing and entrepreneurial orientation in family firms: The moderating role of governance heterogeneity. *Journal of Business Research*, *84*, 312–326. doi:10.1016/j.jbusres.2017.08.014

Poirine, B., Dropsy, V., & Gay, J.-F. (2017). Entrepreneurship and social norms about thrift versus sharing: The Chinese-Tahitian experience. *Asia Pacific Business Review*, *23*(5), 641–657. doi:10.1080/13602381.2017.1290188

Portes, A. (1995). *The economic sociology of immigration: Essays on networks, ethnicity, and entrepreneurship*. Russell Sage Foundation.

Pratt, M. G. (2009). From the editors: For the lack of a boilerplate: Tips on writing up (and reviewing) qualitative research. Academy of Management Journal, 52(5), 856-862.

Ram, M. (1997). Complexity and diversity. *Organization*, *4*(2), 294–296. doi:10.1177/135050849742011

Ram, M., Jones, T., & Villares-Varela, M. (2017). Migrant entrepreneurship: Reflections on research and practice. *International Small Business Journal*, *35*(1), 3–18. doi:10.1177/0266242616678051

Rath, J. (2000). *Immigrant businesses*. Palgrave Macmillan. doi:10.1057/9781403905338

Rath, J. C. (2002). *Unravelling the rag trade: Immigrant entrepreneurship in seven world cities*. Berg. doi:10.2752/9781847888945

Riddle, L., Hrivnak, G. A., & Nielsen, T. M. (2010). Transnational diaspora entrepreneurship in emerging markets: Bridging institutional divides. *Journal of International Management*, *16*(4), 398–411. doi:10.1016/j.intman.2010.09.009

Sanders, J. M., & Nee, V. (1996). Immigrant self-employment: The family as social capital and the value of human capital. *American Sociological Review*, *61*(2), 231–249. doi:10.2307/2096333

Sherrell, H. (2015). *Economic Impact of Migration - Refugee Council of Australia*. https://www.mia.org.au/documents/item/752

Simon, H. A. (1997). *Models of bounded rationality: Empirically grounded economic reason*. MIT Press. doi:10.7551/mitpress/4711.001.0001

Simon-Davies, J. (2018). *Population and migration statistics in Australia*. Department of Parliamentary Services, Parliamentary Library.

Sirmon, D. G., & Hitt, M. A. (2003). Managing resources: Linking unique resources, management, and wealth creation in family firms. *Entrepreneurship Theory and Practice*, *27*(4), 339–358. doi:10.1111/1540-8520.t01-1-00013

Steier, L. (2001). Next-generation entrepreneurs and succession: An exploratory study of modes and means of managing social capital. *Family Business Review*, *14*(3), 259–276. doi:10.1111/j.1741-6248.2001.00259.x

Strauss, A., & Corbin, J. (1998). *Basics of qualitative research: Procedures and techniques for developing grounded theory*. Sage Publications.

Szkudlarek, B., & Wu, S. X. (2018). The culturally contingent meaning of entrepreneurship: Mixed embeddedness and co-ethnic ties. *Entrepreneurship and Regional Development*, *30*(5–6), 585–611. doi:10.1080/08985626.2018.1432701

Tarrius, A., & Péraldi, M. (1995). Marseille et ses étrangers. *Revue Européenne des Migrations Internationales*, *11*(1), 5–132.

Tata, J., & Prasad, S. (2015). Immigrant family businesses: Social capital, network benefits and business performance. *International Journal of Entrepreneurial Behaviour & Research*, *21*(6), 842–866. doi:10.1108/IJEBR-06-2014-0111

Tatli, A., Vassilopoulou, J., Özbilgin, M., Forson, C., & Slutskaya, N. (2014). A Bourdieuan relational perspective for entrepreneurship research. *Journal of Small Business Management*, *52*(4), 615–632. doi:10.1111/jsbm.12122

Thornton, P. H., Ribeiro-Soriano, D., & Urbano, D. (2011). Socio-cultural factors and entrepreneurial activity: An overview. *International Small Business Journal*, *29*(2), 105–118. doi:10.1177/0266242610391930

Useche, D., Miguelez, E., & Lissoni, F. (2019). Highly skilled and well connected: Migrant inventors in cross-border M&As. *Journal of International Business Studies*, *51*(5), 737–763. doi:10.105741267-018-0203-3

Uzzi, B. (1996). The sources and consequences of embeddedness for the economic performance of organizations: The network effect. *American Sociological Review*, *61*(4), 674–698. doi:10.2307/2096399

Uzzi, B. (1997). Social structure and competition in interfirm networks: The paradox of embeddedness. *Administrative Science Quarterly*, *42*(1), 35–67. doi:10.2307/2393808

Uzzi, B., & Gillespie, J. J. (2002). Knowledge spillover in corporate financing networks: Embeddedness and the firm's debt performance. *Strategic Management Journal*, *23*(7), 595–618. doi:10.1002mj.241

Van de Ven, A. H. (1992). Suggestions for studying strategy process: A research note. *Strategic Management Journal*, *13*(S1), 169–188. doi:10.1002mj.4250131013

Van De Ven, A. H. (2011). Building a European community of engaged scholars. *European Management Review*, *8*(4), 189–195. doi:10.1111/j.1740-4762.2011.01019.x

Van de Ven, A. H., & Poole, M. S. (1995). Explaining development and change in organizations. *Academy of Management Review*, *20*(3), 510–540. doi:10.5465/amr.1995.9508080329

Verduijn, K., & Essers, C. (2013). Questioning dominant entrepreneurship assumptions: The case of female ethnic minority entrepreneurs. *Entrepreneurship and Regional Development*, *25*(7–8), 612–630. doi:10.1080/08985626.2013.814718

Villadsen, A. R., & Wulff, J. N. (2018). Is the public sector a fairer employer? Ethnic employment discrimination in the public and private sectors. *Academy of Management Discoveries*, *4*(4), 429–448. doi:10.5465/amd.2016.0029

Villares-Varela, M. (2017). "Not helping out": Classed strategies of the (non) contribution of children in immigrant family businesses. *Ethnic and Racial Studies*, *40*(10), 1758–1775. doi:10.1080/01419870.2016.1206591

Vissak, T., & Zhang, X. (2014). Chinese immigrant entrepreneurs' involvement in internationalization and innovation: Three Canadian cases. *Journal of International Entrepreneurship*, *12*(2), 183–201. doi:10.100710843-014-0128-2

Volery, T. (2007). *Ethnic entrepreneurship: A theoretical framework. In Handbook of research on ethnic minority entrepreneurship (pp. 30–41)*. Unisgh.

Waldinger, R. (1984). Immigrant enterprise in the New York garment industry. *Social Problems*, *32*(1), 60–71. doi:10.2307/800262

Waldinger, R. D., Aldrich, H., & Ward, R. (1990). *Ethnic entrepreneurs: Immigrant business in industrial societies*. Sage Publications.

Wallace, R. L. (1997). *Black wealth through black entrepreneurship*. APU Publishing Group.

Wang, C. L., & Altinay, L. (2012). Social embeddedness, entrepreneurial orientation and firm growth in ethnic minority small businesses in the UK. *International Small Business Journal*, *30*(1), 3–23. doi:10.1177/0266242610366060

Wang, Y., & Poutziouris, P. (2010). Entrepreneurial risk taking: Empirical evidence from UK family firms. *International Journal of Entrepreneurial Behaviour & Research*, *16*(5), 370–388. doi:10.1108/13552551011071841

Wang, Y., & Warn, J. (2018). Chinese immigrant entrepreneurship: Embeddedness and the interaction of resources with the wider social and economic context. *International Small Business Journal*, *36*(2), 131–148. doi:10.1177/0266242617726364

Ward, R., & Jenkins, R. (1984). *Ethnic communities in business: Strategies for economic survival*. Cambridge University Press.

Welter, F. (2011). Contextualizing entrepreneurship—Conceptual challenges and ways forward. *Entrepreneurship Theory and Practice*, *35*(1), 165–184. doi:10.1111/j.1540-6520.2010.00427.x

Wengraf, T. (2011). BNIM short guide bound with the detailed manual. Sage Publications.

Wigren-Kristofersen, C., Korsgaard, S., Brundin, E., Hellerstedt, K., Agnete Alsos, G., & Grande, J. (2019). Entrepreneurship and embeddedness: Dynamic, processual and multi-layered perspectives. *Entrepreneurship and Regional Development*, *31*(9–10), 1011–2015. doi:10.1080/08985626.2019.1656868

Wood, H. (2003). Cultural studies for Oceania. *The Contemporary Pacific*, *15*(2), 340–374. doi:10.1353/cp.2003.0062

You, T., & Zhou, M. (2019). Simultaneous embeddedness in immigrant entrepreneurship: Global forces behind Chinese-owned nail salons in New York City. *The American Behavioral Scientist*, *63*(2), 166–185. doi:10.1177/0002764218793684

Zahra, S. A. (2003). International expansion of US manufacturing family businesses: The effect of ownership and involvement. *Journal of Business Venturing*, *18*(4), 495–512. doi:10.1016/S0883-9026(03)00057-0

Zahra, S. A. (2020). International entrepreneurship (IE) in the age of political turbulence. *Academy of Management Discoveries*, *6*(2), 172–175. doi:10.5465/amd.2019.0076

Zahra, S. A., Wright, M., & Abdelgawad, S. G. (2014). Contextualization and the advancement of entrepreneurship research. *International Small Business Journal*, *32*(5), 479–500. doi:10.1177/0266242613519807

Zolin, R., & Schlosser, F. (2013). Characteristics of immigrant entrepreneurs and their involvement in international new ventures. *Thunderbird International Business Review*, *55*(3), 271–284. doi:10.1002/tie.21543

ENDNOTE

1 Australia has a history of immigrant entrepreneurship that dates back more than a century in the case of Chinese, Greek, Italian and Lebanese immigrants (Collins et al., 1995: 39–46), and some decades for Korean, Indian, Thai, Malaysian, Sri Lankan and other "minority" groups (Collins et al., 1995; Collins, 2008). Their immigration histories and their family background have shaped the landscape of the Australian immigrant entrepreneurship context. As such, Australian immigrant entrepreneurs and their firms are often embedded within family and ethnic networks locally, nationally and internationally, as well as within government regulations and policies (Kloosterman and Rath, 2001).

2 Australia has a history of immigrant entrepreneurship that dates back more than a century in the case of Chinese, Greek, Italian and Lebanese immigrants (Collins et al., 1995: 39–46), and some decades for Korean, Indian, Thai, Malaysian, Sri Lankan and other "minority" groups (Collins et al., 1995; Collins, 2008). Their immigration histories and their family background have shaped the landscape of the Australian immigrant entrepreneurship context. As such, Australian immigrant entrepreneurs and their firms are often embedded within family and ethnic networks locally, nationally and internationally, as well as within government regulations and policies (Kloosterman and Rath, 2001).

3 We thank an anonymous reviewer for this insightful suggestion.

4 Organizational change is defined as "a difference in form, quality, or state over time in an organizational entity" (Van de Ven & Poole, 1995: 512).

5 A document that consists of more than 200 pages of quotes is available from the authors upon request.

Related References

To continue our tradition of advancing information science and technology research, we have compiled a list of recommended IGI Global readings. These references will provide additional information and guidance to further enrich your knowledge and assist you with your own research and future publications.

Abdul Razak, R., & Mansor, N. A. (2021). Instagram Influencers in Social Media-Induced Tourism: Rethinking Tourist Trust Towards Tourism Destination. In M. Dinis, L. Bonixe, S. Lamy, & Z. Breda (Eds.), *Impact of New Media in Tourism* (pp. 135-144). IGI Global. https://doi.org/10.4018/978-1-7998-7095-1.ch009

Abir, T., & Khan, M. Y. (2022). Importance of ICT Advancement and Culture of Adaptation in the Tourism and Hospitality Industry for Developing Countries. In C. Ramos, S. Quinteiro, & A. Gonçalves (Eds.), *ICT as Innovator Between Tourism and Culture* (pp. 30–41). IGI Global. https://doi.org/10.4018/978-1-7998-8165-0.ch003

Abir, T., & Khan, M. Y. (2022). Importance of ICT Advancement and Culture of Adaptation in the Tourism and Hospitality Industry for Developing Countries. In C. Ramos, S. Quinteiro, & A. Gonçalves (Eds.), *ICT as Innovator Between Tourism and Culture* (pp. 30–41). IGI Global. https://doi.org/10.4018/978-1-7998-8165-0.ch003

Abtahi, M. S., Behboudi, L., & Hasanabad, H. M. (2017). Factors Affecting Internet Advertising Adoption in Ad Agencies. *International Journal of Innovation in the Digital Economy*, *8*(4), 18–29. doi:10.4018/IJIDE.2017100102

Afenyo-Agbe, E., & Mensah, I. (2022). Principles, Benefits, and Barriers to Community-Based Tourism: Implications for Management. In I. Mensah & E. Afenyo-Agbe (Eds.), *Prospects and Challenges of Community-Based Tourism and Changing Demographics* (pp. 1–29). IGI Global. doi:10.4018/978-1-7998-7335-8.ch001

Agbo, V. M. (2022). Distributive Justice Issues in Community-Based Tourism. In I. Mensah & E. Afenyo-Agbe (Eds.), *Prospects and Challenges of Community-Based Tourism and Changing Demographics* (pp. 107–129). IGI Global. https://doi.org/10.4018/978-1-7998-7335-8.ch005

Agrawal, S. (2017). The Impact of Emerging Technologies and Social Media on Different Business(es): Marketing and Management. In O. Rishi & A. Sharma (Eds.), *Maximizing Business Performance and Efficiency Through Intelligent Systems* (pp. 37–49). Hershey, PA: IGI Global. doi:10.4018/978-1-5225-2234-8.ch002

Ahmad, A., & Johari, S. (2022). Georgetown as a Gastronomy Tourism Destination: Visitor Awareness Towards Revisit Intention of Nasi Kandar Restaurant. In M. Valeri (Ed.), *New Governance and Management in Touristic Destinations* (pp. 71–83). IGI Global. https://doi.org/10.4018/978-1-6684-3889-3.ch005

Alkhatib, G., & Bayouq, S. T. (2021). A TAM-Based Model of Technological Factors Affecting Use of E-Tourism. *International Journal of Tourism and Hospitality Management in the Digital Age*, *5*(2), 50–67. https://doi.org/10.4018/IJTHMDA.20210701.oa1

Altinay Ozdemir, M. (2021). Virtual Reality (VR) and Augmented Reality (AR) Technologies for Accessibility and Marketing in the Tourism Industry. In C. Eusébio, L. Teixeira, & M. Carneiro (Eds.), *ICT Tools and Applications for Accessible Tourism* (pp. 277-301). IGI Global. https://doi.org/10.4018/978-1-7998-6428-8.ch013

Anantharaman, R. N., Rajeswari, K. S., Angusamy, A., & Kuppusamy, J. (2017). Role of Self-Efficacy and Collective Efficacy as Moderators of Occupational Stress Among Software Development Professionals. *International Journal of Human Capital and Information Technology Professionals*, *8*(2), 45–58. doi:10.4018/IJHCITP.2017040103

Aninze, F., El-Gohary, H., & Hussain, J. (2018). The Role of Microfinance to Empower Women: The Case of Developing Countries. *International Journal of Customer Relationship Marketing and Management, 9*(1), 54–78. doi:10.4018/IJCRMM.2018010104

Antosova, G., Sabogal-Salamanca, M., & Krizova, E. (2021). Human Capital in Tourism: A Practical Model of Endogenous and Exogenous Territorial Tourism Planning in Bahía Solano, Colombia. In V. Costa, A. Moura, & M. Mira (Eds.), *Handbook of Research on Human Capital and People Management in the Tourism Industry* (pp. 282–302). IGI Global. https://doi.org/10.4018/978-1-7998-4318-4.ch014

Arsenijević, O. M., Orčić, D., & Kastratović, E. (2017). Development of an Optimization Tool for Intangibles in SMEs: A Case Study from Serbia with a Pilot Research in the Prestige by Milka Company. In M. Vemić (Ed.), *Optimal Management Strategies in Small and Medium Enterprises* (pp. 320–347). Hershey, PA: IGI Global. doi:10.4018/978-1-5225-1949-2.ch015

Aryanto, V. D., Wismantoro, Y., & Widyatmoko, K. (2018). Implementing Eco-Innovation by Utilizing the Internet to Enhance Firm's Marketing Performance: Study of Green Batik Small and Medium Enterprises in Indonesia. *International Journal of E-Business Research, 14*(1), 21–36. doi:10.4018/IJEBR.2018010102

Asero, V., & Billi, S. (2022). New Perspective of Networking in the DMO Model. In M. Valeri (Ed.), *New Governance and Management in Touristic Destinations* (pp. 105–118). IGI Global. https://doi.org/10.4018/978-1-6684-3889-3.ch007

Atiku, S. O., & Fields, Z. (2017). Multicultural Orientations for 21st Century Global Leadership. In N. Baporikar (Ed.), *Management Education for Global Leadership* (pp. 28–51). Hershey, PA: IGI Global. doi:10.4018/978-1-5225-1013-0.ch002

Atiku, S. O., & Fields, Z. (2018). Organisational Learning Dimensions and Talent Retention Strategies for the Service Industries. In N. Baporikar (Ed.), *Global Practices in Knowledge Management for Societal and Organizational Development* (pp. 358–381). Hershey, PA: IGI Global. doi:10.4018/978-1-5225-3009-1.ch017

Atsa'am, D. D., & Kuset Bodur, E. (2021). Pattern Mining on How Organizational Tenure Affects the Psychological Capital of Employees Within the Hospitality and Tourism Industry: Linking Employees' Organizational Tenure With PsyCap. *International Journal of Tourism and Hospitality Management in the Digital Age*, *5*(2), 17–28. https://doi.org/10.4018/IJTHMDA.2021070102

Ávila, L., & Teixeira, L. (2018). The Main Concepts Behind the Dematerialization of Business Processes. In M. Khosrow-Pour, D.B.A. (Ed.), Encyclopedia of Information Science and Technology, Fourth Edition (pp. 888-898). Hershey, PA: IGI Global. https://doi.org/ doi:10.4018/978-1-5225-2255-3.ch076

Ayorekire, J., Mugizi, F., Obua, J., & Ampaire, G. (2022). Community-Based Tourism and Local People's Perceptions Towards Conservation: The Case of Queen Elizabeth Conservation Area, Uganda. In I. Mensah & E. Afenyo-Agbe (Eds.), *Prospects and Challenges of Community-Based Tourism and Changing Demographics* (pp. 56–82). IGI Global. https://doi.org/10.4018/978-1-7998-7335-8.ch003

Baleiro, R. (2022). Tourist Literature and the Architecture of Travel in Olga Tokarczuk and Patti Smith. In R. Baleiro & R. Pereira (Eds.), *Global Perspectives on Literary Tourism and Film-Induced Tourism* (pp. 202-216). IGI Global. https://doi.org/10.4018/978-1-7998-8262-6.ch011

Barat, S. (2021). Looking at the Future of Medical Tourism in Asia. *International Journal of Tourism and Hospitality Management in the Digital Age*, *5*(1), 19–33. https://doi.org/10.4018/IJTHMDA.2021010102

Barbosa, C. A., Magalhães, M., & Nunes, M. R. (2021). Travel Instagramability: A Way of Choosing a Destination? In M. Dinis, L. Bonixe, S. Lamy, & Z. Breda (Eds.), *Impact of New Media in Tourism* (pp. 173-190). IGI Global. https://doi.org/10.4018/978-1-7998-7095-1.ch011

Bari, M. W., & Khan, Q. (2021). Pakistan as a Destination of Religious Tourism. In E. Alaverdov & M. Bari (Eds.), *Global Development of Religious Tourism* (pp. 1-10). IGI Global. https://doi.org/10.4018/978-1-7998-5792-1.ch001

Bartens, Y., Chunpir, H. I., Schulte, F., & Voß, S. (2017). Business/IT Alignment in Two-Sided Markets: A COBIT 5 Analysis for Media Streaming Business Models. In S. De Haes & W. Van Grembergen (Eds.), *Strategic IT Governance and Alignment in Business Settings* (pp. 82–111). Hershey, PA: IGI Global. doi:10.4018/978-1-5225-0861-8.ch004

Bashayreh, A. M. (2018). Organizational Culture and Organizational Performance. In W. Lee & F. Sabetzadeh (Eds.), *Contemporary Knowledge and Systems Science* (pp. 50–69). Hershey, PA: IGI Global. doi:10.4018/978-1-5225-5655-8.ch003

Bechthold, L., Lude, M., & Prügl, R. (2021). Crisis Favors the Prepared Firm: How Organizational Ambidexterity Relates to Perceptions of Organizational Resilience. In A. Zehrer, G. Glowka, K. Schwaiger, & V. Ranacher-Lackner (Eds.), *Resiliency Models and Addressing Future Risks for Family Firms in the Tourism Industry* (pp. 178–205). IGI Global. https://doi.org/10.4018/978-1-7998-7352-5.ch008

Bedford, D. A. (2018). Sustainable Knowledge Management Strategies: Aligning Business Capabilities and Knowledge Management Goals. In N. Baporikar (Ed.), *Global Practices in Knowledge Management for Societal and Organizational Development* (pp. 46–73). Hershey, PA: IGI Global. doi:10.4018/978-1-5225-3009-1.ch003

Bekjanov, D., & Matyusupov, B. (2021). Influence of Innovative Processes in the Competitiveness of Tourist Destination. In J. Soares (Ed.), *Innovation and Entrepreneurial Opportunities in Community Tourism* (pp. 243–263). IGI Global. https://doi.org/10.4018/978-1-7998-4855-4.ch014

Bharwani, S., & Musunuri, D. (2018). Reflection as a Process From Theory to Practice. In M. Khosrow-Pour, D.B.A. (Ed.), Encyclopedia of Information Science and Technology, Fourth Edition (pp. 1529-1539). Hershey, PA: IGI Global. doi:10.4018/978-1-5225-2255-3.ch132

Bhatt, G. D., Wang, Z., & Rodger, J. A. (2017). Information Systems Capabilities and Their Effects on Competitive Advantages: A Study of Chinese Companies. *Information Resources Management Journal, 30*(3), 41–57. doi:10.4018/IRMJ.2017070103

Bhushan, M., & Yadav, A. (2017). Concept of Cloud Computing in ESB. In R. Bhadoria, N. Chaudhari, G. Tomar, & S. Singh (Eds.), *Exploring Enterprise Service Bus in the Service-Oriented Architecture Paradigm* (pp. 116–127). Hershey, PA: IGI Global. doi:10.4018/978-1-5225-2157-0.ch008

Bhushan, S. (2017). System Dynamics Base-Model of Humanitarian Supply Chain (HSCM) in Disaster Prone Eco-Communities of India: A Discussion on Simulation and Scenario Results. *International Journal of System Dynamics Applications, 6*(3), 20–37. doi:10.4018/IJSDA.2017070102

Binder, D., & Miller, J. W. (2021). A Generations' Perspective on Employer Branding in Tourism. In V. Costa, A. Moura, & M. Mira (Eds.), *Handbook of Research on Human Capital and People Management in the Tourism Industry* (pp. 152–174). IGI Global. https://doi.org/10.4018/978-1-7998-4318-4.ch008

Birch Freeman, A. A., Mensah, I., & Antwi, K. B. (2022). Smiling vs. Frowning Faces: Community Participation for Sustainable Tourism in Ghanaian Communities. In I. Mensah & E. Afenyo-Agbe (Eds.), *Prospects and Challenges of Community-Based Tourism and Changing Demographics* (pp. 83–106). IGI Global. https://doi.org/10.4018/978-1-7998-7335-8.ch004

Biswas, A., & De, A. K. (2017). On Development of a Fuzzy Stochastic Programming Model with Its Application to Business Management. In S. Trivedi, S. Dey, A. Kumar, & T. Panda (Eds.), *Handbook of Research on Advanced Data Mining Techniques and Applications for Business Intelligence* (pp. 353–378). Hershey, PA: IGI Global. doi:10.4018/978-1-5225-2031-3.ch021

Boragnio, A., & Faracce Macia, C. (2021). "Taking Care of Yourself at Home": Use of E-Commerce About Food and Care During the COVID-19 Pandemic in the City of Buenos Aires. In M. Korstanje (Ed.), *Socio-Economic Effects and Recovery Efforts for the Rental Industry: Post-COVID-19 Strategies* (pp. 45–71). IGI Global. https://doi.org/10.4018/978-1-7998-7287-0.ch003

Borges, V. D. (2021). Happiness: The Basis for Public Policy in Tourism. In A. Perinotto, V. Mayer, & J. Soares (Eds.), *Rebuilding and Restructuring the Tourism Industry: Infusion of Happiness and Quality of Life* (pp. 1–25). IGI Global. https://doi.org/10.4018/978-1-7998-7239-9.ch001

Bücker, J., & Ernste, K. (2018). Use of Brand Heroes in Strategic Reputation Management: The Case of Bacardi, Adidas, and Daimler. In A. Erdemir (Ed.), *Reputation Management Techniques in Public Relations* (pp. 126–150). Hershey, PA: IGI Global. doi:10.4018/978-1-5225-3619-2.ch007

Buluk Eşitti, B. (2021). COVID-19 and Alternative Tourism: New Destinations and New Tourism Products. In M. Demir, A. Dalgıç, & F. Ergen (Eds.), *Handbook of Research on the Impacts and Implications of COVID-19 on the Tourism Industry* (pp. 786–805). IGI Global. https://doi.org/10.4018/978-1-7998-8231-2.ch038

Bureš, V. (2018). Industry 4.0 From the Systems Engineering Perspective: Alternative Holistic Framework Development. In R. Brunet-Thornton & F. Martinez (Eds.), *Analyzing the Impacts of Industry 4.0 in Modern Business Environments* (pp. 199–223). Hershey, PA: IGI Global. doi:10.4018/978-1-5225-3468-6.ch011

Buzady, Z. (2017). Resolving the Magic Cube of Effective Case Teaching: Benchmarking Case Teaching Practices in Emerging Markets – Insights from the Central European University Business School, Hungary. In D. Latusek (Ed.), *Case Studies as a Teaching Tool in Management Education* (pp. 79–103). Hershey, PA: IGI Global. doi:10.4018/978-1-5225-0770-3.ch005

Camillo, A. (2021). *Legal Matters, Risk Management, and Risk Prevention: From Forming a Business to Legal Representation.* IGI Global. doi:10.4018/978-1-7998-4342-9.ch004

Căpusneanu, S., & Topor, D. I. (2018). Business Ethics and Cost Management in SMEs: Theories of Business Ethics and Cost Management Ethos. In I. Oncioiu (Ed.), *Ethics and Decision-Making for Sustainable Business Practices* (pp. 109–127). Hershey, PA: IGI Global. doi:10.4018/978-1-5225-3773-1.ch007

Chan, R. L., Mo, P. L., & Moon, K. K. (2018). Strategic and Tactical Measures in Managing Enterprise Risks: A Study of the Textile and Apparel Industry. In K. Strang, M. Korstanje, & N. Vajjhala (Eds.), *Research, Practices, and Innovations in Global Risk and Contingency Management* (pp. 1–19). Hershey, PA: IGI Global. doi:10.4018/978-1-5225-4754-9.ch001

Charlier, S. D., Burke-Smalley, L. A., & Fisher, S. L. (2018). Undergraduate Programs in the U.S: A Contextual and Content-Based Analysis. In J. Mendy (Ed.), *Teaching Human Resources and Organizational Behavior at the College Level* (pp. 26–57). Hershey, PA: IGI Global. doi:10.4018/978-1-5225-2820-3.ch002

Chumillas, J., Güell, M., & Quer, P. (2022). The Use of ICT in Tourist and Educational Literary Routes: The Role of the Guide. In C. Ramos, S. Quinteiro, & A. Gonçalves (Eds.), *ICT as Innovator Between Tourism and Culture* (pp. 15–29). IGI Global. https://doi.org/10.4018/978-1-7998-8165-0.ch002

Dahlberg, T., Kivijärvi, H., & Saarinen, T. (2017). IT Investment Consistency and Other Factors Influencing the Success of IT Performance. In S. De Haes & W. Van Grembergen (Eds.), *Strategic IT Governance and Alignment in Business Settings* (pp. 176–208). Hershey, PA: IGI Global. doi:10.4018/978-1-5225-0861-8.ch007

Damnjanović, A. M. (2017). Knowledge Management Optimization through IT and E-Business Utilization: A Qualitative Study on Serbian SMEs. In M. Vemić (Ed.), *Optimal Management Strategies in Small and Medium Enterprises* (pp. 249–267). Hershey, PA: IGI Global. doi:10.4018/978-1-5225-1949-2.ch012

Daneshpour, H. (2017). Integrating Sustainable Development into Project Portfolio Management through Application of Open Innovation. In M. Vemić (Ed.), *Optimal Management Strategies in Small and Medium Enterprises* (pp. 370–387). Hershey, PA: IGI Global. doi:10.4018/978-1-5225-1949-2.ch017

Daniel, A. D., & Reis de Castro, V. (2018). Entrepreneurship Education: How to Measure the Impact on Nascent Entrepreneurs. In A. Carrizo Moreira, J. Guilherme Leitão Dantas, & F. Manuel Valente (Eds.), *Nascent Entrepreneurship and Successful New Venture Creation* (pp. 85–110). Hershey, PA: IGI Global. doi:10.4018/978-1-5225-2936-1.ch004

David, R., Swami, B. N., & Tangirala, S. (2018). Ethics Impact on Knowledge Management in Organizational Development: A Case Study. In N. Baporikar (Ed.), *Global Practices in Knowledge Management for Societal and Organizational Development* (pp. 19–45). Hershey, PA: IGI Global. doi:10.4018/978-1-5225-3009-1.ch002

De Uña-Álvarez, E., & Villarino-Pérez, M. (2022). Fostering Ecocultural Resources, Identity, and Tourism in Inland Territories (Galicia, NW Spain). In G. Fernandes (Ed.), *Challenges and New Opportunities for Tourism in Inland Territories: Ecocultural Resources and Sustainable Initiatives* (pp. 1-16). IGI Global. https://doi.org/10.4018/978-1-7998-7339-6.ch001

Delias, P., & Lakiotaki, K. (2018). Discovering Process Horizontal Boundaries to Facilitate Process Comprehension. *International Journal of Operations Research and Information Systems, 9*(2), 1–31. doi:10.4018/IJORIS.2018040101

Denholm, J., & Lee-Davies, L. (2018). Success Factors for Games in Business and Project Management. In *Enhancing Education and Training Initiatives Through Serious Games* (pp. 34–68). Hershey, PA: IGI Global. doi:10.4018/978-1-5225-3689-5.ch002

Deshpande, M. (2017). Best Practices in Management Institutions for Global Leadership: Policy Aspects. In N. Baporikar (Ed.), *Management Education for Global Leadership* (pp. 1–27). Hershey, PA: IGI Global. doi:10.4018/978-1-5225-1013-0.ch001

Deshpande, M. (2018). Policy Perspectives for SMEs Knowledge Management. In N. Baporikar (Ed.), *Knowledge Integration Strategies for Entrepreneurship and Sustainability* (pp. 23–46). Hershey, PA: IGI Global. doi:10.4018/978-1-5225-5115-7.ch002

Dezdar, S. (2017). ERP Implementation Projects in Asian Countries: A Comparative Study on Iran and China. *International Journal of Information Technology Project Management*, *8*(3), 52–68. doi:10.4018/IJITPM.2017070104

Domingos, D., Respício, A., & Martinho, R. (2017). Reliability of IoT-Aware BPMN Healthcare Processes. In C. Reis & M. Maximiano (Eds.), *Internet of Things and Advanced Application in Healthcare* (pp. 214–248). Hershey, PA: IGI Global. doi:10.4018/978-1-5225-1820-4.ch008

Dosumu, O., Hussain, J., & El-Gohary, H. (2017). An Exploratory Study of the Impact of Government Policies on the Development of Small and Medium Enterprises in Developing Countries: The Case of Nigeria. *International Journal of Customer Relationship Marketing and Management*, *8*(4), 51–62. doi:10.4018/IJCRMM.2017100104

Durst, S., Bruns, G., & Edvardsson, I. R. (2017). Retaining Knowledge in Smaller Building and Construction Firms. *International Journal of Knowledge and Systems Science*, *8*(3), 1–12. doi:10.4018/IJKSS.2017070101

Edvardsson, I. R., & Durst, S. (2017). Outsourcing, Knowledge, and Learning: A Critical Review. *International Journal of Knowledge-Based Organizations*, *7*(2), 13–26. doi:10.4018/IJKBO.2017040102

Edwards, J. S. (2018). Integrating Knowledge Management and Business Processes. In M. Khosrow-Pour, D.B.A. (Ed.), Encyclopedia of Information Science and Technology, Fourth Edition (pp. 5046-5055). Hershey, PA: IGI Global. doi:10.4018/978-1-5225-2255-3.ch437

Eichelberger, S., & Peters, M. (2021). Family Firm Management in Turbulent Times: Opportunities for Responsible Tourism. In A. Zehrer, G. Glowka, K. Schwaiger, & V. Ranacher-Lackner (Eds.), *Resiliency Models and Addressing Future Risks for Family Firms in the Tourism Industry* (pp. 103–124). IGI Global. https://doi.org/10.4018/978-1-7998-7352-5.ch005

Eide, D., Hjalager, A., & Hansen, M. (2022). Innovative Certifications in Adventure Tourism: Attributes and Diffusion. In R. Augusto Costa, F. Brandão, Z. Breda, & C. Costa (Eds.), *Planning and Managing the Experience Economy in Tourism* (pp. 161-175). IGI Global. https://doi.org/10.4018/978-1-7998-8775-1.ch009

Ejiogu, A. O. (2018). Economics of Farm Management. In *Agricultural Finance and Opportunities for Investment and Expansion* (pp. 56–72). Hershey, PA: IGI Global. doi:10.4018/978-1-5225-3059-6.ch003

Ekanem, I., & Abiade, G. E. (2018). Factors Influencing the Use of E-Commerce by Small Enterprises in Nigeria. *International Journal of ICT Research in Africa and the Middle East*, *7*(1), 37–53. doi:10.4018/IJICTRAME.2018010103

Ekanem, I., & Alrossais, L. A. (2017). Succession Challenges Facing Family Businesses in Saudi Arabia. In P. Zgheib (Ed.), *Entrepreneurship and Business Innovation in the Middle East* (pp. 122–146). Hershey, PA: IGI Global. doi:10.4018/978-1-5225-2066-5.ch007

El Faquih, L., & Fredj, M. (2017). Ontology-Based Framework for Quality in Configurable Process Models. *Journal of Electronic Commerce in Organizations*, *15*(2), 48–60. doi:10.4018/JECO.2017040104

Faisal, M. N., & Talib, F. (2017). Building Ambidextrous Supply Chains in SMEs: How to Tackle the Barriers? *International Journal of Information Systems and Supply Chain Management*, *10*(4), 80–100. doi:10.4018/IJISSCM.2017100105

Fernandes, T. M., Gomes, J., & Romão, M. (2017). Investments in E-Government: A Benefit Management Case Study. *International Journal of Electronic Government Research*, *13*(3), 1–17. doi:10.4018/IJEGR.2017070101

Figueira, L. M., Honrado, G. R., & Dionísio, M. S. (2021). Human Capital Management in the Tourism Industry in Portugal. In V. Costa, A. Moura, & M. Mira (Eds.), *Handbook of Research on Human Capital and People Management in the Tourism Industry* (pp. 1–19). IGI Global. doi:10.4018/978-1-7998-4318-4.ch001

Gao, S. S., Oreal, S., & Zhang, J. (2018). Contemporary Financial Risk Management Perceptions and Practices of Small-Sized Chinese Businesses. In I. Management Association (Ed.), Global Business Expansion: Concepts, Methodologies, Tools, and Applications (pp. 917-931). Hershey, PA: IGI Global. doi:10.4018/978-1-5225-5481-3.ch041

Garg, R., & Berning, S. C. (2017). Indigenous Chinese Management Philosophies: Key Concepts and Relevance for Modern Chinese Firms. In B. Christiansen & G. Koc (Eds.), *Transcontinental Strategies for Industrial Development and Economic Growth* (pp. 43–57). Hershey, PA: IGI Global. doi:10.4018/978-1-5225-2160-0.ch003

Gencer, Y. G. (2017). Supply Chain Management in Retailing Business. In U. Akkucuk (Ed.), *Ethics and Sustainability in Global Supply Chain Management* (pp. 197–210). Hershey, PA: IGI Global. doi:10.4018/978-1-5225-2036-8.ch011

Gera, R., Arora, S., & Malik, S. (2021). Emotional Labor in the Tourism Industry: Strategies, Antecedents, and Outcomes. In V. Costa, A. Moura, & M. Mira (Eds.), *Handbook of Research on Human Capital and People Management in the Tourism Industry* (pp. 73–91). IGI Global. https://doi.org/10.4018/978-1-7998-4318-4.ch004

Giacosa, E. (2018). The Increasing of the Regional Development Thanks to the Luxury Business Innovation. In L. Carvalho (Ed.), *Handbook of Research on Entrepreneurial Ecosystems and Social Dynamics in a Globalized World* (pp. 260–273). Hershey, PA: IGI Global. doi:10.4018/978-1-5225-3525-6.ch011

Glowka, G., Tusch, M., & Zehrer, A. (2021). The Risk Perception of Family Business Owner-Manager in the Tourism Industry: A Qualitative Comparison of the Intra-Firm Senior and Junior Generation. In A. Zehrer, G. Glowka, K. Schwaiger, & V. Ranacher-Lackner (Eds.), *Resiliency Models and Addressing Future Risks for Family Firms in the Tourism Industry* (pp. 126–153). IGI Global. https://doi.org/10.4018/978-1-7998-7352-5.ch006

Glykas, M., & George, J. (2017). Quality and Process Management Systems in the UAE Maritime Industry. *International Journal of Productivity Management and Assessment Technologies, 5*(1), 20–39. doi:10.4018/IJPMAT.2017010102

Glykas, M., Valiris, G., Kokkinaki, A., & Koutsoukou, Z. (2018). Banking Business Process Management Implementation. *International Journal of Productivity Management and Assessment Technologies, 6*(1), 50–69. doi:10.4018/IJPMAT.2018010104

Gomes, J., & Romão, M. (2017). The Balanced Scorecard: Keeping Updated and Aligned with Today's Business Trends. *International Journal of Productivity Management and Assessment Technologies, 5*(2), 1–15. doi:10.4018/IJPMAT.2017070101

Gomes, J., & Romão, M. (2017). Aligning Information Systems and Technology with Benefit Management and Balanced Scorecard. In S. De Haes & W. Van Grembergen (Eds.), *Strategic IT Governance and Alignment in Business Settings* (pp. 112–131). Hershey, PA: IGI Global. doi:10.4018/978-1-5225-0861-8.ch005

Goyal, A. (2021). Communicating and Building Destination Brands With New Media. In M. Dinis, L. Bonixe, S. Lamy, & Z. Breda (Eds.), *Impact of New Media in Tourism* (pp. 1-20). IGI Global. https://doi.org/10.4018/978-1-7998-7095-1.ch001

Grefen, P., & Turetken, O. (2017). Advanced Business Process Management in Networked E-Business Scenarios. *International Journal of E-Business Research, 13*(4), 70–104. doi:10.4018/IJEBR.2017100105

Guasca, M., Van Broeck, A. M., & Vanneste, D. (2021). Tourism and the Social Reintegration of Colombian Ex-Combatants. In J. da Silva, Z. Breda, & F. Carbone (Eds.), *Role and Impact of Tourism in Peacebuilding and Conflict Transformation* (pp. 66-86). IGI Global. https://doi.org/10.4018/978-1-7998-5053-3.ch005

Haider, A., & Saetang, S. (2017). Strategic IT Alignment in Service Sector. In S. Rozenes & Y. Cohen (Eds.), *Handbook of Research on Strategic Alliances and Value Co-Creation in the Service Industry* (pp. 231–258). Hershey, PA: IGI Global. doi:10.4018/978-1-5225-2084-9.ch012

Hajilari, A. B., Ghadaksaz, M., & Fasghandis, G. S. (2017). Assessing Organizational Readiness for Implementing ERP System Using Fuzzy Expert System Approach. *International Journal of Enterprise Information Systems, 13*(1), 67–85. doi:10.4018/IJEIS.2017010105

Haldorai, A., Ramu, A., & Murugan, S. (2018). Social Aware Cognitive Radio Networks: Effectiveness of Social Networks as a Strategic Tool for Organizational Business Management. In H. Bansal, G. Shrivastava, G. Nguyen, & L. Stanciu (Eds.), *Social Network Analytics for Contemporary Business Organizations* (pp. 188–202). Hershey, PA: IGI Global. doi:10.4018/978-1-5225-5097-6.ch010

Hall, O. P. Jr. (2017). Social Media Driven Management Education. *International Journal of Knowledge-Based Organizations, 7*(2), 43–59. doi:10.4018/IJKBO.2017040104

Hanifah, H., Halim, H. A., Ahmad, N. H., & Vafaei-Zadeh, A. (2017). Innovation Culture as a Mediator Between Specific Human Capital and Innovation Performance Among Bumiputera SMEs in Malaysia. In N. Ahmad, T. Ramayah, H. Halim, & S. Rahman (Eds.), *Handbook of Research on Small and Medium Enterprises in Developing Countries* (pp. 261–279). Hershey, PA: IGI Global. doi:10.4018/978-1-5225-2165-5.ch012

Hartlieb, S., & Silvius, G. (2017). Handling Uncertainty in Project Management and Business Development: Similarities and Differences. In Y. Raydugin (Ed.), *Handbook of Research on Leveraging Risk and Uncertainties for Effective Project Management* (pp. 337–362). Hershey, PA: IGI Global. doi:10.4018/978-1-5225-1790-0.ch016

Hass, K. B. (2017). Living on the Edge: Managing Project Complexity. In Y. Raydugin (Ed.), *Handbook of Research on Leveraging Risk and Uncertainties for Effective Project Management* (pp. 177–201). Hershey, PA: IGI Global. doi:10.4018/978-1-5225-1790-0.ch009

Hawking, P., & Carmine Sellitto, C. (2017). Developing an Effective Strategy for Organizational Business Intelligence. In M. Tavana (Ed.), *Enterprise Information Systems and the Digitalization of Business Functions* (pp. 222–237). Hershey, PA: IGI Global. doi:10.4018/978-1-5225-2382-6.ch010

Hawking, P., & Sellitto, C. (2017). A Fast-Moving Consumer Goods Company and Business Intelligence Strategy Development. *International Journal of Enterprise Information Systems, 13*(2), 22–33. doi:10.4018/IJEIS.2017040102

Hawking, P., & Sellitto, C. (2017). Business Intelligence Strategy: Two Case Studies. *International Journal of Business Intelligence Research, 8*(2), 17–30. doi:10.4018/IJBIR.2017070102

Hee, W. J., Jalleh, G., Lai, H., & Lin, C. (2017). E-Commerce and IT Projects: Evaluation and Management Issues in Australian and Taiwanese Hospitals. *International Journal of Public Health Management and Ethics, 2*(1), 69–90. doi:10.4018/IJPHME.2017010104

Hernandez, A. A. (2018). Exploring the Factors to Green IT Adoption of SMEs in the Philippines. *Journal of Cases on Information Technology, 20*(2), 49–66. doi:10.4018/JCIT.2018040104

Hollman, A., Bickford, S., & Hollman, T. (2017). Cyber InSecurity: A Post-Mortem Attempt to Assess Cyber Problems from IT and Business Management Perspectives. *Journal of Cases on Information Technology, 19*(3), 42–70. doi:10.4018/JCIT.2017070104

Ibrahim, F., & Zainin, N. M. (2021). Exploring the Technological Impacts: The Case of Museums in Brunei Darussalam. *International Journal of Tourism and Hospitality Management in the Digital Age, 5*(1), 1–18. https://doi.org/10.4018/IJTHMDA.2021010101

Igbinakhase, I. (2017). Responsible and Sustainable Management Practices in Developing and Developed Business Environments. In Z. Fields (Ed.), *Collective Creativity for Responsible and Sustainable Business Practice* (pp. 180–207). Hershey, PA: IGI Global. doi:10.4018/978-1-5225-1823-5.ch010

Iwata, J. J., & Hoskins, R. G. (2017). Managing Indigenous Knowledge in Tanzania: A Business Perspective. In P. Jain & N. Mnjama (Eds.), *Managing Knowledge Resources and Records in Modern Organizations* (pp. 198–214). Hershey, PA: IGI Global. doi:10.4018/978-1-5225-1965-2.ch012

Jain, P. (2017). Ethical and Legal Issues in Knowledge Management Life-Cycle in Business. In P. Jain & N. Mnjama (Eds.), *Managing Knowledge Resources and Records in Modern Organizations* (pp. 82–101). Hershey, PA: IGI Global. doi:10.4018/978-1-5225-1965-2.ch006

James, S., & Hauli, E. (2017). Holistic Management Education at Tanzanian Rural Development Planning Institute. In N. Baporikar (Ed.), *Management Education for Global Leadership* (pp. 112–136). Hershey, PA: IGI Global. doi:10.4018/978-1-5225-1013-0.ch006

Janošková, M., Csikósová, A., & Čulková, K. (2018). Measurement of Company Performance as Part of Its Strategic Management. In R. Leon (Ed.), *Managerial Strategies for Business Sustainability During Turbulent Times* (pp. 309–335). Hershey, PA: IGI Global. doi:10.4018/978-1-5225-2716-9.ch017

Jean-Vasile, A., & Alecu, A. (2017). Theoretical and Practical Approaches in Understanding the Influences of Cost-Productivity-Profit Trinomial in Contemporary Enterprises. In A. Jean Vasile & D. Nicolò (Eds.), *Sustainable Entrepreneurship and Investments in the Green Economy* (pp. 28–62). Hershey, PA: IGI Global. doi:10.4018/978-1-5225-2075-7.ch002

Joia, L. A., & Correia, J. C. (2018). CIO Competencies From the IT Professional Perspective: Insights From Brazil. *Journal of Global Information Management, 26*(2), 74–103. doi:10.4018/JGIM.2018040104

Juma, A., & Mzera, N. (2017). Knowledge Management and Records Management and Competitive Advantage in Business. In P. Jain & N. Mnjama (Eds.), *Managing Knowledge Resources and Records in Modern Organizations* (pp. 15–28). Hershey, PA: IGI Global. doi:10.4018/978-1-5225-1965-2.ch002

K., I., & A, V. (2018). Monitoring and Auditing in the Cloud. In K. Munir (Ed.), *Cloud Computing Technologies for Green Enterprises* (pp. 318-350). Hershey, PA: IGI Global. https://doi.org/ doi:10.4018/978-1-5225-3038-1.ch013

Kabra, G., Ghosh, V., & Ramesh, A. (2018). Enterprise Integrated Business Process Management and Business Intelligence Framework for Business Process Sustainability. In A. Paul, D. Bhattacharyya, & S. Anand (Eds.), *Green Initiatives for Business Sustainability and Value Creation* (pp. 228–238). Hershey, PA: IGI Global. doi:10.4018/978-1-5225-2662-9.ch010

Kaoud, M. (2017). Investigation of Customer Knowledge Management: A Case Study Research. *International Journal of Service Science, Management, Engineering, and Technology, 8*(2), 12–22. doi:10.4018/IJSSMET.2017040102

Katuu, S. (2018). A Comparative Assessment of Enterprise Content Management Maturity Models. In N. Gwangwava & M. Mutingi (Eds.), *E-Manufacturing and E-Service Strategies in Contemporary Organizations* (pp. 93–118). Hershey, PA: IGI Global. doi:10.4018/978-1-5225-3628-4.ch005

Khan, M. Y., & Abir, T. (2022). The Role of Social Media Marketing in the Tourism and Hospitality Industry: A Conceptual Study on Bangladesh. In C. Ramos, S. Quinteiro, & A. Gonçalves (Eds.), *ICT as Innovator Between Tourism and Culture* (pp. 213–229). IGI Global. https://doi.org/10.4018/978-1-7998-8165-0.ch013

Kinnunen, S., Ylä-Kujala, A., Marttonen-Arola, S., Kärri, T., & Baglee, D. (2018). Internet of Things in Asset Management: Insights from Industrial Professionals and Academia. *International Journal of Service Science, Management, Engineering, and Technology, 9*(2), 104–119. doi:10.4018/IJSSMET.2018040105

Klein, A. Z., Sabino de Freitas, A., Machado, L., Freitas, J. C. Jr, Graziola, P. G. Jr, & Schlemmer, E. (2017). Virtual Worlds Applications for Management Education. In L. Tomei (Ed.), *Exploring the New Era of Technology-Infused Education* (pp. 279–299). Hershey, PA: IGI Global. doi:10.4018/978-1-5225-1709-2.ch017

Kővári, E., Saleh, M., & Steinbachné Hajmásy, G. (2022). The Impact of Corporate Digital Responsibility (CDR) on Internal Stakeholders' Satisfaction in Hungarian Upscale Hotels. In M. Valeri (Ed.), *New Governance and Management in Touristic Destinations* (pp. 35–51). IGI Global. https://doi.org/10.4018/978-1-6684-3889-3.ch003

Kożuch, B., & Jabłoński, A. (2017). Adopting the Concept of Business Models in Public Management. In M. Lewandowski & B. Kożuch (Eds.), *Public Sector Entrepreneurship and the Integration of Innovative Business Models* (pp. 10–46). Hershey, PA: IGI Global. doi:10.4018/978-1-5225-2215-7.ch002

Kumar, J., Adhikary, A., & Jha, A. (2017). Small Active Investors' Perceptions and Preferences Towards Tax Saving Mutual Fund Schemes in Eastern India: An Empirical Note. *International Journal of Asian Business and Information Management, 8*(2), 35–45. doi:10.4018/IJABIM.2017040103

Latusi, S., & Fissore, M. (2021). Pilgrimage Routes to Happiness: Comparing the Camino de Santiago and Via Francigena. In A. Perinotto, V. Mayer, & J. Soares (Eds.), *Rebuilding and Restructuring the Tourism Industry: Infusion of Happiness and Quality of Life* (pp. 157–182). IGI Global. https://doi.org/10.4018/978-1-7998-7239-9.ch008

Lavassani, K. M., & Movahedi, B. (2017). Applications Driven Information Systems: Beyond Networks toward Business Ecosystems. *International Journal of Innovation in the Digital Economy*, *8*(1), 61–75. doi:10.4018/IJIDE.2017010104

Lazzareschi, V. H., & Brito, M. S. (2017). Strategic Information Management: Proposal of Business Project Model. In G. Jamil, A. Soares, & C. Pessoa (Eds.), *Handbook of Research on Information Management for Effective Logistics and Supply Chains* (pp. 59–88). Hershey, PA: IGI Global. doi:10.4018/978-1-5225-0973-8.ch004

Lechuga Sancho, M. P., & Martín Navarro, A. (2022). Evolution of the Literature on Social Responsibility in the Tourism Sector: A Systematic Literature Review. In G. Fernandes (Ed.), *Challenges and New Opportunities for Tourism in Inland Territories: Ecocultural Resources and Sustainable Initiatives* (pp. 169–186). IGI Global. https://doi.org/10.4018/978-1-7998-7339-6.ch010

Lederer, M., Kurz, M., & Lazarov, P. (2017). Usage and Suitability of Methods for Strategic Business Process Initiatives: A Multi Case Study Research. *International Journal of Productivity Management and Assessment Technologies*, *5*(1), 40–51. doi:10.4018/IJPMAT.2017010103

Lee, I. (2017). A Social Enterprise Business Model and a Case Study of Pacific Community Ventures (PCV). In V. Potocan, M. Üngan, & Z. Nedelko (Eds.), *Handbook of Research on Managerial Solutions in Non-Profit Organizations* (pp. 182–204). Hershey, PA: IGI Global. doi:10.4018/978-1-5225-0731-4.ch009

Leon, L. A., Seal, K. C., Przasnyski, Z. H., & Wiedenman, I. (2017). Skills and Competencies Required for Jobs in Business Analytics: A Content Analysis of Job Advertisements Using Text Mining. *International Journal of Business Intelligence Research*, *8*(1), 1–25. doi:10.4018/IJBIR.2017010101

Levy, C. L., & Elias, N. I. (2017). SOHO Users' Perceptions of Reliability and Continuity of Cloud-Based Services. In M. Moore (Ed.), *Cybersecurity Breaches and Issues Surrounding Online Threat Protection* (pp. 248–287). Hershey, PA: IGI Global. doi:10.4018/978-1-5225-1941-6.ch011

Levy, M. (2018). Change Management Serving Knowledge Management and Organizational Development: Reflections and Review. In N. Baporikar (Ed.), *Global Practices in Knowledge Management for Societal and Organizational Development* (pp. 256–270). Hershey, PA: IGI Global. doi:10.4018/978-1-5225-3009-1.ch012

Lewandowski, M. (2017). Public Organizations and Business Model Innovation: The Role of Public Service Design. In M. Lewandowski & B. Kożuch (Eds.), *Public Sector Entrepreneurship and the Integration of Innovative Business Models* (pp. 47–72). Hershey, PA: IGI Global. doi:10.4018/978-1-5225-2215-7.ch003

Lhannaoui, H., Kabbaj, M. I., & Bakkoury, Z. (2017). A Survey of Risk-Aware Business Process Modelling. *International Journal of Risk and Contingency Management, 6*(3), 14–26. doi:10.4018/IJRCM.2017070102

Li, J., Sun, W., Jiang, W., Yang, H., & Zhang, L. (2017). How the Nature of Exogenous Shocks and Crises Impact Company Performance?: The Effects of Industry Characteristics. *International Journal of Risk and Contingency Management, 6*(4), 40–55. doi:10.4018/IJRCM.2017100103

Lopez-Fernandez, M., Perez-Perez, M., Serrano-Bedia, A., & Cobo-Gonzalez, A. (2021). Small and Medium Tourism Enterprise Survival in Times of Crisis: "El Capricho de Gaudí. In D. Toubes & N. Araújo-Vila (Eds.), *Risk, Crisis, and Disaster Management in Small and Medium-Sized Tourism Enterprises* (pp. 103–129). IGI Global. doi:10.4018/978-1-7998-6996-2.ch005

Mahajan, A., Maidullah, S., & Hossain, M. R. (2022). Experience Toward Smart Tour Guide Apps in Travelling: An Analysis of Users' Reviews on Audio Odigos and Trip My Way. In R. Augusto Costa, F. Brandão, Z. Breda, & C. Costa (Eds.), *Planning and Managing the Experience Economy in Tourism* (pp. 255-273). IGI Global. https://doi.org/10.4018/978-1-7998-8775-1.ch014

Malega, P. (2017). Small and Medium Enterprises in the Slovak Republic: Status and Competitiveness of SMEs in the Global Markets and Possibilities of Optimization. In M. Vemić (Ed.), *Optimal Management Strategies in Small and Medium Enterprises* (pp. 102–124). Hershey, PA: IGI Global. doi:10.4018/978-1-5225-1949-2.ch006

Malewska, K. M. (2017). Intuition in Decision-Making on the Example of a Non-Profit Organization. In V. Potocan, M. Ünğan, & Z. Nedelko (Eds.), *Handbook of Research on Managerial Solutions in Non-Profit Organizations* (pp. 378–399). Hershey, PA: IGI Global. doi:10.4018/978-1-5225-0731-4.ch018

Maroofi, F. (2017). Entrepreneurial Orientation and Organizational Learning Ability Analysis for Innovation and Firm Performance. In N. Baporikar (Ed.), *Innovation and Shifting Perspectives in Management Education* (pp. 144–165). Hershey, PA: IGI Global. doi:10.4018/978-1-5225-1019-2.ch007

Marques, M., Moleiro, D., Brito, T. M., & Marques, T. (2021). Customer Relationship Management as an Important Relationship Marketing Tool: The Case of the Hospitality Industry in Estoril Coast. In M. Dinis, L. Bonixe, S. Lamy, & Z. Breda (Eds.), Impact of New Media in Tourism (pp. 39-56). IGI Global. https://doi.org/ doi:10.4018/978-1-7998-7095-1.ch003

Martins, P. V., & Zacarias, M. (2017). A Web-based Tool for Business Process Improvement. *International Journal of Web Portals*, *9*(2), 68–84. doi:10.4018/IJWP.2017070104

Matthies, B., & Coners, A. (2017). Exploring the Conceptual Nature of e-Business Projects. *Journal of Electronic Commerce in Organizations*, *15*(3), 33–63. doi:10.4018/JECO.2017070103

Mayer, V. F., Fraga, C. C., & Silva, L. C. (2021). Contributions of Neurosciences to Studies of Well-Being in Tourism. In A. Perinotto, V. Mayer, & J. Soares (Eds.), *Rebuilding and Restructuring the Tourism Industry: Infusion of Happiness and Quality of Life* (pp. 108–128). IGI Global. https://doi.org/10.4018/978-1-7998-7239-9.ch006

McKee, J. (2018). Architecture as a Tool to Solve Business Planning Problems. In M. Khosrow-Pour, D.B.A. (Ed.), Encyclopedia of Information Science and Technology, Fourth Edition (pp. 573-586). Hershey, PA: IGI Global. doi:10.4018/978-1-5225-2255-3.ch050

McMurray, A. J., Cross, J., & Caponecchia, C. (2018). The Risk Management Profession in Australia: Business Continuity Plan Practices. In N. Bajgoric (Ed.), *Always-On Enterprise Information Systems for Modern Organizations* (pp. 112–129). Hershey, PA: IGI Global. doi:10.4018/978-1-5225-3704-5.ch006

Meddah, I. H., & Belkadi, K. (2018). Mining Patterns Using Business Process Management. In R. Hamou (Ed.), *Handbook of Research on Biomimicry in Information Retrieval and Knowledge Management* (pp. 78–89). Hershey, PA: IGI Global. doi:10.4018/978-1-5225-3004-6.ch005

Melian, A. G., & Camprubí, R. (2021). The Accessibility of Museum Websites: The Case of Barcelona. In C. Eusébio, L. Teixeira, & M. Carneiro (Eds.), *ICT Tools and Applications for Accessible Tourism* (pp. 234–255). IGI Global. https://doi.org/10.4018/978-1-7998-6428-8.ch011

Mendes, L. (2017). TQM and Knowledge Management: An Integrated Approach Towards Tacit Knowledge Management. In D. Jaziri-Bouagina & G. Jamil (Eds.), *Handbook of Research on Tacit Knowledge Management for Organizational Success* (pp. 236–263). Hershey, PA: IGI Global. doi:10.4018/978-1-5225-2394-9.ch009

Menezes, V. D., & Cavagnaro, E. (2021). Communicating Sustainable Initiatives in the Hotel Industry: The Case of the Hotel Jakarta Amsterdam. In F. Brandão, Z. Breda, R. Costa, & C. Costa (Eds.), *Handbook of Research on the Role of Tourism in Achieving Sustainable Development Goals* (pp. 224-234). IGI Global. https://doi.org/10.4018/978-1-7998-5691-7.ch013

Menezes, V. D., & Cavagnaro, E. (2021). Communicating Sustainable Initiatives in the Hotel Industry: The Case of the Hotel Jakarta Amsterdam. In F. Brandão, Z. Breda, R. Costa, & C. Costa (Eds.), *Handbook of Research on the Role of Tourism in Achieving Sustainable Development Goals* (pp. 224-234). IGI Global. https://doi.org/10.4018/978-1-7998-5691-7.ch013

Mitas, O., Bastiaansen, M., & Boode, W. (2022). If You're Happy, I'm Happy: Emotion Contagion at a Tourist Information Center. In R. Augusto Costa, F. Brandão, Z. Breda, & C. Costa (Eds.), *Planning and Managing the Experience Economy in Tourism* (pp. 122-140). IGI Global. https://doi.org/10.4018/978-1-7998-8775-1.ch007

Mnjama, N. M. (2017). Preservation of Recorded Information in Public and Private Sector Organizations. In P. Jain & N. Mnjama (Eds.), *Managing Knowledge Resources and Records in Modern Organizations* (pp. 149–167). Hershey, PA: IGI Global. doi:10.4018/978-1-5225-1965-2.ch009

Mokoqama, M., & Fields, Z. (2017). Principles of Responsible Management Education (PRME): Call for Responsible Management Education. In Z. Fields (Ed.), *Collective Creativity for Responsible and Sustainable Business Practice* (pp. 229–241). Hershey, PA: IGI Global. doi:10.4018/978-1-5225-1823-5.ch012

Monteiro, A., Lopes, S., & Carbone, F. (2021). Academic Mobility: Bridging Tourism and Peace Education. In J. da Silva, Z. Breda, & F. Carbone (Eds.), *Role and Impact of Tourism in Peacebuilding and Conflict Transformation* (pp. 275-301). IGI Global. https://doi.org/10.4018/978-1-7998-5053-3.ch016

Muniapan, B. (2017). Philosophy and Management: The Relevance of Vedanta in Management. In P. Ordóñez de Pablos (Ed.), *Managerial Strategies and Solutions for Business Success in Asia* (pp. 124–139). Hershey, PA: IGI Global. doi:10.4018/978-1-5225-1886-0.ch007

Murad, S. E., & Dowaji, S. (2017). Using Value-Based Approach for Managing Cloud-Based Services. In A. Turuk, B. Sahoo, & S. Addya (Eds.), *Resource Management and Efficiency in Cloud Computing Environments* (pp. 33–60). Hershey, PA: IGI Global. doi:10.4018/978-1-5225-1721-4.ch002

Mutahar, A. M., Daud, N. M., Thurasamy, R., Isaac, O., & Abdulsalam, R. (2018). The Mediating of Perceived Usefulness and Perceived Ease of Use: The Case of Mobile Banking in Yemen. *International Journal of Technology Diffusion, 9*(2), 21–40. doi:10.4018/IJTD.2018040102

Naidoo, V. (2017). E-Learning and Management Education at African Universities. In N. Baporikar (Ed.), *Management Education for Global Leadership* (pp. 181–201). Hershey, PA: IGI Global. doi:10.4018/978-1-5225-1013-0.ch009

Naidoo, V., & Igbinakhase, I. (2018). Opportunities and Challenges of Knowledge Retention in SMEs. In N. Baporikar (Ed.), *Knowledge Integration Strategies for Entrepreneurship and Sustainability* (pp. 70–94). Hershey, PA: IGI Global. doi:10.4018/978-1-5225-5115-7.ch004

Naumov, N., & Costandachi, G. (2021). Creativity and Entrepreneurship: Gastronomic Tourism in Mexico. In J. Soares (Ed.), *Innovation and Entrepreneurial Opportunities in Community Tourism* (pp. 90–108). IGI Global. https://doi.org/10.4018/978-1-7998-4855-4.ch006

Nayak, S., & Prabhu, N. (2017). Paradigm Shift in Management Education: Need for a Cross Functional Perspective. In N. Baporikar (Ed.), *Management Education for Global Leadership* (pp. 241–255). Hershey, PA: IGI Global. doi:10.4018/978-1-5225-1013-0.ch012

Nedelko, Z., & Potocan, V. (2017). Management Solutions in Non-Profit Organizations: Case of Slovenia. In V. Potocan, M. Üngan, & Z. Nedelko (Eds.), *Handbook of Research on Managerial Solutions in Non-Profit Organizations* (pp. 1–22). Hershey, PA: IGI Global. doi:10.4018/978-1-5225-0731-4.ch001

Nedelko, Z., & Potocan, V. (2017). Priority of Management Tools Utilization among Managers: International Comparison. In V. Wang (Ed.), *Encyclopedia of Strategic Leadership and Management* (pp. 1083–1094). Hershey, PA: IGI Global. doi:10.4018/978-1-5225-1049-9.ch075

Nedelko, Z., Raudeliūnienė, J., & Črešnar, R. (2018). Knowledge Dynamics in Supply Chain Management. In N. Baporikar (Ed.), *Knowledge Integration Strategies for Entrepreneurship and Sustainability* (pp. 150–166). Hershey, PA: IGI Global. doi:10.4018/978-1-5225-5115-7.ch008

Nguyen, H. T., & Hipsher, S. A. (2018). Innovation and Creativity Used by Private Sector Firms in a Resources-Constrained Environment. In S. Hipsher (Ed.), *Examining the Private Sector's Role in Wealth Creation and Poverty Reduction* (pp. 219–238). Hershey, PA: IGI Global. doi:10.4018/978-1-5225-3117-3.ch010

Obicci, P. A. (2017). Risk Sharing in a Partnership. In *Risk Management Strategies in Public-Private Partnerships* (pp. 115–152). Hershey, PA: IGI Global. doi:10.4018/978-1-5225-2503-5.ch004

Obidallah, W. J., & Raahemi, B. (2017). Managing Changes in Service Oriented Virtual Organizations: A Structural and Procedural Framework to Facilitate the Process of Change. *Journal of Electronic Commerce in Organizations, 15*(1), 59–83. doi:10.4018/JECO.2017010104

Ojo, O. (2017). Impact of Innovation on the Entrepreneurial Success in Selected Business Enterprises in South-West Nigeria. *International Journal of Innovation in the Digital Economy, 8*(2), 29–38. doi:10.4018/IJIDE.2017040103

Okdinawati, L., Simatupang, T. M., & Sunitiyoso, Y. (2017). Multi-Agent Reinforcement Learning for Value Co-Creation of Collaborative Transportation Management (CTM). *International Journal of Information Systems and Supply Chain Management, 10*(3), 84–95. doi:10.4018/IJISSCM.2017070105

Olivera, V. A., & Carrillo, I. M. (2021). Organizational Culture: A Key Element for the Development of Mexican Micro and Small Tourist Companies. In J. Soares (Ed.), *Innovation and Entrepreneurial Opportunities in Community Tourism* (pp. 227–242). IGI Global. doi:10.4018/978-1-7998-4855-4.ch013

Ossorio, M. (2022). Corporate Museum Experiences in Enogastronomic Tourism. In R. Augusto Costa, F. Brandão, Z. Breda, & C. Costa (Eds.), Planning and Managing the Experience Economy in Tourism (pp. 107-121). IGI Global. https://doi.org/ doi:10.4018/978-1-7998-8775-1.ch006

Ossorio, M. (2022). Enogastronomic Tourism in Times of Pandemic. In G. Fernandes (Ed.), *Challenges and New Opportunities for Tourism in Inland Territories: Ecocultural Resources and Sustainable Initiatives* (pp. 241–255). IGI Global. https://doi.org/10.4018/978-1-7998-7339-6.ch014

Özekici, Y. K. (2022). ICT as an Acculturative Agent and Its Role in the Tourism Context: Introduction, Acculturation Theory, Progress of the Acculturation Theory in Extant Literature. In C. Ramos, S. Quinteiro, & A. Gonçalves (Eds.), *ICT as Innovator Between Tourism and Culture* (pp. 42–66). IGI Global. https://doi.org/10.4018/978-1-7998-8165-0.ch004

Pal, K. (2018). Building High Quality Big Data-Based Applications in Supply Chains. In A. Kumar & S. Saurav (Eds.), *Supply Chain Management Strategies and Risk Assessment in Retail Environments* (pp. 1–24). Hershey, PA: IGI Global. doi:10.4018/978-1-5225-3056-5.ch001

Palos-Sanchez, P. R., & Correia, M. B. (2018). Perspectives of the Adoption of Cloud Computing in the Tourism Sector. In J. Rodrigues, C. Ramos, P. Cardoso, & C. Henriques (Eds.), *Handbook of Research on Technological Developments for Cultural Heritage and eTourism Applications* (pp. 377–400). Hershey, PA: IGI Global. doi:10.4018/978-1-5225-2927-9.ch018

Papadopoulou, G. (2021). Promoting Gender Equality and Women Empowerment in the Tourism Sector. In F. Brandão, Z. Breda, R. Costa, & C. Costa (Eds.), Handbook of Research on the Role of Tourism in Achieving Sustainable Development Goals (pp. 152-174). IGI Global. https://doi.org/ doi:10.4018/978-1-7998-5691-7.ch009

Papp-Váry, Á. F., & Tóth, T. Z. (2022). Analysis of Budapest as a Film Tourism Destination. In R. Baleiro & R. Pereira (Eds.), *Global Perspectives on Literary Tourism and Film-Induced Tourism* (pp. 257-279). IGI Global. https://doi.org/10.4018/978-1-7998-8262-6.ch014

Patiño, B. E. (2017). New Generation Management by Convergence and Individual Identity: A Systemic and Human-Oriented Approach. In N. Baporikar (Ed.), *Innovation and Shifting Perspectives in Management Education* (pp. 119–143). Hershey, PA: IGI Global. doi:10.4018/978-1-5225-1019-2.ch006

Patro, C. S. (2021). Digital Tourism: Influence of E-Marketing Technology. In M. Dinis, L. Bonixe, S. Lamy, & Z. Breda (Eds.), *Impact of New Media in Tourism* (pp. 234-254). IGI Global. https://doi.org/10.4018/978-1-7998-7095-1.ch014

Pawliczek, A., & Rössler, M. (2017). Knowledge of Management Tools and Systems in SMEs: Knowledge Transfer in Management. In A. Bencsik (Ed.), *Knowledge Management Initiatives and Strategies in Small and Medium Enterprises* (pp. 180–203). Hershey, PA: IGI Global. doi:10.4018/978-1-5225-1642-2.ch009

Pejic-Bach, M., Omazic, M. A., Aleksic, A., & Zoroja, J. (2018). Knowledge-Based Decision Making: A Multi-Case Analysis. In R. Leon (Ed.), *Managerial Strategies for Business Sustainability During Turbulent Times* (pp. 160–184). Hershey, PA: IGI Global. doi:10.4018/978-1-5225-2716-9.ch009

Perano, M., Hysa, X., & Calabrese, M. (2018). Strategic Planning, Cultural Context, and Business Continuity Management: Business Cases in the City of Shkoder. In A. Presenza & L. Sheehan (Eds.), *Geopolitics and Strategic Management in the Global Economy* (pp. 57–77). Hershey, PA: IGI Global. doi:10.4018/978-1-5225-2673-5.ch004

Pereira, R., Mira da Silva, M., & Lapão, L. V. (2017). IT Governance Maturity Patterns in Portuguese Healthcare. In S. De Haes & W. Van Grembergen (Eds.), *Strategic IT Governance and Alignment in Business Settings* (pp. 24–52). Hershey, PA: IGI Global. doi:10.4018/978-1-5225-0861-8.ch002

Pérez-Uribe, R. I., Torres, D. A., Jurado, S. P., & Prada, D. M. (2018). Cloud Tools for the Development of Project Management in SMEs. In R. Perez-Uribe, C. Salcedo-Perez, & D. Ocampo-Guzman (Eds.), *Handbook of Research on Intrapreneurship and Organizational Sustainability in SMEs* (pp. 95–120). Hershey, PA: IGI Global. doi:10.4018/978-1-5225-3543-0.ch005

Petrisor, I., & Cozmiuc, D. (2017). Global Supply Chain Management Organization at Siemens in the Advent of Industry 4.0. In L. Saglietto & C. Cezanne (Eds.), *Global Intermediation and Logistics Service Providers* (pp. 123–142). Hershey, PA: IGI Global. doi:10.4018/978-1-5225-2133-4.ch007

Pierce, J. M., Velliaris, D. M., & Edwards, J. (2017). A Living Case Study: A Journey Not a Destination. In N. Silton (Ed.), *Exploring the Benefits of Creativity in Education, Media, and the Arts* (pp. 158–178). Hershey, PA: IGI Global. doi:10.4018/978-1-5225-0504-4.ch008

Pipia, S., & Pipia, S. (2021). Challenges of Religious Tourism in the Conflict Region: An Example of Jerusalem. In E. Alaverdov & M. Bari (Eds.), *Global Development of Religious Tourism* (pp. 135-148). IGI Global. https://doi.org/10.4018/978-1-7998-5792-1.ch009

Poulaki, P., Kritikos, A., Vasilakis, N., & Valeri, M. (2022). The Contribution of Female Creativity to the Development of Gastronomic Tourism in Greece: The Case of the Island of Naxos in the South Aegean Region. In M. Valeri (Ed.), *New Governance and Management in Touristic Destinations* (pp. 246–258). IGI Global. https://doi.org/10.4018/978-1-6684-3889-3.ch015

Radosavljevic, M., & Andjelkovic, A. (2017). Multi-Criteria Decision Making Approach for Choosing Business Process for the Improvement: Upgrading of the Six Sigma Methodology. In J. Stanković, P. Delias, S. Marinković, & S. Rochhia (Eds.), *Tools and Techniques for Economic Decision Analysis* (pp. 225–247). Hershey, PA: IGI Global. doi:10.4018/978-1-5225-0959-2.ch011

Radovic, V. M. (2017). Corporate Sustainability and Responsibility and Disaster Risk Reduction: A Serbian Overview. In M. Camilleri (Ed.), *CSR 2.0 and the New Era of Corporate Citizenship* (pp. 147–164). Hershey, PA: IGI Global. doi:10.4018/978-1-5225-1842-6.ch008

Raghunath, K. M., Devi, S. L., & Patro, C. S. (2018). Impact of Risk Assessment Models on Risk Factors: A Holistic Outlook. In K. Strang, M. Korstanje, & N. Vajjhala (Eds.), *Research, Practices, and Innovations in Global Risk and Contingency Management* (pp. 134–153). Hershey, PA: IGI Global. doi:10.4018/978-1-5225-4754-9.ch008

Raman, A., & Goyal, D. P. (2017). Extending IMPLEMENT Framework for Enterprise Information Systems Implementation to Information System Innovation. In M. Tavana (Ed.), *Enterprise Information Systems and the Digitalization of Business Functions* (pp. 137–177). Hershey, PA: IGI Global. doi:10.4018/978-1-5225-2382-6.ch007

Rao, Y., & Zhang, Y. (2017). The Construction and Development of Academic Library Digital Special Subject Databases. In L. Ruan, Q. Zhu, & Y. Ye (Eds.), *Academic Library Development and Administration in China* (pp. 163–183). Hershey, PA: IGI Global. doi:10.4018/978-1-5225-0550-1.ch010

Ravasan, A. Z., Mohammadi, M. M., & Hamidi, H. (2018). An Investigation Into the Critical Success Factors of Implementing Information Technology Service Management Frameworks. In K. Jakobs (Ed.), *Corporate and Global Standardization Initiatives in Contemporary Society* (pp. 200–218). Hershey, PA: IGI Global. doi:10.4018/978-1-5225-5320-5.ch009

Rezaie, S., Mirabedini, S. J., & Abtahi, A. (2018). Designing a Model for Implementation of Business Intelligence in the Banking Industry. *International Journal of Enterprise Information Systems, 14*(1), 77–103. doi:10.4018/IJEIS.2018010105

Richards, V., Matthews, N., Williams, O. J., & Khan, Z. (2021). The Challenges of Accessible Tourism Information Systems for Tourists With Vision Impairment: Sensory Communications Beyond the Screen. In C. Eusébio, L. Teixeira, & M. Carneiro (Eds.), *ICT Tools and Applications for Accessible Tourism* (pp. 26–54). IGI Global. https://doi.org/10.4018/978-1-7998-6428-8.ch002

Rodrigues de Souza Neto, V., & Marques, O. (2021). Rural Tourism Fostering Welfare Through Sustainable Development: A Conceptual Approach. In A. Perinotto, V. Mayer, & J. Soares (Eds.), *Rebuilding and Restructuring the Tourism Industry: Infusion of Happiness and Quality of Life* (pp. 38–57). IGI Global. https://doi.org/10.4018/978-1-7998-7239-9.ch003

Romano, L., Grimaldi, R., & Colasuonno, F. S. (2017). Demand Management as a Success Factor in Project Portfolio Management. In L. Romano (Ed.), *Project Portfolio Management Strategies for Effective Organizational Operations* (pp. 202–219). Hershey, PA: IGI Global. doi:10.4018/978-1-5225-2151-8.ch008

Rubio-Escuderos, L., & García-Andreu, H. (2021). Competitiveness Factors of Accessible Tourism E-Travel Agencies. In C. Eusébio, L. Teixeira, & M. Carneiro (Eds.), *ICT Tools and Applications for Accessible Tourism* (pp. 196–217). IGI Global. https://doi.org/10.4018/978-1-7998-6428-8.ch009

Rucci, A. C., Porto, N., Darcy, S., & Becka, L. (2021). Smart and Accessible Cities?: Not Always – The Case for Accessible Tourism Initiatives in Buenos Aries and Sydney. In C. Eusébio, L. Teixeira, & M. Carneiro (Eds.), *ICT Tools and Applications for Accessible Tourism* (pp. 115–145). IGI Global. https://doi.org/10.4018/978-1-7998-6428-8.ch006

Ruhi, U. (2018). Towards an Interdisciplinary Socio-Technical Definition of Virtual Communities. In M. Khosrow-Pour, D.B.A. (Ed.), Encyclopedia of Information Science and Technology, Fourth Edition (pp. 4278-4295). Hershey, PA: IGI Global. doi:10.4018/978-1-5225-2255-3.ch371

Ryan, L., Catena, M., Ros, P., & Stephens, S. (2021). Designing Entrepreneurial Ecosystems to Support Resource Management in the Tourism Industry. In V. Costa, A. Moura, & M. Mira (Eds.), *Handbook of Research on Human Capital and People Management in the Tourism Industry* (pp. 265–281). IGI Global. https://doi.org/10.4018/978-1-7998-4318-4.ch013

Sabuncu, I. (2021). Understanding Tourist Perceptions and Expectations During Pandemic Through Social Media Big Data. In M. Demir, A. Dalgıç, & F. Ergen (Eds.), *Handbook of Research on the Impacts and Implications of COVID-19 on the Tourism Industry* (pp. 330–350). IGI Global. https://doi.org/10.4018/978-1-7998-8231-2.ch016

Safari, M. R., & Jiang, Q. (2018). The Theory and Practice of IT Governance Maturity and Strategies Alignment: Evidence From Banking Industry. *Journal of Global Information Management*, *26*(2), 127–146. doi:10.4018/JGIM.2018040106

Sahoo, J., Pati, B., & Mohanty, B. (2017). Knowledge Management as an Academic Discipline: An Assessment. In B. Gunjal (Ed.), *Managing Knowledge and Scholarly Assets in Academic Libraries* (pp. 99–126). Hershey, PA: IGI Global. doi:10.4018/978-1-5225-1741-2.ch005

Saini, D. (2017). Relevance of Teaching Values and Ethics in Management Education. In N. Baporikar (Ed.), *Management Education for Global Leadership* (pp. 90–111). Hershey, PA: IGI Global. doi:10.4018/978-1-5225-1013-0.ch005

Sambhanthan, A. (2017). Assessing and Benchmarking Sustainability in Organisations: An Integrated Conceptual Model. *International Journal of Systems and Service-Oriented Engineering*, *7*(4), 22–43. doi:10.4018/IJSSOE.2017100102

Sambhanthan, A., & Potdar, V. (2017). A Study of the Parameters Impacting Sustainability in Information Technology Organizations. *International Journal of Knowledge-Based Organizations*, *7*(3), 27–39. doi:10.4018/IJKBO.2017070103

Sánchez-Fernández, M. D., & Manríquez, M. R. (2018). The Entrepreneurial Spirit Based on Social Values: The Digital Generation. In P. Isaias & L. Carvalho (Eds.), *User Innovation and the Entrepreneurship Phenomenon in the Digital Economy* (pp. 173–193). Hershey, PA: IGI Global. doi:10.4018/978-1-5225-2826-5.ch009

Sanchez-Ruiz, L., & Blanco, B. (2017). Process Management for SMEs: Barriers, Enablers, and Benefits. In M. Vemić (Ed.), *Optimal Management Strategies in Small and Medium Enterprises* (pp. 293–319). Hershey, PA: IGI Global. doi:10.4018/978-1-5225-1949-2.ch014

Sanz, L. F., Gómez-Pérez, J., & Castillo-Martinez, A. (2018). Analysis of the European ICT Competence Frameworks. In V. Ahuja & S. Rathore (Eds.), *Multidisciplinary Perspectives on Human Capital and Information Technology Professionals* (pp. 225–245). Hershey, PA: IGI Global. doi:10.4018/978-1-5225-5297-0.ch012

Sarvepalli, A., & Godin, J. (2017). Business Process Management in the Classroom. *Journal of Cases on Information Technology*, *19*(2), 17–28. doi:10.4018/JCIT.2017040102

Saxena, G. G., & Saxena, A. (2021). Host Community Role in Medical Tourism Development. In M. Singh & S. Kumaran (Eds.), *Growth of the Medical Tourism Industry and Its Impact on Society: Emerging Research and Opportunities* (pp. 105–127). IGI Global. https://doi.org/10.4018/978-1-7998-3427-4.ch006

Saygili, E. E., Ozturkoglu, Y., & Kocakulah, M. C. (2017). End Users' Perceptions of Critical Success Factors in ERP Applications. *International Journal of Enterprise Information Systems, 13*(4), 58–75. doi:10.4018/IJEIS.2017100104

Saygili, E. E., & Saygili, A. T. (2017). Contemporary Issues in Enterprise Information Systems: A Critical Review of CSFs in ERP Implementations. In M. Tavana (Ed.), *Enterprise Information Systems and the Digitalization of Business Functions* (pp. 120–136). Hershey, PA: IGI Global. doi:10.4018/978-1-5225-2382-6.ch006

Schwaiger, K. M., & Zehrer, A. (2021). The COVID-19 Pandemic and Organizational Resilience in Hospitality Family Firms: A Qualitative Approach. In A. Zehrer, G. Glowka, K. Schwaiger, & V. Ranacher-Lackner (Eds.), *Resiliency Models and Addressing Future Risks for Family Firms in the Tourism Industry* (pp. 32–49). IGI Global. https://doi.org/10.4018/978-1-7998-7352-5.ch002

Scott, N., & Campos, A. C. (2022). Cognitive Science of Tourism Experiences. In R. Augusto Costa, F. Brandão, Z. Breda, & C. Costa (Eds.), Planning and Managing the Experience Economy in Tourism (pp. 1-21). IGI Global. https://doi.org/ doi:10.4018/978-1-7998-8775-1.ch001

Seidenstricker, S., & Antonino, A. (2018). Business Model Innovation-Oriented Technology Management for Emergent Technologies. In M. Khosrow-Pour, D.B.A. (Ed.), Encyclopedia of Information Science and Technology, Fourth Edition (pp. 4560-4569). Hershey, PA: IGI Global. doi:10.4018/978-1-5225-2255-3.ch396

Selvi, M. S. (2021). Changes in Tourism Sales and Marketing Post COVID-19. In M. Demir, A. Dalgıç, & F. Ergen (Eds.), *Handbook of Research on the Impacts and Implications of COVID-19 on the Tourism Industry* (pp. 437–460). IGI Global. doi:10.4018/978-1-7998-8231-2.ch021

Senaratne, S., & Gunarathne, A. D. (2017). Excellence Perspective for Management Education from a Global Accountants' Hub in Asia. In N. Baporikar (Ed.), *Management Education for Global Leadership* (pp. 158–180). Hershey, PA: IGI Global. doi:10.4018/978-1-5225-1013-0.ch008

Sensuse, D. I., & Cahyaningsih, E. (2018). Knowledge Management Models: A Summative Review. *International Journal of Information Systems in the Service Sector*, *10*(1), 71–100. doi:10.4018/IJISSS.2018010105

Seth, M., Goyal, D., & Kiran, R. (2017). Diminution of Impediments in Implementation of Supply Chain Management Information System for Enhancing its Effectiveness in Indian Automobile Industry. *Journal of Global Information Management*, *25*(3), 1–20. doi:10.4018/JGIM.2017070101

Seyal, A. H., & Rahman, M. N. (2017). Investigating Impact of Inter-Organizational Factors in Measuring ERP Systems Success: Bruneian Perspectives. In M. Tavana (Ed.), *Enterprise Information Systems and the Digitalization of Business Functions* (pp. 178–204). Hershey, PA: IGI Global. doi:10.4018/978-1-5225-2382-6.ch008

Shaqrah, A. A. (2018). Analyzing Business Intelligence Systems Based on 7s Model of McKinsey. *International Journal of Business Intelligence Research*, *9*(1), 53–63. doi:10.4018/IJBIR.2018010104

Sharma, A. J. (2017). Enhancing Sustainability through Experiential Learning in Management Education. In N. Baporikar (Ed.), *Management Education for Global Leadership* (pp. 256–274). Hershey, PA: IGI Global. doi:10.4018/978-1-5225-1013-0.ch013

Shetty, K. P. (2017). Responsible Global Leadership: Ethical Challenges in Management Education. In N. Baporikar (Ed.), *Innovation and Shifting Perspectives in Management Education* (pp. 194–223). Hershey, PA: IGI Global. doi:10.4018/978-1-5225-1019-2.ch009

Sinthupundaja, J., & Kohda, Y. (2017). Effects of Corporate Social Responsibility and Creating Shared Value on Sustainability. *International Journal of Sustainable Entrepreneurship and Corporate Social Responsibility*, *2*(1), 27–38. doi:10.4018/IJSECSR.2017010103

Škarica, I., & Hrgović, A. V. (2018). Implementation of Total Quality Management Principles in Public Health Institutes in the Republic of Croatia. *International Journal of Productivity Management and Assessment Technologies*, *6*(1), 1–16. doi:10.4018/IJPMAT.2018010101

Skokic, V. (2021). How Small Hotel Owners Practice Resilience: Longitudinal Study Among Small Family Hotels in Croatia. In A. Zehrer, G. Glowka, K. Schwaiger, & V. Ranacher-Lackner (Eds.), *Resiliency Models and Addressing Future Risks for Family Firms in the Tourism Industry* (pp. 50–73). IGI Global. doi:10.4018/978-1-7998-7352-5.ch003

Smuts, H., Kotzé, P., Van der Merwe, A., & Loock, M. (2017). Framework for Managing Shared Knowledge in an Information Systems Outsourcing Context. *International Journal of Knowledge Management, 13*(4), 1–30. doi:10.4018/IJKM.2017100101

Sousa, M. J., Cruz, R., Dias, I., & Caracol, C. (2017). Information Management Systems in the Supply Chain. In G. Jamil, A. Soares, & C. Pessoa (Eds.), *Handbook of Research on Information Management for Effective Logistics and Supply Chains* (pp. 469–485). Hershey, PA: IGI Global. doi:10.4018/978-1-5225-0973-8.ch025

Spremic, M., Turulja, L., & Bajgoric, N. (2018). Two Approaches in Assessing Business Continuity Management Attitudes in the Organizational Context. In N. Bajgoric (Ed.), *Always-On Enterprise Information Systems for Modern Organizations* (pp. 159–183). Hershey, PA: IGI Global. doi:10.4018/978-1-5225-3704-5.ch008

Steenkamp, A. L. (2018). Some Insights in Computer Science and Information Technology. In *Examining the Changing Role of Supervision in Doctoral Research Projects: Emerging Research and Opportunities* (pp. 113–133). Hershey, PA: IGI Global. doi:10.4018/978-1-5225-2610-0.ch005

Stipanović, C., Rudan, E., & Zubović, V. (2022). Reaching the New Tourist Through Creativity: Sustainable Development Challenges in Croatian Coastal Towns. In M. Valeri (Ed.), *New Governance and Management in Touristic Destinations* (pp. 231–245). IGI Global. https://doi.org/10.4018/978-1-6684-3889-3.ch014

Tabach, A., & Croteau, A. (2017). Configurations of Information Technology Governance Practices and Business Unit Performance. *International Journal of IT/Business Alignment and Governance, 8*(2), 1–27. doi:10.4018/IJITBAG.2017070101

Talaue, G. M., & Iqbal, T. (2017). Assessment of e-Business Mode of Selected Private Universities in the Philippines and Pakistan. *International Journal of Online Marketing, 7*(4), 63–77. doi:10.4018/IJOM.2017100105

Tam, G. C. (2017). Project Manager Sustainability Competence. In *Managerial Strategies and Green Solutions for Project Sustainability* (pp. 178–207). Hershey, PA: IGI Global. doi:10.4018/978-1-5225-2371-0.ch008

Tambo, T. (2018). Fashion Retail Innovation: About Context, Antecedents, and Outcome in Technological Change Projects. In I. Management Association (Ed.), Fashion and Textiles: Breakthroughs in Research and Practice (pp. 233-260). Hershey, PA: IGI Global. https://doi.org/ doi:10.4018/978-1-5225-3432-7.ch010

Tantau, A. D., & Frăţilă, L. C. (2018). Information and Management System for Renewable Energy Business. In *Entrepreneurship and Business Development in the Renewable Energy Sector* (pp. 200–244). Hershey, PA: IGI Global. doi:10.4018/978-1-5225-3625-3.ch006

Teixeira, N., Pardal, P. N., & Rafael, B. G. (2018). Internationalization, Financial Performance, and Organizational Challenges: A Success Case in Portugal. In L. Carvalho (Ed.), *Handbook of Research on Entrepreneurial Ecosystems and Social Dynamics in a Globalized World* (pp. 379–423). Hershey, PA: IGI Global. doi:10.4018/978-1-5225-3525-6.ch017

Teixeira, P., Teixeira, L., Eusébio, C., Silva, S., & Teixeira, A. (2021). The Impact of ICTs on Accessible Tourism: Evidence Based on a Systematic Literature Review. In C. Eusébio, L. Teixeira, & M. Carneiro (Eds.), *ICT Tools and Applications for Accessible Tourism* (pp. 1–25). IGI Global. doi:10.4018/978-1-7998-6428-8.ch001

Trad, A., & Kalpić, D. (2018). The Business Transformation Framework, Agile Project and Change Management. In M. Khosrow-Pour, D.B.A. (Ed.), Encyclopedia of Information Science and Technology, Fourth Edition (pp. 620-635). Hershey, PA: IGI Global. https://doi.org/ doi:10.4018/978-1-5225-2255-3.ch054

Trad, A., & Kalpić, D. (2018). The Business Transformation and Enterprise Architecture Framework: The Financial Engineering E-Risk Management and E-Law Integration. In B. Sergi, F. Fidanoski, M. Ziolo, & V. Naumovski (Eds.), *Regaining Global Stability After the Financial Crisis* (pp. 46–65). Hershey, PA: IGI Global. doi:10.4018/978-1-5225-4026-7.ch003

Trengereid, V. (2022). Conditions of Network Engagement: The Quest for a Common Good. In R. Augusto Costa, F. Brandão, Z. Breda, & C. Costa (Eds.), *Planning and Managing the Experience Economy in Tourism* (pp. 69-84). IGI Global. https://doi.org/10.4018/978-1-7998-8775-1.ch004

Turulja, L., & Bajgoric, N. (2018). Business Continuity and Information Systems: A Systematic Literature Review. In N. Bajgoric (Ed.), *Always-On Enterprise Information Systems for Modern Organizations* (pp. 60–87). Hershey, PA: IGI Global. doi:10.4018/978-1-5225-3704-5.ch004

Vargas-Hernández, J. G. (2017). Professional Integrity in Business Management Education. In N. Baporikar (Ed.), *Management Education for Global Leadership* (pp. 70–89). Hershey, PA: IGI Global. doi:10.4018/978-1-5225-1013-0.ch004

Varnacı Uzun, F. (2021). The Destination Preferences of Foreign Tourists During the COVID-19 Pandemic and Attitudes Towards: Marmaris, Turkey. In M. Demir, A. Dalgıç, & F. Ergen (Eds.), *Handbook of Research on the Impacts and Implications of COVID-19 on the Tourism Industry* (pp. 285–306). IGI Global. https://doi.org/10.4018/978-1-7998-8231-2.ch014

Vasista, T. G., & AlAbdullatif, A. M. (2017). Role of Electronic Customer Relationship Management in Demand Chain Management: A Predictive Analytic Approach. *International Journal of Information Systems and Supply Chain Management*, *10*(1), 53–67. doi:10.4018/IJISSCM.2017010104

Vieru, D., & Bourdeau, S. (2017). Survival in the Digital Era: A Digital Competence-Based Multi-Case Study in the Canadian SME Clothing Industry. *International Journal of Social and Organizational Dynamics in IT*, *6*(1), 17–34. doi:10.4018/IJSODIT.2017010102

Vijayan, G., & Kamarulzaman, N. H. (2017). An Introduction to Sustainable Supply Chain Management and Business Implications. In M. Khan, M. Hussain, & M. Ajmal (Eds.), *Green Supply Chain Management for Sustainable Business Practice* (pp. 27–50). Hershey, PA: IGI Global. doi:10.4018/978-1-5225-0635-5.ch002

Vlachvei, A., & Notta, O. (2017). Firm Competitiveness: Theories, Evidence, and Measurement. In A. Vlachvei, O. Notta, K. Karantininis, & N. Tsounis (Eds.), *Factors Affecting Firm Competitiveness and Performance in the Modern Business World* (pp. 1–42). Hershey, PA: IGI Global. doi:10.4018/978-1-5225-0843-4.ch001

Wang, C., Schofield, M., Li, X., & Ou, X. (2017). Do Chinese Students in Public and Private Higher Education Institutes Perform at Different Level in One of the Leadership Skills: Critical Thinking?: An Exploratory Comparison. In V. Wang (Ed.), *Encyclopedia of Strategic Leadership and Management* (pp. 160–181). Hershey, PA: IGI Global. doi:10.4018/978-1-5225-1049-9.ch013

Wang, J. (2017). Multi-Agent based Production Management Decision System Modelling for the Textile Enterprise. *Journal of Global Information Management, 25*(4), 1–15. doi:10.4018/JGIM.2017100101

Wiedemann, A., & Gewald, H. (2017). Examining Cross-Domain Alignment: The Correlation of Business Strategy, IT Management, and IT Business Value. *International Journal of IT/Business Alignment and Governance, 8*(1), 17–31. doi:10.4018/IJITBAG.2017010102

Wolf, R., & Thiel, M. (2018). Advancing Global Business Ethics in China: Reducing Poverty Through Human and Social Welfare. In S. Hipsher (Ed.), *Examining the Private Sector's Role in Wealth Creation and Poverty Reduction* (pp. 67–84). Hershey, PA: IGI Global. doi:10.4018/978-1-5225-3117-3.ch004

Yablonsky, S. (2018). Innovation Platforms: Data and Analytics Platforms. In *Multi-Sided Platforms (MSPs) and Sharing Strategies in the Digital Economy: Emerging Research and Opportunities* (pp. 72–95). Hershey, PA: IGI Global. doi:10.4018/978-1-5225-5457-8.ch003

Yaşar, B. (2021). The Impact of COVID-19 on Volatility of Tourism Stocks: Evidence From BIST Tourism Index. In M. Demir, A. Dalgıç, & F. Ergen (Eds.), *Handbook of Research on the Impacts and Implications of COVID-19 on the Tourism Industry* (pp. 23–44). IGI Global. https://doi.org/10.4018/978-1-7998-8231-2.ch002

Yusoff, A., Ahmad, N. H., & Halim, H. A. (2017). Agropreneurship among Gen Y in Malaysia: The Role of Academic Institutions. In N. Ahmad, T. Ramayah, H. Halim, & S. Rahman (Eds.), *Handbook of Research on Small and Medium Enterprises in Developing Countries* (pp. 23–47). Hershey, PA: IGI Global. doi:10.4018/978-1-5225-2165-5.ch002

Zacher, D., & Pechlaner, H. (2021). Resilience as an Opportunity Approach: Challenges and Perspectives for Private Sector Participation on a Community Level. In A. Zehrer, G. Glowka, K. Schwaiger, & V. Ranacher-Lackner (Eds.), *Resiliency Models and Addressing Future Risks for Family Firms in the Tourism Industry* (pp. 75–102). IGI Global. https://doi.org/10.4018/978-1-7998-7352-5.ch004

Zanin, F., Comuzzi, E., & Costantini, A. (2018). The Effect of Business Strategy and Stock Market Listing on the Use of Risk Assessment Tools. In *Management Control Systems in Complex Settings: Emerging Research and Opportunities* (pp. 145–168). Hershey, PA: IGI Global. doi:10.4018/978-1-5225-3987-2.ch007

Zgheib, P. W. (2017). Corporate Innovation and Intrapreneurship in the Middle East. In P. Zgheib (Ed.), *Entrepreneurship and Business Innovation in the Middle East* (pp. 37–56). Hershey, PA: IGI Global. doi:10.4018/978-1-5225-2066-5.ch003

About the Authors

Meena Chavan, BCom, MCom, PhD (International Business/Entrepreneurship), is a Senior Fellow of the Higher Education Academy (SFHEA), Fellow of the Intercultural Academy of Intercultural Research (IAIR), and Ambassador Australia – International Entrepreneurship Network. Dr. Meena Chavan is an ardent, broad-spectrum Business/ Management academic at Macquarie University. Her core research interests lie at the intersection of International Business & International Entrepreneurship. She is an interculturalist and scholar in the field of Intercultural Management and Managing Diversity. Within this stream, Dr. Chavan's focus has been on developing intercultural competence and cross-cultural leadership and entrepreneurship development. Her PhD research has produced the first Australian model for Ethnic Migrant Business Creation, "The Productive Diversity Model", which is specific to Australia and measures the value of a multicultural migrant workforce to bolster "International Business" and export earnings through links to their country of origin. Dr Chavan's research has been published in top-tier national and international peer-reviewed journals and she has presented at Global Conference. She has published a book on *Intercultural Management in Practice: Learning to Lead Diverse Global Organisations* (Emerald Publications).

Sheba Nandkeolyar is a proud migrant from India. She is a leading Australian marketer and a global diversity leader. She is the Founder & CEO of MultiConnexions Group, Australia's leading Marketing, Advertising, Digital, PR & Social Media company, a full service 360 company which works with multicultural and diaspora audiences in Australia and abroad. Sheba is passionate about bilateral business and international trade. She was the first woman National Chair of Australia India Business Council (AIBC) and is the current National Chair of AIBC Women in Business Chapter. A great believer in diversity, she has recently been inducted into the Global Board (headquartered in US) of International Advertising Association (IAA) as the Global Vice President of Diversity, Equity & Inclusion (DE&I). As the Chair of the IAA DE&I Council, Sheba leads DE&I marcoms initiatives across 56 countries. She is engaged in mentoring and assisting start-ups in Australia and in the bilateral space. A frequent guest lecturer, she is often invited to share her business and industry experience at business schools. Sheba believes in migration. She believes in celebrating migrants' contributions towards creating a richer social and economic fabric in Australia.

Research Assistants
Sapna Khiani Kumar & Katrina Hall.

Index

I

K

L

M

N

O

P

R

S

T

V

www.ingramcontent.com/pod-product-compliance
Lightning Source LLC
LaVergne TN
LVHW061535290926
849162LV00004B/800